Additional Praise for
The Executive Guide to Boosting Cash Flow and Shareholder Value

"Jones has written a thoughtful, thorough, and practical guide focusing on the key element of shareholder value creation—creating long term, sustainable cash flow. His diagnoses and prescriptions will make business leaders better stewards of capital. For those business leaders operating under private equity ownership, this book is a must read; for those who are not, Jones' book is a glimpse at the playbook that private equity firms employ."

—**John Almeida, Jr.**
General Partner,
Welsh, Carson, Anderson & Stowe

"Having spent the bulk of my career in media and communications and now in a non-profit enterprise, I believe the precepts of value creation I first learned several years ago from Jones apply across the range of business types. The key, pointed out in this seminal book, is in market strategy focused on long-term cash flow; which empowers corporate leaders to achieve outsized results for stakeholders. I highly recommend *The Executive Guide to Boosting Cash Flow and Shareholder Value* to anyone seeking a better understanding of what it takes to create real value in the modern corporate enterprise."

—**William W. Airy**
COO, The Inspiration Networks
and formerly, CMO, Liberty Livewire

"This book uniquely fills a void between classical financial analyses and the recent focus on execution. Providing the insight of market strategy as a path to shareholder value creation is intuitively obvious, but often obfuscated by the proliferation of short-term tactics that result when classic financial analysis is the only input for an executive focused on execution. As an executive that has led businesses within public companies and private equity owned companies, I highly recommend this book to business leaders searching for the "why" and "how" to boost cash flow and create long-term shareholder value."

—**Jeffrey S. Henderson**
SVP, Strategy and Business Development
Avago Technologies

"I am very impressed by this book and the intellectual foundation on which it sits. Cash is no longer king. It is emperor. In a sea of business books, this one delivers what it promises. *The Executive Guide* is your roadmap for capturing untapped pools of cash for your business."

—**Marvin Zonis**
Economics Professor,
Graduate School of Business, University of Chicago

"Jones has crafted a distinctive and valuable synthesis of the best thinking in economic value analysis, market focused investment, and strategic management. It is a practical and highly useable guide for operating executives, consultants, and investment professionals for examining existing and future businesses and building their careers."

— **Vincent C. Perro**
President, Leadership Consulting Division
Heidrick & Struggles

"To create and keep long-term client relationships, service providers must align services with the ultimate goals of those they serve. In serving business organizations that means helping business leaders drive value growth—and this book makes it crystal clear what's needed. It prioritizes the issues facing C-suite executives and their information needs—market, financial, and organizational. Senior executives in service organizations will find this book an essential tool in their tool kit, one that gives insight into the true needs of their clients."

—**Jay D. Norman**
President, Diamond Cluster International
and, recognized as a Top 25 Consultant for 2006

"Few books make running a successful business seem so easy. In an age when how-to manuals abound, it is refreshing to read a book that actually provides sound and actionable advice. As someone who has worked intimately with many companies as both operator and investor, I am impressed with Jones' ability to identify the key attributes for delivering shareholder value. *The Executive Guide* does more than simply expose the common pitfalls of managing an enterprise—it provides a useful framework for C-level executives to refocus on the oft-obscured task at hand; generating cash profits over the long-term."

—**David J. Roux**
Cofounder and Co-CEO,
Silver Lake Partners

"Typical financial accounting systems can be a huge roadblock to really understanding a business and making good decisions. In this book, Jones shows why cash-based profitability and investment information at a granular level is a critical key to managing for value growth; it tells you where to allocate capital and grow, where to rationalize, and how to manage products and services in markets. He lays out an approach to do this effectively, while avoiding the many hidden traps—like incorrectly allocated costs—which lead to very misleading conclusions and poor business decisions. C-suite executives operating under PE ownership, and those contemplating it, will find that this book provides invaluable insights and tools aligned with cash and value growth."

—**Howard D. Morgan**
Senior Managing Director
Castle Harlan, Inc.

"Jones does a great job explaining why these ideas and approaches are critical to driving shareholder value—however, unlike many other business books, he also includes very practical guidance on 'the how.' The initial chapters provide insightful and useful explanations for CEOs and division heads looking to create a well-organized team and to set the path forward. Following that, Jones shifts the emphasis to address specifics for marketers, strategists, finance executives and others to use this book as a primer to their work."

—**Eric G. Rodli**
GM and Executive VP, Entertainment, Macrovision
and formally, President, Entertainment Imaging, Eastman Kodak

"Jones has adopted a pragmatic approach, making the concepts of economic profit and market profit pools available to all businesses. He has brought to life, in a usable and readable manner, the best of economic profit and cash generation practices, and has taken the dry world of accounting and shown CFOs a real way to add value to their organizations. The result is a practical guide on how to set your business on the path to sustainable value growth, and illustrating how every day historical accounting can help a market-led growth strategy. It shows how opportunities to boost cash flow permeate throughout the organization—from innovation to business model structure—and makes it clear that growing value is the responsibility of all managers in the business. It outlines the tools needed in a way that everyone can readily grasp and deploy; those business leaders who implement the principles of this book will outperform competitors."

—**James McLauchlan**
Chief Financial Officer
Skyy Spirits (a Gruppo Campari company)

"In a world where intense competition and everyday demands consume more and more of a marketers time, this book brings sharp clarity to what really matters in business—and the critical role marketers play in delivering it. In addition to providing a primer on new core concepts, it sets out very practical steps marketers can take to ensure market actions have a positive and dramatic impact to long-term results and business value. This high-level viewpoint is as refreshing as it is clarifying—and I recommend it as a critical input for all functional executives interested in strengthening their overall business leadership and effectiveness."

—**James Taschetta**
Senior Vice President,
Marketing, Strategy & Planning,
Visa, Inc.

The Executive Guide to Boosting Cash Flow and Shareholder Value

The Profit Pool Approach

V. RORY JONES

John Wiley & Sons, Inc.

Copyright © 2008 by V. Rory Jones. All rights reserved.

Published by John Wiley & Sons, Inc., Hoboken, New Jersey.
Published simultaneously in Canada.

No part of this publication may be reproduced, stored in a retrieval system, or transmitted in any form or by any means, electronic, mechanical, photocopying, recording, scanning, or otherwise, except as permitted under Section 107 or 108 of the 1976 United States Copyright Act, without either the prior written permission of the Publisher, or authorization through payment of the appropriate per-copy fee to the Copyright Clearance Center, Inc., 222 Rosewood Drive, Danvers, MA 01923, (978) 750-8400, fax (978) 646-8600, or on the Web at www.copyright.com. Requests to the Publisher for permission should be addressed to the Permissions Department, John Wiley & Sons, Inc., 111 River Street, Hoboken, NJ 07030, (201) 748-6011, fax (201) 748-6008, or online at http://www.wiley.com/go/permissions.

Limit of Liability/Disclaimer of Warranty: While the publisher and author have used their best efforts in preparing this book, they make no representations or warranties with respect to the accuracy or completeness of the contents of this book and specifically disclaim any implied warranties of merchantability or fitness for a particular purpose. No warranty may be created or extended by sales representatives or written sales materials. The advice and strategies contained herein may not be suitable for your situation. You should consult with a professional where appropriate. Neither the publisher nor author shall be liable for any loss of profit or any other commercial damages, including but not limited to special, incidental, consequential, or other damages.

For general information on our other products and services or for technical support, please contact our Customer Care Department within the United States at (800) 762-2974, outside the United States at (317) 572-3993 or fax (317) 572-4002.

Wiley also publishes its books in a variety of electronic formats. Some content that appears in print may not be available in electronic formats. For more information about Wiley products, visit our Web site at www.wiley.com.

Library of Congress Cataloging-in-Publication Data:

Jones, V. Rory, 1962–
   The executive guide to boosting cash flow and shareholder value : the profit pool approach / V. Rory Jones.
     p. cm.
   Includes bibliographical references and index.
   ISBN 978-0-470-13896-0 (cloth)
  1. Business enterprises–Valuation.   2. Corporations–Valuation.   3. Cash flow–Management.   I. Title.
   HG4028.V3J665   2008
   658.15′2–dc22

2007034462

Printed in the United States of America.

10 9 8 7 6 5 4 3 2 1

To my wife, Janet, and our son, Miles.

Contents

List of Examples		xiii
Acknowledgments		xiv
About the Author		xv
Introduction		1
PART I	THE SHORTCUT TO HIGH PERFORMANCE	5
CHAPTER 1	So You Want a High-Performing Business?	7
	Deliver Great Returns and the Rest Will Maximize	7
	Cash Became Emperor	8
	Market Strategy Is the 80:20 Rule of Cash Flow	14
	Throw Away the Old Playbook!	21
CHAPTER 2	Profit Pools *Market Strategy on Steroids*	25
	What Makes a *Real* Profit Pool?	26
	Profit Pools and Business Models	27
	Internal Profit Pools	28
	Market Profit Pools	31
	Summary	38
CHAPTER 3	You Just Can't See Them	39
	Accounting Systems Don't Actually Report a Useful Profitability	39
	Market Profitability Information Is Difficult to Come By	47
	Businesses Aren't Configured to Get and Process Timely Cash-Based Profitability Information	52

	New Markets Are Difficult to Envision	53
	Getting It Done	55
PART II	**YOUR GUIDE TO EARLY RESULTS**	57
CHAPTER 4	Know Your Own ACTUAL PERFORMANCE	59
	Cut through the GAAP and Other Information Obfuscation	60
	Reconstitute the Numbers and See the Internal Profit Pools Emerge	79
	Now It's Time to Act: Neutralize Your Drains and Boost Your Sources	80
	Got It, What's Next?	91
CHAPTER 5	Get a STRATEGIC VIEW of Markets	93
	What's in a Strategic View?	94
	Estimating Market Profit Pool Values	100
	Strategic Fit: What It Takes to Play	123
	Synthesizing Your Strategic View	130
	Your Summarized Strategic View	130
CHAPTER 6	Define a Path That Exploits REAL OPPORTUNITIES	133
	Business Value and Making Strategic Choices	134
	Task 1: List and Define Opportunities	140
	Task 2: Flesh Out and Map Opportunities	143
	Task 3: Characterize Outcomes	151
	Task 4: Evaluate the Economics	160
	Task 5: Define the Path Forward	167
	Task 6: Plan and Execute	175
	Return on Effort	176
PART III	**SUSTAINING VALUE GROWTH**	177
CHAPTER 7	Corporate Renewal and New Business Management With *Jim McCreary*	179
	How Is Sustained Value Growth Achieved?	180

	Why Sustaining High Value Growth Is Such a Challenge	181
	Five Basic Rules for Sustaining High Value Growth	183
	It *Is* Possible to Sustain High Value Growth Performance	187
	Reconfiguring New Business Development to Deliver Value Growth and Corporate Renewal	190
	In Conclusion...	206
CHAPTER 8	Value-Maximizing the Existing Business	207
	Business Specialization	208
	Focusing on Your Sources of Value	212
	Extending Your Sources of Value	219
Appendix A	***Unwinding, Line Item by Line Item***	223
	Revenue	223
	Expenses	226
	Capital Investments and Charges	232
Appendix B	***The Monte Carlo Simulation***	237
	What Problem Does It Solve?	237
	What Does It Do?	238
	What Do You Have to Do to Use It?	238
Appendix C	***Using Real Options***	
	The Binomial Lattice Approach	239
	What the Binomial Lattice Does	240
	How the Binomial Lattice Works	241
	Beyond This Example	247

Bibliography 249

Index 251

List of Examples

EXAMPLE 5.1	A Traditional Strategic View	95
EXAMPLE 5.2	Market Profit Pool Values	97
EXAMPLE 5.3	Pioneer Market Opportunities	99
EXAMPLE 5.4	Historical Market Inflexion Events	103
EXAMPLE 5.5	Future Market Inflexion Events	105
EXAMPLE 5.6	Making Quantitative Forecasts	107
EXAMPLE 5.7	Completed Demand Forecast	109
EXAMPLE 5.8	Competitive Environment Assessment	113
EXAMPLE 5.9	MIE Sequencing and Timing Summary	115
EXAMPLE 5.10	Estimating Future Cash Flow	117
EXAMPLE 5.11	Uncertainty in Market Profit Pools	118
EXAMPLE 5.12	Profiling Market Value Uncertainty	120
EXAMPLE 5.13	Forecast Events Summary	122
EXAMPLE 5.14	Success Requirements: Offering	125
EXAMPLE 5.15	Success Requirements: Brand	126
EXAMPLE 5.16	Success Requirements: Distribution	128
EXAMPLE 5.17	Success Requirements: Operations/Suppliers	129
EXAMPLE 5.18	Summary Strategic View	131
EXAMPLE 6.1	Introducing Samsung's Current Situation	139
EXAMPLE 6.2	Listing Market Strategy Opportunities	141
EXAMPLE 6.3	Example Outcomes by Branch/Variant	154
EXAMPLE 6.4	Example Capital Investments Needs	155
EXAMPLE 6.5	Summary of Samsung's Opportunities	168

Acknowledgments

Although as the author I may have spent the most hours writing this book, intellectual contribution and insight are really the most appropriate measures of value-add. Using those measures, the following deserve great tribute:

Jim McCreary, an old friend and colleague from my days at Marakon Associates. Beyond the great amount of shareholder value creation 'technology' that Jim has imparted to me over the years, to a large extent, this book was a night job for him for many months also.

David Schneider, Eric Peterson, and Bill Eichhorn, all business strategy consulting partners from PricewaterhouseCoopers. Each in his own way played a powerful role in freeing me from the numbers that often consume anyone who tries to drive shareholder value.

Consulting colleagues, who have always been there to show the way, as well as point out issues and identify mistakes (including in drafting this book!): John Almieda, Saul Berman, Chris Fox, Scott Gillis, Mike Hecht, Jeff Kelly, Leslie Kues, Larry Leisure, Spencer Lin, Steve Malloy, Tom McKay, Graham Wik, and many others.

Clients, without whom there would be little to pass on at all; most notably AT&T, Blue Cross Blue Shield, BP/Amoco, Boots, Caremark, Diageo, Encyclopedia Britannica, Hewlett-Packard, IBM, Liberty, Nordstrom, PEPCO, Samsung, Shaklee/Harry & David, and a wide array of mid-cap and early-stage businesses.

The University of Chicago faculty. Those who taught me and with whom I have worked—Gary Becker, Robert Gertner, Steven Kaplan, Marc Knez, Milind Lele, Marvin Zonis, to name a few; and those whose intellectual capital this book draws on extensively: Fischer Black, Milton Friedman, Harry Markowitz, Merton Miller, and Myron Scholes.

Finally, my wife Janet and son Miles, who have put up with me as I have attended to my work life over the years. They have carried the true burden along the way, including the unsociable hours, my impatience and intolerance, and my generally high level of distraction. I am both thankful to them and humbled by their patience.

About the Author

Leveraging market strategy to rapidly boost cash flow and business value has become a life's work for Rory. Since the 1980s he has helped a wide range of clients use this technique to quickly deliver billions of dollars in additional cash flow and shareholder value.

Rory co-founded Business Intelligence Associates with two partners in 2002, a management consultancy explicitly focused on value-driven market strategies. Previously, he was a partner in PricewaterhouseCoopers' (PwC) strategy consulting business, where he led the practice in shareholder value consulting in the United States. Before joining PwC, Rory was with consultants Marakon Associates, and prior to that, he held senior positions with Thorn EMI and Thomson Consumer Electronics in Europe.

Rory earned his MBA in strategy and finance from the University of Chicago, and his BSc in electronic engineering from the City University in London. He has published many papers and speaks regularly on shareholder value creation and technology markets.

V. Rory Jones, BSc, MBA
Partner, Business Intelligence Associates LLC

Introduction

Ever had that feeling you've got a great business, but that it's not delivering the results it really deserves? More likely than not, you *do* have a great business—the problem is simply that all its strengths are not being directed toward the right opportunities, or that those opportunities are not being properly exploited.

This book provides a new and refreshing approach to creating shareholder value and driving share price performance. As a business leader, a key aspect of your modus operandi is the need to get to the bottom line as quickly and efficiently as possible; issues must be prioritized, as must be the resources marshaled to address each of them—even your own time. We have written this book in a highly prioritized and nontechnical manner to deliver the key messages on how to drive shareholder value performance. The result is a very practical path for business leaders to travel, one that rapidly creates substantial amounts of shareholder value and maintains that higher level of value-creation performance over time.

Rapidly Create Lots of Shareholder Value

As we shall see, this tall order can be achieved by focusing on, and adopting a new approach to, market strategy, a component of business strategy that has the greatest impact on the intrinsic value of a business—by several orders of magnitude. Specifically, we take a long-term, economically oriented view of market strategy, one that is centered on *cash-based* profit pools. With this approach, and with an integration of marketing and finance skills, your organization can rapidly deliver large, previously untapped sources of cash flow.

In fact, we have found this approach is intuitively very appealing to business leaders and shareholders alike. Why, one might wonder, is it not already a part of management doctrine? The answer to this is mostly due to management's inability to recognize two major issues and opportunities:

1. Most businesses have a very poor vision of their own *internal* profit pools, for two reasons.
   a. The right information is simply not available. Most businesses do not have usefully granular views of profitability by customer, channel, offering, or geography. What information does exist is grossly insufficient in granularity and is not well integrated with other performance measures.
   b. The accounting profession, through generally accepted accounting principles (GAAP), heavily distorts the profit picture: Large noncash and other adjustments, poor expense allocations, and the exclusion of substantive costs make GAAP-based measures of profit essentially unusable for management purposes, and in many cases they are actually misleading.
2. Management is not prioritizing opportunities based on the *market's* potential to deliver economic returns, again for two reasons.
   a. Management does not explicitly orient investment decisions around market long-term profit potential.
   b. Market profitability information is not readily available. Market profitability is dependent on understanding the profitability achieved by competitors, customer economics, and alternative business models that may be adopted to serve customers. This is complicated by the need to obtain future views. Businesses typically expend very little effort to cultivate this forward-looking, economically based view of the market and its opportunities.

Almost all businesses are organized in functional silos—a finance group, a separate marketing group, and many other functional groups—a structure that is mostly driven by the skills needs of day-to-day operations. As a consequence, however, there tend to be few cross-skills in each silo; finance recruits and trains accountants, while marketing develops product managers (for the most part). Insightful dissection of markets in order to understand long-term cash profitability requires a blend of both skills—cutting through GAAP is itself a challenge, to say nothing of properly segmenting a market in an actionable and measurable way. Layered on top are other familiar inhibitors: differing motives (GAAP/financial reporting in finance, revenue in marketing), differing incentives, turf stakes, and other issues—all driving a separation between marketing and finance.

The net result? Businesses are not able to take a long-term, economic view of their market choices and positioning.

This one weakness opens the door for savvy competitors to gain superior economic strength and win—in the product markets first, and then in the capital markets. This book points out these high-value issues and opportunities, illustrates them, and outlines how to address them.

We advocate an approach to market strategy that stems from an integrated set of tested intellectual capital on the topic. We have packaged it all in a relatively simple and easy-to-communicate notion—that of inviting business leaders to recognize, focus on, and exploit *profit pools*.

Who Are You?

Long-term cash flow and business value is a subject very close to the hearts (and wallets) of C-suite managers in most complex businesses. As a result, our primary audience is C-suite management and those aspiring to join them. As agents of shareholders, you have the awesome responsibility of maximizing the shareholder value creation capability of the business you have been entrusted with. In short, we outline what the right opportunities are, how to find them, and how to fully leverage their potential.

In serving C-suite managers we also hope to help shareholders, their advocates (such as boards, etc.), and debt holders gain a greater understanding of business economics and market management, and the interaction between the two. We hope that, armed with this understanding, they will be more focused in their demands for information, and become better informed as they provide guidance to C-suite managers.

Policy makers and information industry vendors will also gain from an improved picture of what business leaders and others need from their reporting systems. Policy makers need an improved picture of the information needs of business leaders; state and federal lawmakers' understanding of business information needs is currently grounded in GAAP, which, as this book reveals, is tremendously difficult and inefficient to use as an effective basis for business decisions. Information vendors (particularly enterprise resource planning and business process software providers) also need greater insight into the specific information needs of C-level managers, so they can enhance the utility (and attractiveness) of their offering.

Other professionals (accountants, consultants, academics, and the like) will also get an improved picture of the economic and other issues involved in market strategy, and what business leaders need from their reporting systems; they need to understand the limitations and shortcomings of the accounting/information systems they utilize and oversee. As a result they will also be better positioned to advise clients on business issues and information systems.

The Path We'll Take You On

In recognition of your need to rapidly get to the bottom line, we have organized this work to efficiently deliver highly usable management notions and practical steps.

Part One sets out the premise that a profit pool–driven market strategy provides leaders in most businesses with a shortcut to rapidly create shareholder value—and to sustain higher levels of value creation over time. Chapter 1 sets out the basics, briefly addressing what the various kinds of business value are, and outlining the dominating impact of market strategy on value. Chapter 2 introduces profit pools, examines them and their characteristics at a high level, and shows how they can be applied to market strategy with great effect. Lastly, in Chapter 3, we identify some of the issues management has in seeing profit pools (both internal and market profit pools), and provide insights on why these issues exist and how they might be dealt with.

Part Two outlines a path management can adopt to secure results rapidly and efficiently. Chapter 4 advocates starting with a review of internal profit pools to identify areas for immediate action, and to identify opportunities and issues for further consideration as the process unfolds. Chapter 5 takes an external perspective—gathering a fact base of information on existing and potential markets, and leveraging that fact base to put together a strategic view of those markets (including a view of market profit pools). Chapter 6 pulls this strategic view together with traditional and advanced market strategy and economic analysis tools to chart a path forward for the business. It also sets out how to deal with the uncertainties involved, such that the business is able to chart the value-maximizing path—no matter how the uncertainties actually unfold.

Finally, Part Three provides tips and insights needed for sustained higher performance in value creation. Chapter 7 discusses the importance and challenges of corporate renewal, and outlines best practices the new business development organization can adopt. Chapter 8 reviews the impact of organizational configuration on value creation, and sets out breakthrough structures that help focus the organization and maximize value.

In short, you will walk away with a concise set of insights and management approaches—highly focused on maximizing the value of your business, while prioritized to make good use of your time.

PART I

The Shortcut to High Performance

In Part One we set the field for management action by recasting the fundamentals of shareholder value creation in an understandable and practical light. This action orientation is achieved by focusing on the linkages between creating value and those things that management can use to drive that value. This is done in three easy-to-digest chapters:

- Chapter 1 starts with a quick review of the basic tenets of business management. All managers (not just business leaders) have the responsibility to maximize shareholder returns, and it is all but universally accepted that the way to achieve that is to maximize long-term cash flow and intrinsic value. The secret to doing this massively and quickly is to focus on market strategy.
- Chapter 2 runs with this last point on the dominating impact of market strategy and focuses on the relationship it has with business economics. The underpinning and intermediary notion is that of *profit pools*, a new view of markets and performance that includes an assessment of economic attractiveness in addition to other, perhaps more traditional, views.
- Chapter 3 closes this part of the book by taking a look at why today's business leaders aren't already acting to drive shareholder value in the way we suggest, despite the fact that there is such a clear duty to do so and that today's managers are well trained and solidly experienced. In short, it turns out that information visibility is very poor in today's business, due to existing accounting standards and hopelessly poor software systems, and organizations are traditionally structured in a way that divides information, time-perspectives, and responsibilities at just the wrong points.

CHAPTER 1

So You Want a High-Performing Business?

Who do you think of when asked for examples of high-performing companies? What is a high-performing company? These questions seem to have become difficult to answer as business management and our economies have become more complex. With that said, the answer is as simple today as it was in the industrial revolution, even back in ancient times:

> *Businesses and their leaders* must be *evaluated based on their ability to deliver financial returns to investors.*

We need to be unequivocal in asserting this viewpoint; it is the cornerstone of all the insights, tips, and even philosophical outlook that you will read in this book. It is true that there are other possible objectives for businesses, but for most, this is the overriding reason for their existence. Certainly for public companies, management has this one fiduciary responsibility (in addition to certain limitations and guides, such as operating in accordance with the law and other ethical obligations). The exceptions may only exist in privately owned businesses, where owners *might* decide to operate toward one or more other objectives—for example, a physicians' practice, where there may be a number of philanthropic or other motives that exist among the ownership group. Even here, though, it is unlikely that investor returns is not one of the principal objectives.

Deliver Great Returns and the Rest Will Maximize

Investors and business managers are in business to make money, and they should not be shy about it. In fact, one of the most socially compelling ideas about maximizing investor returns is that it comes with superior performance in all other areas—in product markets, in employment markets, in supply markets, in addition to the capital markets themselves. Notably, and conversely, success in those noninvestor areas drives investor returns. The system is optimized, such that noninvestor areas are all maximized, only as long as the overriding goal is to maximize investor returns.

Today, most people call this view of business performance "managing for shareholder returns" or "value," referring to the equity investors (shareholders) in the business. We discuss this singling out of equity investors, in contrast to debt holders and other investors, in the following section. The companies that lead the intuitive list of high-performing businesses of all time are the ones that have delivered on their ability to continually increase the value of their shareholders' equity; GE, IBM, Microsoft, and a multitude of others. Further, the intuitive list of the fallen are also notable for the reversal in their fortunes for shareholder returns: AT&T (until it was bought by SBC and the name was assumed by the new entity), General Motors, Kodak, Xerox, and others.

This book is premised on the understanding that you, as a business leader, recognize your obligation to maximize shareholder returns, and that you believe that doing so results in optimized performance in all aspects of the business in your industry area—from performance in the various product markets, to staff pay and satisfaction, to customer value and satisfaction, and elsewhere. If you do not subscribe to this basic tenet, this book is not for you.

Cash Became Emperor

Cash became king in the 1970s, when Alfred Rappaport, building on work at the University of Chicago, published his theory that the market value of a business could be reliably predicted using a technique known today as *discounted cash flow* (DCF). The technique begins by estimating a business's cash profits in future years (called *free cash flow*, or simply *cash flow*), then discounting each year's cash flow to its value today, and simply summing up these discounted values.

We do not review the subject of cash flow and business valuation in this book; there have been many very good works on that subject, most notably *Valuation* by McKinsey & Company, Inc., Tim Koller, Mark Goedhart, and David Wessels (Wiley & Sons, 2005, 4th ed.). In this book we aim to serve the needs of business leaders rather than finance practitioners. Nevertheless, we must recognize the basics. Those already familiar with the principals of DCF valuation and intrinsic value may want to skip the next few pages.

So You Want a High-Performing Business?

In essence, cash flow simply refers to the *cash* profits that the business is left with in a given period. This is in contrast to accounting/GAAP-based profits, which have been subjected to much manipulation by the accounting profession (Chapter 3 discusses problems this manipulation causes and how management must get around them). Since most people are familiar with GAAP terminology and statements, Figure 1.1 sets out what comprises cash flow at a high level by outlining the key steps needed to unwind a GAAP income statement. Figure 1.2 shows the basic technique of taking each future year's estimated cash flow, discounting it to get its value today, and estimating the intrinsic value of that cash flow stream (that is, how much someone should be willing to pay for it).

Interestingly, it is the proverbial mom-and-pop business that most readily recognizes cash profitability and the need to measure performance by it. The larger and more complex the business becomes, the more difficult it seems to become to understand the need for, and to determine, cash profits, particularly at any useful level. These difficulties are driven in larger complex businesses by the compounding effect of regulations, operational

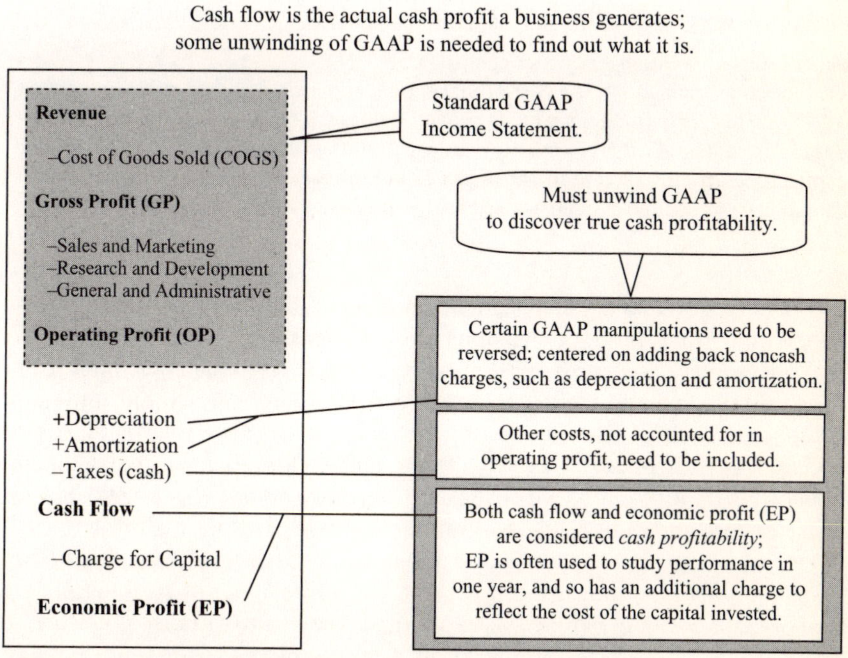

Cash flow is the actual cash profit a business generates; some unwinding of GAAP is needed to find out what it is.

Revenue
−Cost of Goods Sold (COGS)
Gross Profit (GP)
−Sales and Marketing
−Research and Development
−General and Administrative
Operating Profit (OP)

+Depreciation
+Amortization
−Taxes (cash)
Cash Flow

−Charge for Capital
Economic Profit (EP)

Standard GAAP Income Statement.

Must unwind GAAP to discover true cash profitability.

Certain GAAP manipulations need to be reversed; centered on adding back noncash charges, such as depreciation and amortization.

Other costs, not accounted for in operating profit, need to be included.

Both cash flow and economic profit (EP) are considered *cash profitability*; EP is often used to study performance in one year, and so has an additional charge to reflect the cost of the capital invested.

FIGURE 1.1 What Is Cash Flow?
Source: Business Intelligence Associates LLC.

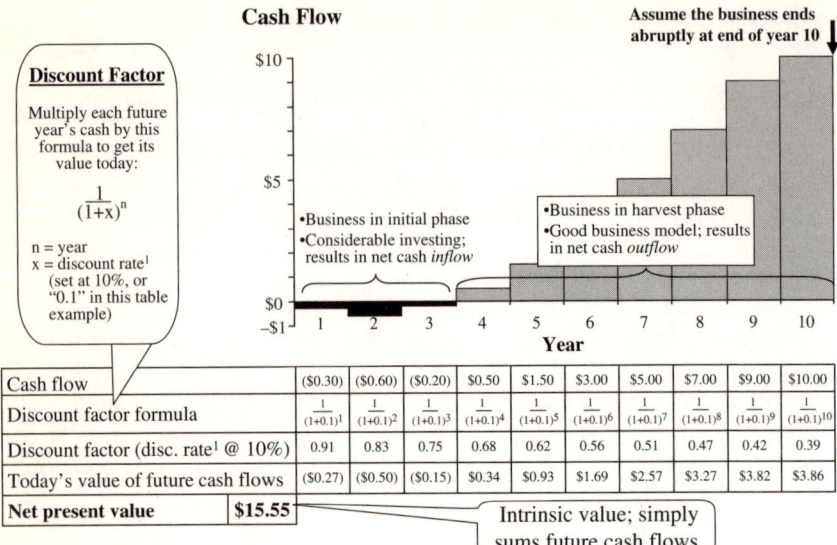

FIGURE 1.2 What Is Present Value of Future Cash Flows?
Source: Business Intelligence Associates LLC.
[1] The discount rate equals the cost of that capital and is basically its opportunity cost. All capital has its own rate, set by its provider; it typically varies by type (the rate for debt is usually lower than for equity), industry, and other risk factors. Where several capital types are invested in the business, as in the case of enterprise or business valuations, a weighted average is used as the discount rate.

complexity, and management's intellectual separation from cash profitability (since individuals and organizations tend to specialize).

The related sidebar discussion outlines the relationships between business value (sometimes called enterprise value), shareholder value, and debt value, and each of their associated cash flows. Because this book is not concerned with financial strategy (how much debt to have, what equity structure to adopt, etc.), we focus on cash flow *before* it is parsed out to shareholders and debt holders—in other words, *operating* cash flow.

Consequently, throughout the remainder of this book, the term *cash flow* refers to operating cash flow, and the term *business value* refers to the operating value of the business. *Cash-based profitability* collectively refers to cash flow or economic profit (per Figure 1.1, economic profit is simply cash flow with a further charge for the cost of capital invested in that business).

Relationships between Business, Enterprise, Shareholder, and Debt Cash Flows and Values

Businesses generate three types of cash flow, and each stream of cash flow has its own value. Operating cash flow is the cash a business throws off to both shareholders and debt holders, and its present value represents the warranted value of the entire business (commonly known as the *operating value* or *enterprise value*). Shareholder cash flow goes to shareholders, and its present value represents the warranted value of the business's equity (known as *shareholder value*, used to value each share). Interest goes to debt holders, and its present value represents the warranted value of the business's debt.

Naturally, each cash flow type has its own expected rate of return, used as its discount factor in valuations. Shareholder cash flows use the shareholder expected rate of return (k), and debt holder cash flows use the debt's interest rate (i); these are weight-averaged together to create the *weighted average cost of capital* (WACC), which is used to discount operating cash flow to determine business value.

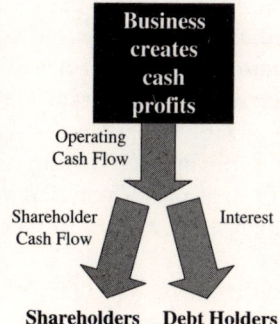

Type of Cash Flow	Who Gets Cash Flow	Value of Cash Flow	Cash Flow Discount Rate
Operating cash flow	Both investor types	Operating value	Weighted average cost of capital (WACC)
Shareholder cash flow	Shareholders	Shareholder value	Shareholder expected rate of return
Interest	Debt holders	Debt value	Interest rate

Source: Business Intelligence Associates LLC.

Look After Intrinsic Value, and Market Values Will Look After Themselves

It is worth noting that Rappaport's perspective on business value is now almost universally accepted by economists. Today, most think of Rappaport's valuation result as the *intrinsic* value of a business. This is not the same as market value, which is based on the price at which investors actually buy and sell the business's shares or debt or other investment instruments. These market values are subject to capital market volatility arising from imperfect information, and macroeconomic and other near-term market factors.

This volatility and the factors that drive it result in a difference between market and intrinsic value at any point in time, though over the long run these values track each other very closely (we will see evidence for this later). Intrinsic value, however, is an immediately available and tangible connection between operational performance and business value, and thus is an invaluable tool for business leaders to forecast the impact of decisions. It is interesting to note that before cash flow, quarterly earnings per share (EPS) growth was deemed the best connection between performance and value, and business leaders gained very poor reputations for short-term decision making as they managed business operations toward EPS growth each quarter. That has now changed as financial reporting increasingly supplements GAAP measures of profit and includes cashlike profit measures, such as earnings before interest, taxes, depreciation, and amortization (EBITDA).

The Elevation to Emperor

Cash has been elevated from king to emperor over the course of the past 10 years. Simply put, its relationship with value has been recognized to the point where most investments are now oriented around cash flow expectations and their related valuations. We can see this in the fit between Rappaport's approach to predicted value and the actual valuations found in the liquid investment markets (and increasingly in private transactions as well); that fit has tightened considerably. The R^2 (a measure of correlation fit) in Rappaport's analysis was 0.71, and in our analysis in 2004 we found that it was 0.88 (see Figure 1.3).

What happened in the intervening period to heighten this fit? Well, investors have become increasingly sophisticated in their valuation techniques and have been adopting the DCF valuation approach. Control of investment capital has shifted from individuals to major institutions, including investment funds, investment banks, and other professional entities. The extent of this shift is shown in Figure 1.4; in 1956 only one-tenth of U.S. equity funds were controlled by institutions, but by 1996, this had risen to fully one-half of all U.S. equity funds. These institutional entities have the scale to apply sophisticated tools and skills (such as DCF valuations) to their capital deployment decisions, and competition between them has become more acute as their own performance is more tightly measured and scrutinized. Furthermore, capital markets have become more liquid, and individual investors are freer to choose and move capital between investment vehicles.

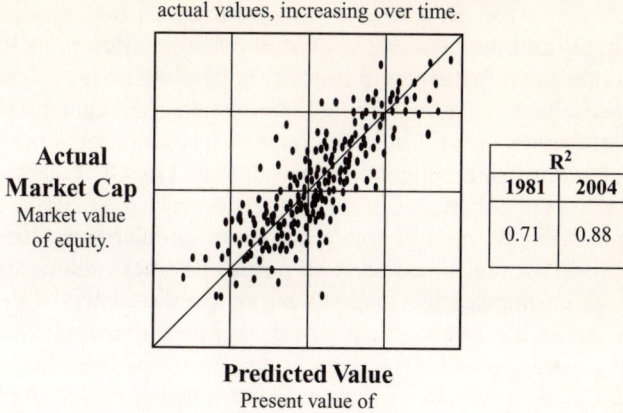

FIGURE 1.3 Fit between Predicted and Actual Equity Values

Source: Alfred Rappaport, *Creating Shareholder Value: The New Standard for Business Performance* (New York: Free Press, 1986); Business Intelligence Associates LLC.

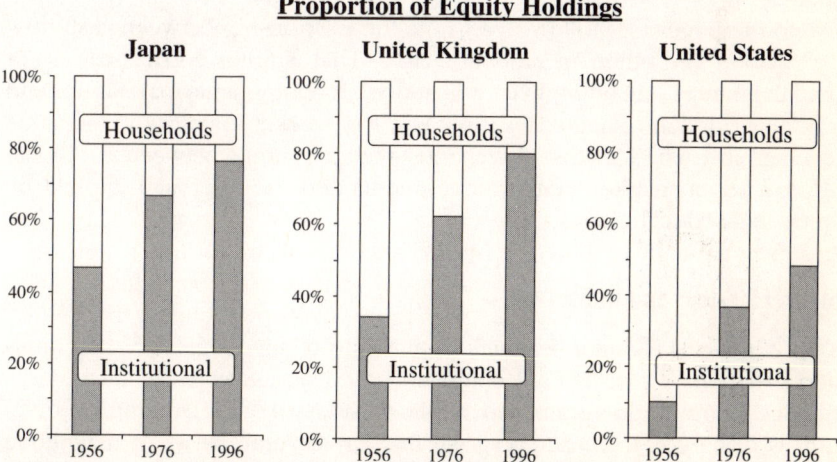

FIGURE 1.4 The Shift in Control of Investment Funds to Institutions

Source: Japanese Ministry for Finance and the National Conference for Stock Exchanges, U.K. Central Statistics Office, U.S. Federal Reserve.

In addition, the estimation of future cash flow has itself become more accurate. Large public companies, in particular, are increasingly helping investors cut through standard accounting reporting schemes, such as GAAP in the United States, to understand historical cash flow by reporting EBITDA and related results. Market forecasting has also become much more accurate as professional investors and business leaders recognize its importance and are more focused on it, driving an entire industry of product market analysts and information collection.

The net effect of these changes has been circular. Investors increasingly use expected future cash flow to predict business value, and market valuations increasingly reflect the valuations predicted by DCF valuation techniques. All of this comes together to put pressure on business leaders to focus on generating cash flow in the long term. Now, with both investors and business leaders switched on to the importance of measuring and managing toward cash-based profitability, cash rules the capitalist empire.

The question for today's business leader is, "What can be done to drive future cash flow?"

Market Strategy Is the 80:20 Rule of Cash Flow

This is where the proverbial rubber hits the road for business leaders interested in maximizing business value. The fact is that no other aspect of business strategy has a greater impact on future cash flow than market strategy.

In the pages that follow, we gauge the relationship between cash flow and market and other operational factors. That is followed by a review of market strategy, including what it is and what components make it up, and a framework that characterizes three levels of market strategy and the value leverage in each. We close the chapter with a contrast between traditional approaches to market strategy investments and the approach implied by value-focused techniques.

Market Strategy and Impact

Take a look at Figure 1.5, which depicts the relative impact of key operational factors on cash flow (compiled based on a composite of the economics of 50 randomly chosen public businesses). The striking observation is that two factors impact cash flow by several orders of magnitude more than the others; and those two—unit sales and price, called *top-line* factors—are almost entirely governed by market strategy.

The power of these two top-line factors makes intuitive sense. All other things being equal, an absolute increase in price goes almost directly to the

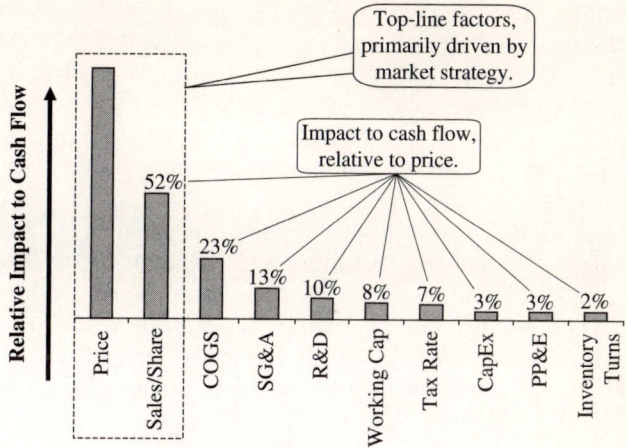

FIGURE 1.5 Relative Impact of Key Business Economics Factors on Cash Flow
Source: Business Intelligence Associates LLC.

bottom line—in cash. As more of those profitable (or unprofitable) units are sold, it adds (or removes) additional profits directly.

We formally define market strategy as it is used in this book in the next subsection. But even without that definition, it is obvious that the more competitive the offer is, and the more relative value it delivers to customers, the more likely it is that price can be set higher. Those very same drivers also have a direct bearing on unit sales. In existing lines of business, market strategy is a question of crafting actions and approaches to the market that drive increases in unit sales and price, and balancing the two to optimize results.

Furthermore, market strategy also has much greater scope to make large, discrete changes in the business and its economics than do other areas of business strategy (such as operational strategy, financial strategy, or other internal viewpoints and planning perspectives). For example, it may bring the business into totally new areas, each bringing with them entirely new streams of cash flow, whereas other more internal and functional strategies are limited to dealing within existing business areas, and the scope of the cash flow that they can influence is limited to some portion of those existing streams.

The implications of the high-leverage relationship between future cash flow and market strategy are dramatic. In terms of returns on invested resources, business leaders get considerably more bang for the buck from mapping out a savvy market strategy than from all other strategizing combined. This is not to say that other areas of business strategy should be neglected or abandoned—they obviously shouldn't be. However, recognizing the relative impact of market strategy is a very useful input for business leaders as they deploy their most valuable resources—their own time and their investors' capital.

In fact, to a large extent it isn't possible to separate market strategy from internally focused decisions and strategies. Famously, Dell's operations strategy dramatically reduces production costs, contributing substantially to cash flow, while also enabling its market strategy by delivering a unique market offering: built-to-order PCs delivered to customers in just a couple of days. With that said, the market leads the way in defining how any business will compete. If the business isn't substantially market-driven, it isn't likely to be serving the value-maximization agenda.

So What Is Market Strategy?

A powerful and useful by-product of having one well-defined business objective (such as maximizing value) is that it brings focus. In turn, this brings a need for business managers to be precise, clear, and thoughtful in order to achieve that objective (in contrast to days gone by, when business leaders of complex organizations would boast how they used their insightful intuition as the basis for business decision making). A key first step is to figure out what to be precise, clear, and thoughtful *about*. This leads us to market strategy—let's have a look at a useful way of thinking about it.

MARKET STRATEGY DEFINED Market strategy is often confused with marke*ting* strategy, which is an immediate, battle plan–like approach to the existing market, addressing merchandising, advertising, messaging, and the like. Market strategy is very different. Working with higher-level options and using a longer-term view, it is defined as follows:

> *A plan that sets out which market areas the business will participate in, and how it will compete in those market areas, in order to achieve a well-defined (set of) business objective(s).*

The two principle components of market strategy are outlined in Figure 1.6. The first, market targeting and participation, sets out *where* the business will compete—specifying which market areas the business will

Market strategy—a plan setting out:
- Which market areas the business will target and participate in.
- How it will compete in each area, in terms of differentiation, price, and economics.

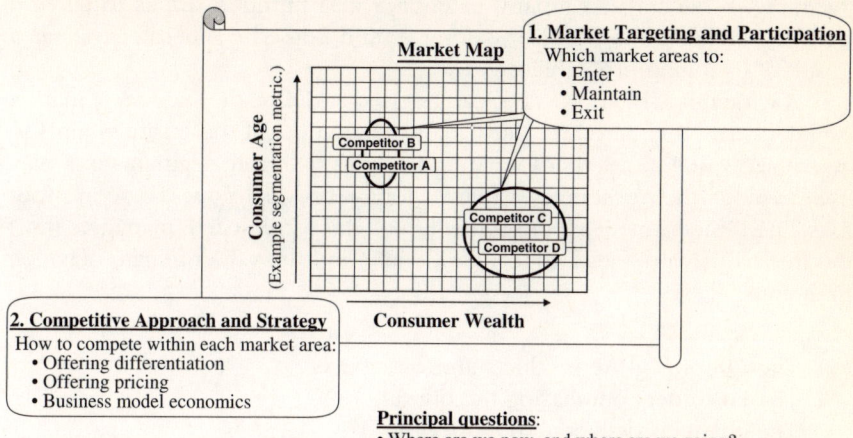

FIGURE 1.6 Key Aspects of Market Strategy
Source: Business Intelligence Associates LLC.

enter and the route it will take, which market areas the business will exit, and in which market areas the business will maintain its presence.

The second component, competitive approach and strategy, sets out *how* the business will compete in its chosen market areas, specifying what the business will deliver in the three key areas of market competition: how the offering will be differentiated, at what price it will be offered, and what the business model and its economics will look like.

An advanced discussion of how to use market strategy to drive business value is the primary topic of Chapter 6. However, we introduce some key notions of market strategy here to illustrate their impact on and relationship with long-term cash flows.

Market Targeting and Participation At a macro level, market participation decisions are exemplified by IBM's decision in the early 1990s to exit most of its hardware businesses and to orient itself around services. At the time, most parts of IBM's hardware business were an increasing profit drain, while services were seen as a relatively new phenomenon with high growth and profitability prospects. This growth in demand for services was largely driven by increasingly complex information systems in large and small businesses.

In making the shift, IBM was moving to an entirely new sector, and in many ways was (and still is) defining those new areas as it proceeded. Most market entry/exit decisions are, however, at a much more micro level—for example, a beverage company extending into nutrition drinks to serve a growing senior population, or exiting certain bottled water categories as a result of changing profitability.

A wide range of approaches can be used to define the borders of market segments to be targeted for participation; however, if the business aims to maximize value, borderlines have to be set to delineate segments in a way that exploits their potential to deliver long-term cash flow. There are four baseline dimensions used to segment markets; within each, managers must be free to use any measure to first identify and then discriminate between segments:

1. The offerings—the products and/or services.
2. The customers purchasing the offering.
3. The channels delivering the offering.
4. The geography in which the offering is transacted.

In fact, the way markets are segmented has a tremendous impact on how the business thinks about the market and how much value it is able to create as a result. Among other things, the carving up of markets needs to be based on the behavior of customers, addressing the various groups, and being able to measure the results in terms of offering and pricing.

Have you ever wondered how it is possible that the price of your airline ticket can be four or five times that of the person you're sitting next to? The answer is that you are a business traveler and can afford more. The airline has used time—that is, short notice to departure—to discriminate between you and the family of four next to you who are traveling on a shoestring.

Competitive Approach and Strategy Marketing professionals tend to focus the most here, albeit with a very near-term lens, making incremental adjustments to some baseline position. By contrast, at the market strategy level we are interested in the strategic and long-term baseline positioning itself—concerned with differentiation and pricing *at the highest level*, and the associated economics.

Differentiation needs to be discrete and sustainably separated from competitors. Two good examples of this are Sony's historical position as first to market with usable technologies, and Samsung's recent repositioning as a hip brand of technology gear. These types of differentiation carry with them the chance to drive relatively higher pricing, though clearly low pricing can itself be a point of differentiation with customers.

The business model delivering this differentiation determines the economics that can be achieved, and so is also a primary area of concern in competitiveness and market strategy. Ultimately, the level of profitability that can be achieved determines the attractiveness of that business and our level of interest in it. Note how we deliberately separate business economics from pricing, which is decided by the market, and the share and unit sales that will be achieved as a result of customer demand elasticity. Southwest Airlines is a salient example of a business configured for an absolute minimum in costs, while it is priced only sufficiently below competitors to capture a full capacity of low-budget customers on its routes (taking some capacity from market competitors and bringing new customers into the market). Costs are operations-based, prices are market-based. In 2006, despite being the low-price player, Southwest has an equity value greater than that of all other U.S. airlines added together.

In every case there is an interrelationship between market targeting and competitive strategies. How can you deliver an offering to a market without the right operating model? In some cases this interrelationship is driven by operational issues, such as Pepsi's move into snacks with its acquisition of Lay's to take advantage of the market power and economics of Lay's' distribution system. Such interrelationships may also be driven by market advantage issues, as in that flexible production system used by Dell to allow it to rapidly deliver its built-to-order PCs.

In fact, interrelationships between market targeting and competitive strategies change over time as customer preferences and technologies change, altering the possibilities in exploiting synergies. At one time, technology companies found it necessary to possess most parts of the supply chain in-house, including semiconductor production, board assemblies, and so forth; and yet now most of these inputs are produced by external vendors. Those same original equipment manufacturers (OEMs) are now entering businesses that once seemed ridiculous, such as Sony's entrée into movies to bring entertainment content in-house.

Market Strategy and Value Leverage

So how much value can you get out of market strategy, anyway? While the answer to this is obviously situation-specific, the framework in Figure 1.7 is very useful for delineating three levels of value leverage. In it, management's options are separated out in two dimensions that are critically influential in driving economic returns: changes in markets served (both customers and channels), and changes in the game played (a *game* may be an offering or an approach to delivering it through the business and/or operating model).

Now, a business's options in both of these dimensions are (1) to remain where it is; (2) to enter a field that is new to it, though not to other

Market strategy has three levels of risk/reward profile.

Market
A customer set; consumers, businesses or channels with common needs and wants.

- The existing business: **A known quantity**
- Enhancements are limited in potential returns.

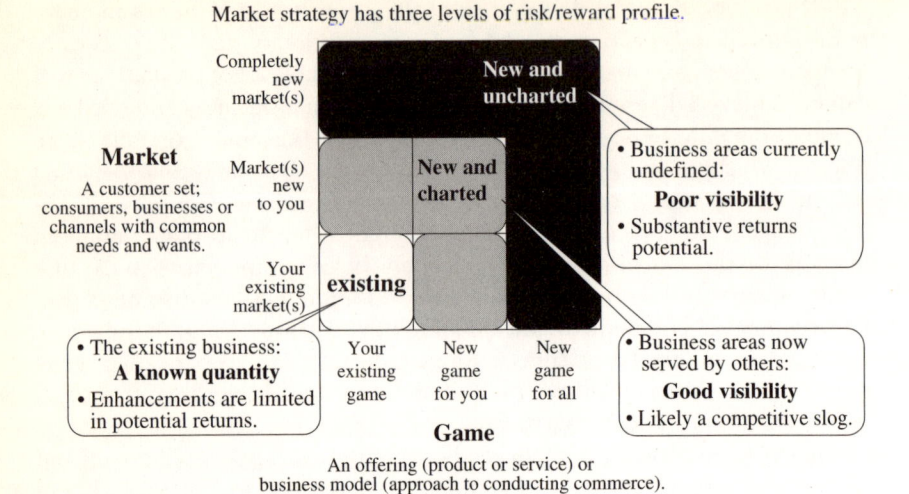

- Business areas currently undefined: **Poor visibility**
- Substantive returns potential.

- Business areas now served by others: **Good visibility**
- Likely a competitive slog.

	Your existing game	New game for you	New game for all
Completely new market(s)			New and uncharted
Market(s) new to you		New and charted	
Your existing market(s)	existing		

Game
An offering (product or service) or business model (approach to conducting commerce).

FIGURE 1.7 Levels of Market Strategy Leverage
Source: Business Intelligence Associates LLC.

competitors; or (3) to enter a field that is new to everyone, both itself and all other players. Let's have a look at each of these three levels.

1. *Existing.* Clearly, the most accessible level of market move is simply not to move—that is, to continue to do what you are currently doing, deploying an existing game in an existing market, perhaps just doing it better. Notably, we find that this is the area where most businesses focus the largest proportion of their market management efforts along with ongoing and investment capital. Unfortunately, this also happens to be the level of market strategy that has the least potential for economic returns, no matter how much is invested in it. It is limited to existing cash flow streams, and the opportunity to increase those streams is usually limited as a result of established and tight competitive pressures. In focusing on it so much, the business basically restricts itself to eking out small, incremental enhancements to business performance.
2. *New and charted.* This second level of market strategy is an increment to the existing business. In this case, the business takes the existing game into a new market/segment, or expands its servicing of an existing market/segment with a new game (offering or business model). Of course, it could do both, and move into a new market with a new game. Notably, since this level has already been charted by others, competitors already exist, together with an established competitive structure and

market regime, making it very hard for new entrants to extract significant incremental returns at all.
3. *New and uncharted.* This third level of market strategy refers to a business making some kind of move into completely uncharted areas. Little is known or established before entering these new markets and/or games; either there is low familiarity with customer needs, or the offering/business model has not been tried before, or both. Frequently, this level receives the least attention from business leaders, despite its potential to deliver returns that are orders of magnitude beyond the first two levels. As you can imagine, these returns are accompanied by elevated risks, a topic that is discussed in Chapter 6 along with approaches business leaders can adopt to heighten returns and mitigate risks.

In short, the third level almost always offers the most value-creation potential (unless the existing play is in an early, high-growth situation), and yet it typically receives comparatively trivial amounts of management time and effort. Business leaders interested in maximizing value would get good leverage from increasing the effort they and their subordinates devote to market strategy. They would probably get the most leverage if that increase was directed specifically at level 3 market strategy.

Throw Away the Old Playbook!

A couple of cautionary comments are due at this point. We find most businesses orient investments (capital, marketing expenditures, and management time) around revenue performance. Considerable emphasis is often placed on historic revenues, though some weight is given to positioning issues, such as share, top x positioning, and the like. One such example was a technology client we served several years ago. Figure 1.8 shows what we found when we matched their historic investments with their recent revenue results by offering. (This business offered a wide mix of technology-based products and services to business customers also in the technology sector).

The business's propensity to invest in large-revenue markets (the shaded part of the chart's columns represent the business's own revenues) is clear and obvious. This is a relatively common approach; almost applying the 80:20 rule, where 20 percent of offerings generate 80 percent of today's revenue—and so (mistakenly) deserve 80 percent of investments. As we shall see in Figure 1.9 and in the next chapter, there were other areas that better deserved both these capital and operational investments.

In fact, markets with the largest revenue opportunity very often do not offer the best long-term profit opportunity. Frequently, large-revenue markets have many players in them and profitability has declined; smaller

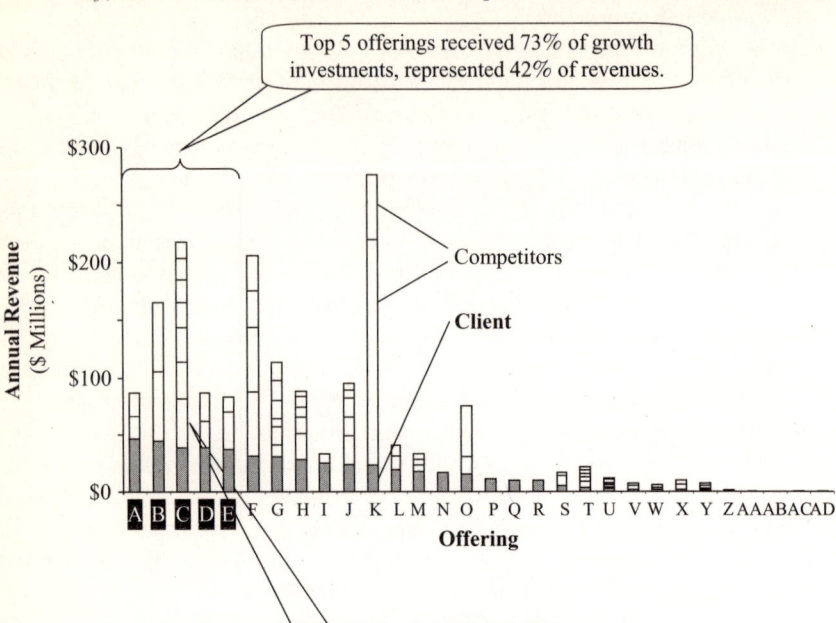

Today, most businesses still base investment priorities on revenue considerations.

> Top 5 offerings received 73% of growth investments, represented 42% of revenues.

> Competitors

> Client

> Some investing consideration given to market share position/potential.

FIGURE 1.8 Typical Investing Strategy

Source: Market research, Business Intelligence Associates LLC.

markets become more attractive. Remember how Southwest's equity capitalization was greater than all other U.S. airlines combined? Its focus on just positive-profit air routes yielded huge returns. There is a lot to be said for a targeting and participation strategy that simply avoids market areas that drain value.

Returning to our technology business example, we started our work with them by taking an alternative view, oriented around the business's internal cash-based profitability performance. In particular, we figured out the economic profit for each part of the business, and arrayed that profitability performance across all the capital invested in the business. The result is shown in Figure 1.9. Basically, the size of each shaded box is proportional to the economic profit produced by that part of the business. The striking insight revealed was that 40 percent of invested capital was not even earning its cost of capital; in fact, around 20 percent of invested capital was actually losing cash! Of the five offerings previously favored for growth investment resources, only one represented an attractive opportunity.

How should the business be investing its resources?

Economic Profit Margin
(EP/Invested Capital, or EROI)

> The 2 offerings receiving most investment actually contribute very little (4% of total EP).

> 2 of the top 5 offerings are actually draining cash, VALUE DESTRUCTION accelerates as they are grown.

> Only 1 of the top 5 offerings delivers substantive amounts of cash to the business.

Invested Capital ($ Millions)

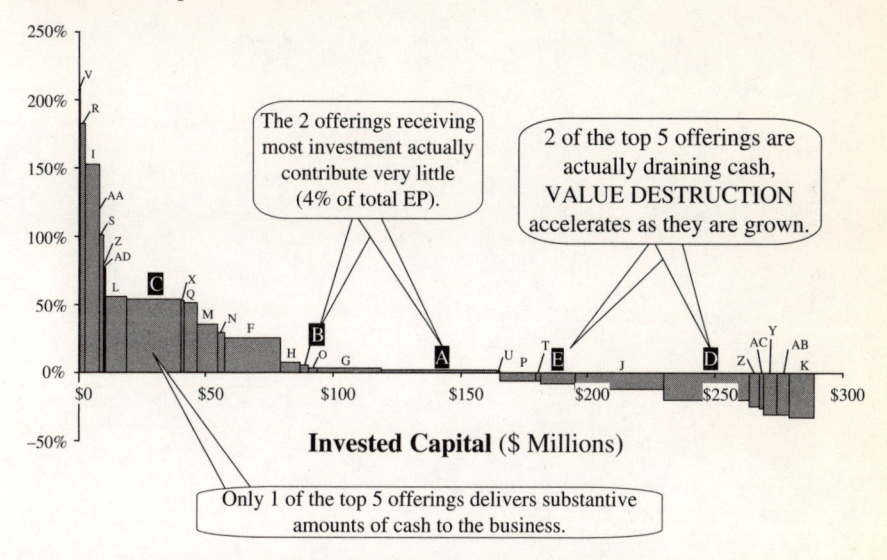

FIGURE 1.9 Reprioritization around Internal Cash-Based Profitability
Source: Company reports, Business Intelligence Associates LLC.

It must be reiterated that the view of the offering portfolio in Figure 1.9 is very limited: It is a single-period, historical, and internally focused view, and is oriented only around offerings; other views that need to be looked at include cash-based profitability by customer, channel, and geography. It is, however, an insightful first step to seeing how the business can be fine-tuned for superior returns. With this information, and information on interdependencies between the various offerings and markets, business leaders are in a far better position to make informed decisions on where to invest to grow profitably, and where to manage other lines of businesses to limit losses, at a minimum. How these tasks are accomplished is addressed in greater depth in Part Two.

CHAPTER 2

Profit Pools
Market Strategy on Steroids

If market strategy is the most powerful lever management has to impact cash flow generation—both positively *and* negatively—then large, deep profit pools need to be the beacons guiding market strategy for any business leader interested in maximizing shareholder value.

So what exactly is a profit pool? The definition is remarkably simple:

A profit pool is a portion of a market or business that delivers some sort of economic return.

Briefly, an attractive profit pool is some part of a market or business that offers a large amount of profit. A less attractive profit pool offers less profit, while an unattractive profit pool offers only net losses.

Market profit pools refer to the profit *generated by each market segment*; this profit is available to all competitors in those segments. Generally, market profit pools are considered in terms of a profit stream going into the future; that is, the profit expected from each market segment today and in the years ahead. *Internal* profit pools refer only to *the profits your business receives* from each segment. Internal profit pools can be defined to focus only on profit performance in a single period (such as this year) or on the profit stream your business is expected to receive over future years.

This chapter walks through the concept of profit pools and how they are used. We start with an outline of what makes a real profit pool, since there are several ways to define profit, and then we look at the role business operations and economics play in determining profit pool attractiveness. After that, we take a closer look at both internal and market profit pools, examining how they are used to boost performance and value.

What Makes a *Real* Profit Pool?

To be useful, profit pools must give business leaders an accurate view of value creation opportunities at hand. As we point out in Chapter 3, not only are there several definitions of profitability, but those profit measures defined using generally accepted accounting principles (GAAP) actually turn out to be highly misleading.

The GAAP-based measures of profit exclude swaths of costs and expenses, and are subject to the inappropriate charges of poor allocation methods and distorted accounting. In one of these distortions, depreciation of investments in plant and other fixed assets is artificially charged against profit; this investment capital is charged as an operating expense in small lumps over arbitrarily set time periods. In most cases, these time periods have very little to do with the life of the equipment they relate to, and their durations are actually guided by the tax code. Moreover, the approaches used by GAAP to allocate shared costs and expenses are, more often than not, totally unrelated to how those costs are consumed.

One thing GAAP does not do is charge profit for the capital that investors actually do have tied up in the business. This is a critical omission; investors sustain an opportunity cost for that capital (they could invest it elsewhere and get a return), and so the business needs to know what minimum profitability it must generate to justify its use of that capital. (Note: This charge for capital is only important in measuring profit performance in specific periods, such as a year; when looking across many periods, as in present value calculations, it is best dealt with differently and is usually not charged against cash flow.)

With these issues, profit pool attractiveness cannot be determined by GAAP-based profit measures. Real profit pool attractiveness can only be figured out using cash-based profit (that is, after unwinding GAAP) and must include a charge for capital invested.

Finally, the degree to which businesses can recognize opportunities is very dependent on how and where the boundaries are drawn to segment profit pools. Consequently, it is vitally important to investigate profit pools using several segmentation schemes, including offerings, customers, channels, geographies, and situation-specific factors.

For example, in a recent review of its internal profit pools, a pipe manufacturer segmented a range of steel valve models by offering, and observed very similar profitability across the board. When segmented by channel, however, the unattractiveness of the chain retailing channel became very clear and was far outweighed by the attractiveness of independents. Furthermore, the metric used in segmentation is also highly influential; the profitability profile of customer groups segmented by revenue size, for example, was very different from that of groups segmented by industry.

Profit Pools and Business Models

A profit pool cannot exist without an associated business model. Why? Because it is the economics of business itself that generates profits. Business models create value in product or service markets, and then translate that value into cash flow to the capital markets. We define the business model as follows:

The combined operational, market, and economic formula a business utilizes to create and sell its offerings and deliver financial returns.

From this definition we can see that a business model encompasses two high-level aspects of business:

- The *operating model*—the internal processes that, together, execute all tasks needed by the business, such as production, sales, human resources, finance, and others.
- The *commercial model*—incorporating the market value proposition (including offering differentiation, pricing, and others) and the economic model, the flow of cash through the business, arriving at profitability.

Take the corner grocer as an example—a focused and relatively simple business model. Operationally, goods arrive at the store and are unloaded, put into display shelves, and subsequently sold in small quantities. Commercially, the grocer adds value by providing the customer with a (nice) location to buy goods, and so is able to add a premium to the cost of the goods and pass the proceeds on to the storekeeper.

Now, a profit pool's attractiveness is as dependent on the characteristics of the business models delivering the offerings as it is on the characteristics of customers and demand. For instance, when there are several competitors in a market profit pool, each with different business models of differing profitability, the total profit available in that profit pool will change as market shares change. A similar result occurs with internal profit pools; when the business model serving a particular segment is altered, the profit from that segment will also change.

The intimate relationship between profit pools and the business models creating them is important, since business model changes can dramatically alter the nature of a profit pool. An insightful illustration of this relationship occurred in the late 1980s and 1990s, when Michael Dell suspended his studies at the University of Texas to focus on a small business he had going in his dorm, building PCs to order. The business was different from that of major PC vendors in that he didn't make PCs months in advance in standard configurations. His PCs were uniquely configured for each customer and reflected their needs and pricing elasticity much more closely and currently. They were also able to be priced lower, since they were made from components purchased now, not six to nine months ago (a critical capability given the huge annual declines in electronic component prices). Then, as now, Dell's business model was unique, one that returned several percentage points in profit margin above all other competitors

If, today, we define the PC market as a market profit pool within the computing sector, its value would be much greater with Dell than if Dell did not exist. This is because Dell sales dominate market share, and its business model returns high profitability. If it wasn't there, the market would return to comprising many similar cutthroat competitors, each with razor-thin margins, and the market profit pool would be very unattractive. Furthermore, if one or more competitors successfully copied Dell's business model, total market profits would dip dramatically then, too—since Dell's profitability would evaporate as more serious, price-based competition set in. To date, Dell investors appear to be betting this will not happen.

The business model is a critical consideration in interpreting profit pools. It deserves significant recognition and attention from business leaders as they digest opportunities, consider their options, and formulate market strategy.

So far, we have reviewed the fundamental concepts underlying profit pools, including how they are defined, what metrics can and cannot be used to measure them, and the role business models have in influencing their attractiveness. From here, we take a closer look at the two basic types—internal profit pools and market profit pools.

Internal Profit Pools

The term *internal profit pools* refers to cash-based profits generated by your own business only, in each of its various segments (the profitability of other players in the market is not addressed). Internal profit pools can be profiled in two ways:

1. With a focus on *current* profitability—that is, profitability in just the most recent period (perhaps profiling some history, also); and,
2. By plotting out cash flows expected in *future* periods.

For the moment we focus on the first of these, current internal profit pools. Since this view of profit performance is based entirely on current information from your own organization, it can be highly accurate and granular. As a result, it is able to unlock very useful insights on how to boost near-term cash flow. While it might be reasonably expected that a business is already extracting all the profits that it can from its existing markets, it turns out that this is not the case at all. Internal profit pool reviews are actually a surprisingly rich source of additional cash flow.

In fact, most businesses have a very limited knowledge of their own performance in extracting cash-based profits from markets. Four factors create this situation (Chapter 3 reviews these issues in greater depth, together with the steps management can take to address them):

1. GAAP distorts the real (cash-based) profit picture, as we have seen.
2. The right information is simply not readily available.
   - Not enough granularity, and very limited views by customer, channel, offering, or geography.
   - Poor/inaccurate expense allocations.
   - Limited competitor and partner information.
3. The right skills are not together at the right place.
4. Management does not explicitly focus on profit pools.

These forces come together with devastating effect. The lack of visibility causing a business not to focus on the good profit pools would be one thing, but the reality is it also causes the business to serve and grow areas where the profit pools are actually negative! The result is a cash flow drain and an opportunity cost for the capital deployed to those areas.

In our client work, we observe this unfortunate situation with boring regularity. Value-creating effort expended at one end of the business is actually being wasted by losses—at the same end of the business! All of it is a result of overserving the wrong parts of the market. On average, in most businesses, 20 to 40 percent of invested capital is in areas where there is a net profit drain.

Figure 2.1 revisits the technology business we discussed at the end of Chapter 1, and recasts Figure 1.8 in terms of the actions its business leaders need to consider, as they look to get the most out of the capital they have invested.

Note that the internal profit pools in Figure 2.1 are given in terms of offerings, in this case groups of various technology products and services. Alternatively, they could be delineated by customer, channel, or geography. The chart has been structured to place the most profitable capital on the left, with the remaining capital trailing to the right in order of declining economic profit productivity.

Current internal profit pools can be separated into three groups, as they are in Figure 2.1. Generally, those grouped together on the left are candidates for growth; those in the middle are candidates for performance improvement; while those on the right are also candidates for performance

Economic Profit Margin
(EP/Invested Capital, or EROI)

Candidates for Growth	Candidates for Performance Improvement	Candidates for Neutralization or Capital Redeployment
Also find out what drives such good performance; take lessons elsewhere.	Must identify the reasons for poor performance and find ways to limit capital deployment in these profit pools.	Need to understand interrelationships between profit pools (products and services in this case) and likely effects of exiting or deemphasizing some markets.

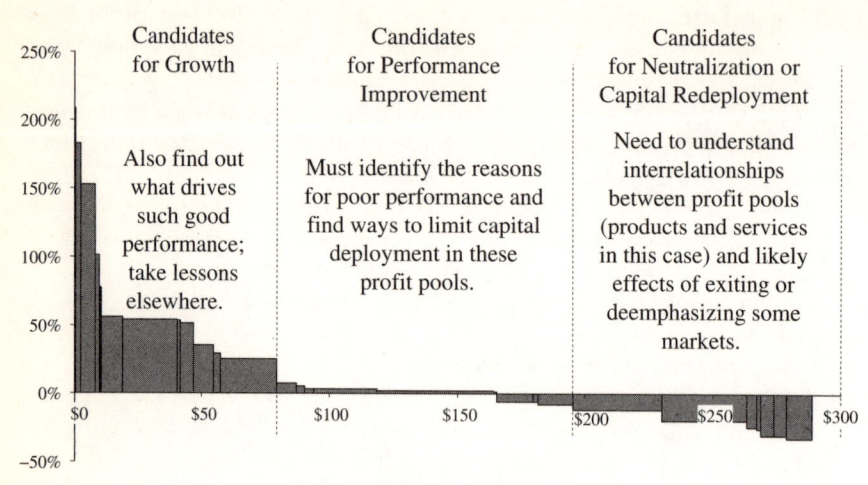

Invested Capital ($ Millions)

FIGURE 2.1 View of Current Internal Profit Pools by Offering
Source: Company reports, Business Intelligence Associates LLC.

improvement, though their role as profit drains must be neutralized in the very near term. Exactly what management should do in each case in the long term is a subject of Part Two of this book. The answers are largely a function of specific market conditions and opportunities, and the interrelationships between the various segments; they are found through an understanding of each segment's demand, competitive dynamics, and economics, now and into the future.

It is worth pausing here to get a sense of the potential of this profit pool–driven approach. In the case of the technology business examined here, we developed only one view of internal profit pools, that of the offering portfolio. Yet, even with just this one view, we can see that a neutralization of, say, just a quarter of the loss-making offerings (which is one of three potential actions available) will enhance this business's cash flow by over 10 percent—a dramatic impact by any measure and, in our experience, not at all unusual.

The current internal cash-based profitability discussed here is a useful insight into, though not a substitute for, an understanding of market opportunities and issues. While some changes to the business's portfolios (offerings, customers, channels, and geographies) to improve near-term performance are possible and desirable, major adjustments must not be undertaken without a much deeper view of market factors. Changes at this stage might include eliminating, or beginning the process to eliminate, very poorly performing segments *with few interdependencies*; growing high-performing segments; or enhancing the performance of large capital investments. Suffice it to say, the returns on efforts to identify and weed out negative profit pools are very high; these steal the results of positive profit pools and deprive investors of the opportunity to invest loss-making capital elsewhere. Chapter 4 addresses these options in more detail.

As luck would have it, this understanding that we need regarding markets happens to be exactly what's needed to build a picture of market profit pools, discussed next. Market profit pools are based on the future cash flow of all competitors in each market segment, including the business we control. As a result, market profit pools are closely related to the second type of internal profit pool, which is based on future cash flows from our business only. The approaches and factors used to determine both these types of future-oriented profit pools are very similar, as are the strategic and tactical issues, as we see next.

Market Profit Pools

A *market profit pool* is simply the sum of the future cash flows of all business models serving that market segment. As with internal profit pools, business leaders interested in maximizing cash flow will be attracted to market profit pools that are positive—clearly, the more positive the better. While this might seem obvious, as we saw in Chapter 1, few growth plans are oriented around long-term cash-based profitability; Chapter 3 discusses how a lack of visibility and other issues perpetuate this situation.

The framework of the three levels of market strategy outlined in Figure 1.7 is a useful tool for thinking about the risk/return profile of market opportunities. This market profit pool approach adds a great deal of insight to that profile and can be a powerful cornerstone to market strategy formulation, a topic addressed in detail in Chapters 5 and 6. In the following material, we discuss market profit pools in the first two levels of the framework, *existing* and *charted*, together as a group. New, *uncharted* market profit pools of the third level are discussed separately since they refer to markets with undeveloped structures, whereas the first two levels deal with markets that already exist.

Existing and Charted Market Profit Pools

Existing and charted market segments have already been penetrated by one or more market players; as such they have an existing market structure with working business models, and there is information available to help determine their attractiveness. This information makes it a lot easier for market entrants to mitigate risk, since they (should) know what they are getting into.

To characterize market profit pools that already exist, we simply need to understand the economics of existing players in the subject segments, now and into the future. The present value of future cash flow from each segment quantifies the attractiveness of each respective market profit pool.

Now, achieving growth in markets that you already serve is usually a question of gaining share and/or increased penetration. Unfortunately, gaining share in a stable market has a strong chance of disrupting the existing competitive order, which in turn alters the nature and attractiveness of the profit pool. So an understanding of competitors to characterize a profit pool is not enough, since the state of the profit pool *after* the enactment of a change (such as your new strategy) is also needed, together with expected competitive responses and endgame market economics. In fact, efforts to change share are not the only market factors that might alter the existing competitive order. Changes in supply markets and customer demand can also do this, and with it change the characteristics of market profit pools. This need for a broader understanding of market issues and conditions is addressed here and in Chapters 5 and 6.

In Chapter 5 we study an example of how new entrants to printing press markets (equipment to print newspapers, books, and the like) completely change the attractiveness of the market's profit pools. These new entrants introduce digital printing, which requires large amounts of highly profitable supplies. This boosts the future cash flow expectations of the various market segments by several orders of magnitude, completely restructuring the starting view of each segment's attractiveness.

As previously noted, the second important attribute of charted market profit pools is that there is a market structure and commercial model already in existence in those markets, which means there is less scope for new entrants to define the market to their terms and strengths. In addition, the presence of an existing competitor set will undoubtedly make the market difficult to break into, and first-mover rewards are long gone. New, uncharted market areas are different from established ones, as they do not have these limitations, though they do have issues of their own.

New, Uncharted Market Profit Pools

Naturally, one way to increase cash flow and business value is to create and grow profitable revenues, and one of the most powerful ways to achieve this is to create new markets. As we discussed in Chapter 1, the ability to add significant amounts of additional revenue streams is one of the key points of leverage that market strategy offers to boost cash flow and business value.

Again, uncharted market profit pools differ from the established, charted ones in three important respects:

1. There is no existing market structure or commercial model in use.
2. First-mover opportunities are very much an attraction.
3. There is only very rudimentary market information available (usually limited to high-level ethnography and addressable market size type information).

In fact, this situation is almost a mirror reflection of established/charted market profit pools; the uncertainty due to reduced information is high, as are potential returns (since first-mover rewards are available, together with the opportunity to define the market and its structure). The profit pool approach has been designed to address these two issues: to help management focus market targeting on high-return markets, and to increase the information gathered on the key drivers of long-term cash flow, thereby enabling a better informed investment decision process and reducing risk.

With that said, business leaders considering uncharted market profit pools need to compile the same types of information as in the preceding discussion of established market profit pools, including the economics of potential business models, market demand, and the others. Obviously, there is much greater uncertainty in this information for uncharted market areas, making it much more important to understand the probabilities of outcomes and to develop well-considered contingencies and their associated triggers. Again, these subjects are studied in more detail in Chapters 5 and 6.

Characterizing Market Profit Pools

So how do you develop a picture of market profit pool attractiveness? Although developing such a picture is the core deliverable in Chapter 5, it is worth taking a brief tour here to see how it is done at a high-level. Let's return to the technology sector business we looked at previously and develop a view of its current and prospective market profit pools.

The first step is to characterize current profitability of each market segment. Since that comprises the profitability of all players serving those segments, we run a competitive review oriented around profiling competitor economics. In most cases, this can be a surprisingly rudimentary process, yet can be highly insightful to understanding competitor behavior. In existing markets, the business models operated by the competition are usually very similar to yours (unlike the Dell situation described earlier). Also, since there is always a movement of people and information within markets, it is usually easy to see the key differences in operating parameters and costs between competitors. When put together, these give a reasonably accurate picture of competitor income statements and balance sheets. Figure 2.2 gives us a (disguised) graphical example for four segments of our technology sector example.

These estimates of competitor profitability don't have to be very precise, since we are only estimating aggregate market segment level profitability. Order-of-magnitude differences are all that are needed to compare attractiveness between market profit pools. In our case, for Figure 2.2, we chose a relatively high degree of preciseness, just for illustrative purposes. In that process, the client's economics were used as a baseline, and differences in competitor operations were used to estimate differences in each line item. For example, it was known that Competitor 1's unit distribution costs in Segment C were two thirds that of the client's. Also, a product breakdown indicated unit material costs of about 80 percent of the client's. With simple assessments like these, a robust view of aggregate market segment profitability, including capital employed, is easily compiled.

Next, total economic profit (EP) for each segment is simply this aggregate market segment EP multiplied by its volume of sales. With that, we

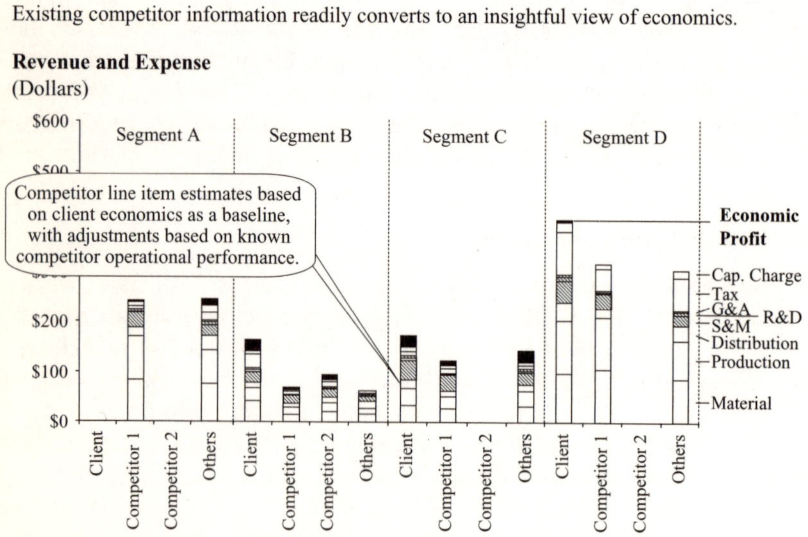

Existing competitor information readily converts to an insightful view of economics.

FIGURE 2.2 Estimated Competitor Economics

Source: Analyst reports, client engineering, supply chain participants, Business Intelligence Associates LLC.

assemble a view of *current* market profit pools, as exemplified in Figure 2.3. Because this is only current information, it is not of any use in strategy, since it tells us little of where profitability is *going to be* (though it is very useful as a starting point from which to build a forecast).

Notice that in Figure 2.3, the offerings are arrayed in the same order as the original investment prioritization made by management (ordered left to right by size of revenue; see Figure 1.7). Interestingly, the top five markets originally slated for growth investments do not even offer the greatest current EP. In fact, of the original top five priority markets, only one offered a substantially attractive profit pool, while two were actually unattractive (growth in these last two is actually driving *value destruction*).

However, we are really interested in the *future* cash flows of market segments, since we use their present values to quantify the attractiveness of each market profit pool. Again, forecasting is dealt with in Chapter 5, where we use new and traditional tools to develop future cash flow estimates for each market segment. Figure 2.4 shows the final result for our technology

Economic Profit Margin
(EP/Invested Capital, or EROI)

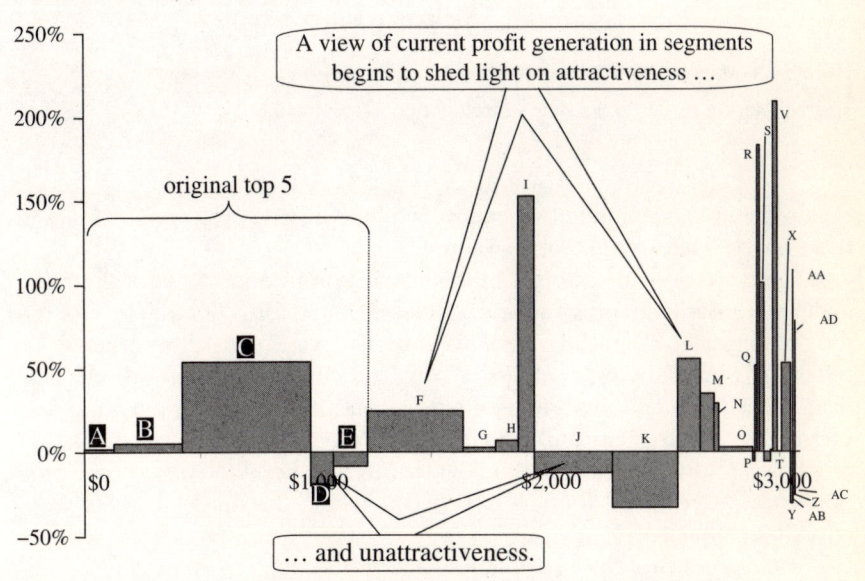

FIGURE 2.3 View of Current Market Profit Pools
Source: Market research, Business Intelligence Associates LLC.

Net Present Value of Future Cash Flows
($ Billions)

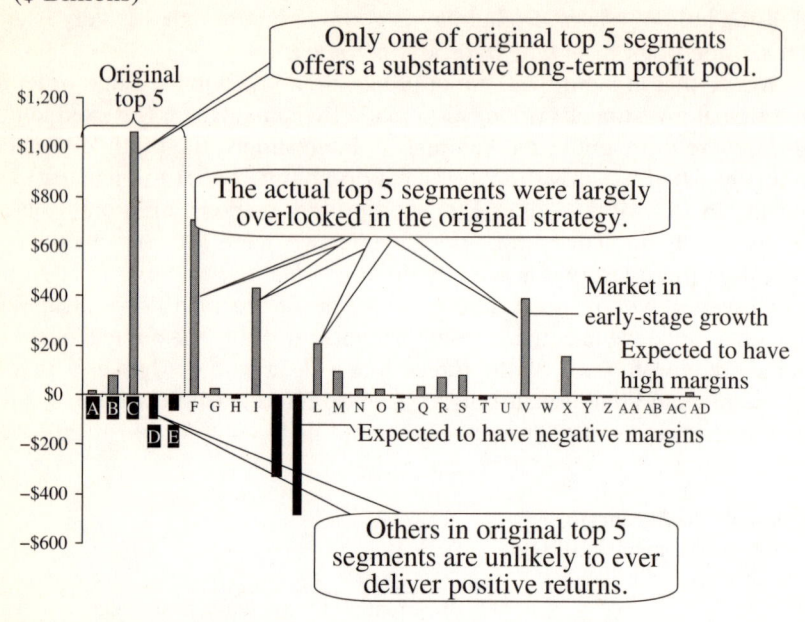

[Chart: Bar chart showing NPV values ranging from -$600 to $1,200 across segments labeled A through AD. Callouts indicate:
- "Original top 5" (pointing to bars A, B, C, D, E)
- "Only one of original top 5 segments offers a substantive long-term profit pool."
- "The actual top 5 segments were largely overlooked in the original strategy."
- "Market in early-stage growth"
- "Expected to have high margins"
- "Expected to have negative margins"
- "Others in original top 5 segments are unlikely to ever deliver positive returns."]

FIGURE 2.4 Market Profit Pools
Source: Market research, Business Intelligence Associates LLC.

sector example: a comparative lineup of all the market profit pools assessed (also ordered left to right, as in Figure 1.7).

There are several surprises in this market profit pool view for the management of our technology sector business. First, it turns out that four of the top five most economically attractive markets were not in the original list of top five investment priorities; in fact, several of them were a long way from receiving much investment at all. Second, two of the original top five offering segments (D and E) actually have little prospect of ever delivering a positive return. A year-by-year review in cases like this may show some opportunistic rewards, though it turned out here that these markets were entirely unattractive.

The market profit pool approach is robust enough to allow direct comparisons of economic attractiveness between market segments, even though there are very different circumstances and forces at work in each. For example, in our technology sector example, several segments are actually in decline, while others are in their early growth stages. In addition, one segment that is currently very profitable is expected to become highly competitive; in the end, it turns out to be much less attractive than mature segments with currently lower profitability. In short, each market profit pool valuation captures a great deal of market understanding and brings it all to a single metric that can be readily used for comparisons in market strategy formulation.

Finally, we must hasten to add that this economic prioritization must be moderated for use in market strategy formulation, which also needs to incorporate issues of strategic fit, operational ability, and other factors. There is also little need to achieve great preciseness, particularly in uncharted market areas, since—as forecasts—the estimates are somewhat blunt and uncertain, and comparisons are most usable in terms of relative orders of magnitude. Indeed, much of the value of the exercise is in understanding markets, thinking through their economics and uncertainties, and drafting exploitive strategies and contingencies.

Next, we briefly look at market profit pools as they exist vertically—that is, along an industry's value chain.

Profit Pools in the Value Chain

Another way to look at profit pools in markets is along the value chain—that is, down the path an offering takes as it makes its way from a raw material to delivery to the end customer. This perspective was explored most notably by Orit Gadiesh and James L. Gilbert in their article "Profit Pools: A Fresh Look at Strategy" (*Harvard Business Review*, May–June 1998). Figure 2.5 provides a view of vertical market profit pools along an industry value chain—in this case, a conceptual view across the auto industry.

A very interesting set of insights and market strategy possibilities arise with this view. First, vertical market profit pools tend to accumulate at various points along the value chain, called *choke points*, depending on where power structures exist; these may be driven by supply constraints, powerful market players (with power in relationships, scale, etc.), or some other similar issue.

With a view of profit accumulations comes a better understanding of the merits of an integration strategy, backwards or forwards along the value chain. This leads us to the second important use for this vertical view: to better understand the economic incentives of other participants in the value chain. In particular, are they making profits in a way that is aligned with your interests? Your distributor, for example, may be making a healthy profit from a product that is actually a profit drain for you. Or he may be losing on one of your best earners, and so he is downplaying its growth. Either way, with visibility into vertical market profit pools, you are in a position to see these economic incentives and take steps to adjust them.

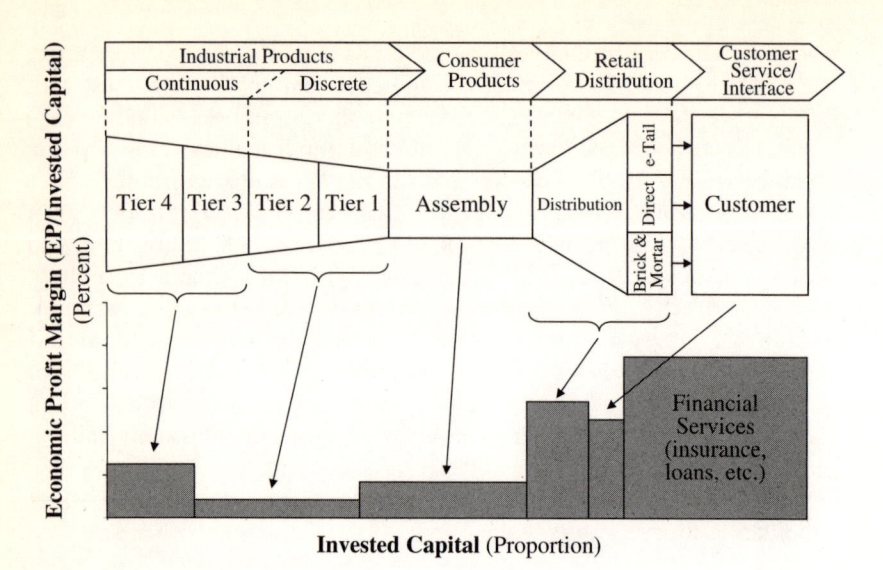

FIGURE 2.5 The Value Chain View of Market Profit Pools
Source: Business Intelligence Associates LLC.

Summary

In this chapter we have introduced the profit pool and seen the range of ways it can be defined and used. Its primary role is to help guide market strategy in a way that boosts business value. With this in mind, it may seem odd that business leaders are not already driving hard after them; but the truth is, while profit pools are powerfully useful, they are also difficult to see—as we find out in Chapter 3. Something that is difficult to see, however, is also a potential source of competitive advantage.

CHAPTER 3

You Just Can't See Them

Profit pools make intuitive sense and they appeal to the most base of entrepreneurial thinking. So why aren't business leaders already chasing them down with great vigor?

It turns out one of the greatest inhibitors is that profit pools are very difficult for today's business to see and properly comprehend. There are four main reasons this is so:

1. Accounting systems don't actually report a useful profitability
2. *Market* profitability information is difficult to come by
3. Businesses aren't configured to get and process the needed profitability information in a timely manner
4. New markets are difficult to envision

In this chapter we look at each of these in turn, reserving for Part Two the task of deciding what to do about what we find.

Accounting Systems Don't Actually Report a Useful Profitability

It seems incredible that with so much invested in information technology (IT) even in the smallest of businesses, management still does not have access to the most basic of business information: a value-oriented measure of profitability. Yet the simple fact is they don't. Today's information systems deliver three broad groups of information:

1. Day-to-day operational information (such as production planning, marketing logistics, etc.).
2. Accounting records and capital markets investment and profitability information.
3. Other regulatory information for tax, environment, and other mandates.

More or less, management tends to view these sets of information in this order of importance. Notice that tucked in the accounting line is a mention of profitability—but also notice how it is oriented to the needs of others, namely capital market regulators. In fact, most businesses use that *external reporting* information system for *business management* purposes. And why not? It is precise (with audits and other mandated quality control measures), it comes mostly complete, and it is well developed (with billions of tested implementations over time).

Unfortunately, external reporting–based information systems do not give business leaders the information needed for them to see cash-based profit contributions and to properly manage the business for the purpose of maximizing long-term cash flow. So what do business leaders need? They need information that is granular enough to give meaningful insight and cash-based profit measures for all the good reasons set out in Chapter 1.

Sufficient Granularity to Spot Issues and Opportunities

This is a question of gaining insights into your own business. In most businesses today, information systems do not parse out profit or other performance information in terms of offer (that is, products and services), customer set, channel, and geography in sufficient detail. More often than not, the business can only see performance in one or two of these dimensions (typically product and geography), and even then it is only available at the most limited levels of granularity.

The result? As we saw in Chapter 2, good, positive-profit parts of the business, such as certain products or customers, are flowing significant amounts of energy and capital into negative-profit parts of the business, bringing overall returns down substantially. Business leaders, totally unaware of such profit drains, actively invest in and attempt to grow both areas, even though every bit of increase in profit drains further neutralizes the fruits of positive contributors and wastes the opportunity in the capital invested.

Again, it is not unusual to find 20 to 40 percent of invested capital driving negative returns. For example, the following profile of an auto parts company's product portfolio is reasonably typical. A high-level review of cash-based profitability at the product family indicated that it was almost entirely a positively contributing business. However, further study at the stock-keeping unit (SKU) level revealed the results shown in Table 3.1.

Looking at the extremes, the top 5 percent of SKUs drove nearly three-quarters of the business's total cash-based profitability, while the bottom 20 percent of SKUs *drained* nearly a quarter of it. Notably, from a market point of view, less than half of the 20 percent of the SKUs draining profit had any strategic or tactical value (such as serving within a bundle or

TABLE 3.1 Cash-Based Profitability Profile of Auto Parts Company's Product Portfolio

Proportion of SKUs	Proportion of Profitability Driven by SKUs
5 percent	71 percent
40 percent	53 percent
35 percent	0 percent
20 percent	−24 percent

as a customer draw/loss leader), while the remainder simply lost profit and clogged operations with added complexity. Since management did not have such granular visibility, it was completely unaware of the problem. With that said, this problem quickly became an opportunity, sufficient to increase cash flow by 13 percent (and driving intrinsic business value up by a similar amount)!

The techniques used to resolve such problems are outlined in Part Two. In this case many market withdrawals of nonstrategic products began with price hikes; while the strategic products, primarily brake and suspension systems and their periphery, were redesigned or replaced to neutralize their drain on profit. In addition, further investing in segments that were ongoing profit drains was almost completely halted.

Profit Measured in Real Money (Cash)

This is where the accounting profession comes in for some considerable criticism. While they are doing a great job of accounting for the comings and goings of money in the business and reporting it to external parties, they are not giving business leaders *information* that is useful for driving cash flow. To some extent they are just doing the bidding of Congress and various regulators, though it must also be said that their influence on those powers is quite considerable (as evident in the recent gains they secured as an industry, in terms of billable hours, from the enactment of Sarbanes-Oxley).

Generally accepted accounting principles (GAAP) statements are not geared to help business leaders track cash flow within their business; and in any case, they are entirely oriented around looking at the past. *At best*, we find that managers in today's businesses have access to operating profit (OP), though in most cases they are only able to use gross profit (GP) or even revenue to make critical investment decisions and steer the business at any appreciable level of granularity.

The most egregious example that we have observed of this kind of flying blind was IBM's use of *blue dollar* revenue in its decision making, and as of just a few years ago it was still using the approach. Here, the information systems leader on the planet was not able to see real revenue (which they called *green dollars*) in terms of offering or customer type; all they could see was double- and triple-counted blue dollar revenue numbers, which was acquired through their sales incentive systems. So the business had only a very poor view of revenue at a granular level and had no way of knowing profitability, since expense information was structured differently and tracked separately. IBM was reduced to applying margin *estimates* to adjusted blue dollars.

Today, most businesses rely almost exclusively on GAAP-based systems for business information, despite their poor and usually misleading information. In the discussions that follow, we look at the primary GAAP-based measures of profit, GP and OP, and profile the merits of using economic profit (EP). After that, we turn to management's need for information on the marketplace, both existing and uncharted markets.

What's Wrong with Gross Profit?

On the surface, GP has some very good traits. Among them are the accuracy with which it is reported and the *potential* granularity it can be taken to. Gross profit basically reports revenue with production costs (otherwise known as *cost of goods*) removed. In most reporting systems, these costs are identified and attributed to each item sold through a process called *standard costs*. Fortunately, standard costs are tracked relatively closely by GAAP procedures, which has a couple of positive outcomes. First, production-based costs can be determined to a good level of granularity in terms of offering and geography, and can be relatively easily manipulated to get GP in terms of customer and channel. Second, detailed tracking usually results in a reasonably accurate reflection of the costs actually used in production to create each respective offering, and so is likely reliable.

The problem is that GP is literally only part of the picture—often a small part. While it includes cost of goods, it excludes all other costs! The issue is most pronounced in financial and other services, raw material production, even pharmaceuticals and software industries. In most businesses, research and development (R&D), sales, marketing, and general and administrative (G&A) costs, which are below the GP line, represent *over half* of cash outgoings. Figure 3.1 shows the relative magnitude of cost of goods and other expenses across 12 industries, as a proportion of revenues.

Importantly, below-the-GP-line costs vary dramatically within and between offerings, customers, channels, and geographies. As a result, investing in and growing a part of the business with a good GP is a very risky

Proportion of Revenues
(Percent)

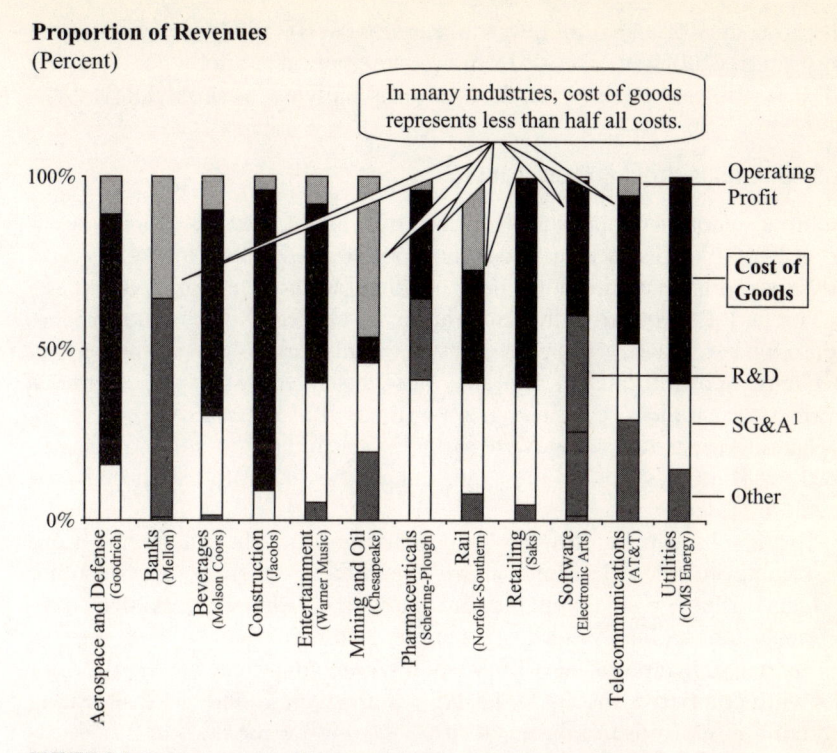

FIGURE 3.1 Representative Income Statement Structures for 12 Industries
Source: Yahoo! Finance; Business Intelligence Associates LLC.
Note: All example companies selected to have revenues between $3 billion and $10 billion, clustered around $6 billion.
[1] Sales, General & Administrative (includes marketing).

proposition, since that product or customer may be drawing a relatively large slice of one of these costs and may actually be net negative in profit generation.

A simple and widely recognized illustration of this is in the PC sector. The same PC sold to large and small corporate customers has similar GPs for both customer types (the slightly lower GP for large customers stems only from the slightly lower average prices they have negotiated). However, as a result of scale economies, sales expenses are considerably lower for large customers. A GP view does not capture this critical difference, leading business leaders to treat and grow each business equally (as many vendors seem to be doing even today).

In addition, GAAP makes many artificial adjustments to cost of goods, such as depreciation. As we saw before, such arbitrary adjustments do not reflect transfers of actual money and therefore serve as a significant source of distortion, shifting cash costs from one time period to another and leaving both investors and business leaders with no real view of profitability.

Surely Operating Profit is Okay, Isn't It?

The other major profit measure delivered by GAAP-based systems is operating profit (OP). This measure does incorporate R&D, sales, marketing, and G&A costs in its makeup, but it has considerable problems of its own.

First, OP is very rarely available at any useful level of granularity. Second, to the extent it has any granularity, it usually turns out to be thoroughly inaccurate. Why? Because it allocates these costs across business segments (products, customers, etc.) using approaches that are almost completely unrelated to the way resources are actually consumed. Just about all GAAP-based reporting systems do the same thing—they allocate expenses based on volume sales or revenues.

The results can be stunningly misleading. Take the following example: Two approaches to the allocation of marketing expenses in a consumer products business were compared, one using the business's GAAP-based reporting system and the other using simple customer counts (which tracked with actual staff time usage to a 95 percent accuracy rate). When the results were compared, the GAAP-based systems were found to be allocating marketing costs (mostly salaries) to products with error rates in thousands of percent! Some products needed very little marketing but were being charged substantive sums, while others benefited from very small charges while soaking up huge amounts of staff time. Allocations can substantively change the profitability picture, and as a result are examined more closely in Chapter 4.

With such inappropriate allocations, business leaders are back to the same problems cited for GP—though possibly in a worse position, since with OP they have a measure that incorporates more costs, and so they are more confident in investment decisions and prioritizations.

It is worth adding that even with such inaccuracies sorted out, OP would still be a poor yardstick because it also omits a number of nontrivial costs, including tax and financing costs, among others. These are sufficient to drive the profit results of parts of the portfolio into negative territory, such that unattractive parts of the business actually appear attractive (if allocated appropriately).

There is no escaping it. Business leaders will only know the true profit contribution of their businesses at a granular level if they make a specific effort to get that information. And only then will they properly see which parts of the business are really profit contributors and warrant investments for growth, and which parts of the business they should limit.

So What about Economic Profit?

Economic profit (EP) is not a measure of profit recognized by GAAP. Nevertheless, it is a measure of profit well recognized by finance experts, economists, sophisticated investors, and even accountants. When properly implemented, it has three key attributes:

1. It reports a cash-based view of profitability that includes *all* relevant costs and expenses and is not subject to accounting distortions.
2. It reports on the business's economics at a usefully fine level of granularity with accurate allocations (it is a *management* reporting tool).
3. It includes a charge for the cost of capital invested.

The first attribute simply goes around standard accounting practices aimed at smoothing profit reporting to investors—it unwinds GAAP's distortions to get to cash profit. The second attribute takes the level of cash profit detail to a point where management gets some very insightful information into the sources and drivers of value creation within the segment portfolios.

However, when evaluating performance in just a few reporting periods (such as one or two years), even cash profit is not enough. It is useful for measuring operations performance, but business leaders also need to know the opportunity cost of capital invested across their segment portfolios if they are to make effective investment decisions. That is where the third attribute makes a difference: the incorporation of a charge for the capital invested. This concept is often associated with *economic value-add* (EVA), a variant of economic profit contrived by Joel Stern and G. Bennett Stewart. Capital deployment to each segment of the business, within each of the dimensions—offering, customer, channel, and geography—must be appropriately charged so that business leaders can see those opportunity cost trade-offs.

To some, the issue of the cost of capital is somewhat arcane, even academic. The fact is it makes a significant difference. Some products require dramatically greater amounts of fixed asset investment than others, and some customers and channels have dramatically differing accounts receivable and working capital needs than others. Even regulatory and other factors drive differences in capital investments between geographies.

Let's look at how important this issue is. If you invested a million dollars in a business prospect, and it did not deliver the level of returns it would have if invested in an S&P 500 index fund, then you'd be out of pocket in a very real way. The loss is not simply an obscure phenomenon in financial theory called *opportunity cost*; if you didn't receive the return at the end of the period and it was expected, that is no different than having it taken away. Besides being very real to investors, these costs are nontrivial to say the least; the average annual return on equity investments in the post-war period is approximately 12 percent, which in the case of that $1 million investment is an expectation of $120,000—every year.

Is it right then, that this business prospect should not recognize the cost investors sustain when it does not deliver the level of returns expected? Of course not. Investors expect their capital to work for them, and when their capital is not performing well enough, they will see that fact and redeploy their capital elsewhere—reducing demand for shares and bringing down the business's value. Any business hoping to meet investor expectations must manage returns on invested capital—and, as with profitability, that can only be achieved when done at a granular level.

Economic profit provides exactly the information needed: The capital employed by the business's various segments is first delineated, and the cash profits from each of those segments is charged for the cost of that capital. The amount charged is simply the value of the capital multiplied by the rate of return investors expect from it.

Now, if investors are prepared to redeploy capital when it is not performing, management needs fair warning, right? In fact, charging for capital would be part of the capital markets reporting system, given its relevance to investors. Well, you'd think so. Again, the accounting profession and regulators come in for some criticism here also. While on one hand they try to smooth profitability by spreading capital investments over time with non-cash charges, they completely fail to incorporate the only noncash charge really needed—that of investor opportunity cost. As a result, even GAAP's end result at the aggregate business level, net income, is not a useful measure for business leaders. Those using GAAP-based systems could be forgiven for assuming that a positive net income is a good thing, but the reality is, being positive may well not be good enough. Net income doesn't even indicate whether the cost of capital has been met.

How Bad Can It Get?

Profit information is at its most useful when it is used to prioritize and direct investments and growth as well as to limit losses. GAAP-based profit measures differ substantially from cash-based measures and can significantly mislead business leaders. Figure 3.2 takes the technology sector business we discussed in Chapters 1 and 2 and overlays gross profit, operating profit, and economic profit for each offering family, so that we can see the differences. Note that GAAP-based profit measures are not available at this level of granularity, and additional parsing was needed (past the business's system's capability) to get the GAAP-based information to a compatible level of granularity.

There are two clear messages from this comparison. First, business leaders are being encouraged to grow offerings that GAAP measures indicate

Profit Margin
(Profit/Invested Capital, or X-ROI)

— Gross Profit (GP)
— Operating Profit (OP)
— Economic Profit (EP)

Both GP and OP give misleading indications of investment returns and prioritization.

Both GP and OP indicate unprofitable offerings are worth growing.

Invested Capital ($ Millions)

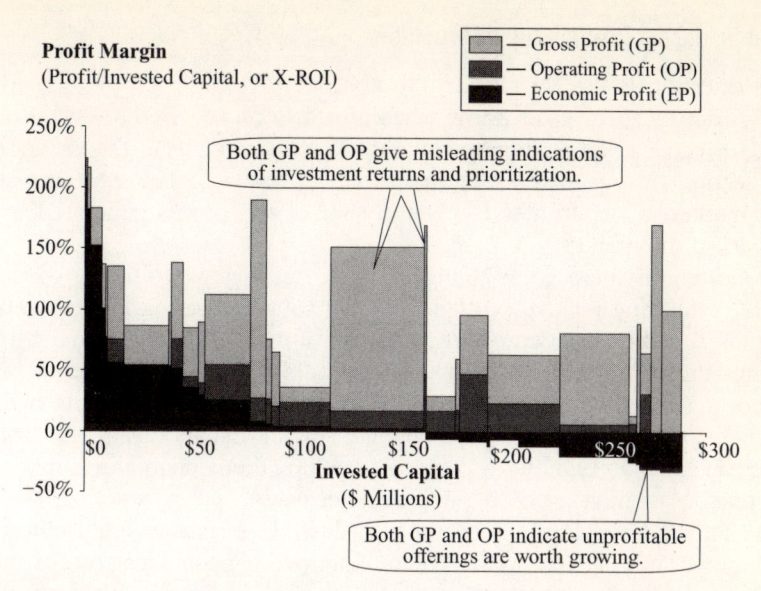

FIGURE 3.2 Example Comparison of Gross Profit, Operating Profit, and Economic Profit

Source: Company reports, BIA analysis.

are profitable, although they are actually profit drains (toward the right of the chart). Second, the priorities for investment are ordered highest on the left and lowest on the right, according to the cash-based measure, EP. If either gross profit or operating profit were used for prioritization, the picture would look very different, and the result would be much lower returns on the amounts invested.

Market Profitability Information Is Difficult to Come By

To some extent it is obvious, and should be of no surprise, that market profitability information is difficult to come by. By implication, it requires insight into the profitability of all that is sold into the subject market—which means understanding the economics of all competitors in the market.

To add another layer of complexity, two sets of market profitability are actually needed: what it is and what it could be. Understanding the differing business models and associated economics of today's competitors addresses what market profitability is now; understanding how they are likely to be configured is necessary for making forecasts.

In this discussion we identify what market information is needed to evaluate profit pools, subsequently turning to where and how the right information can be compiled.

What Is Market Profitability Information?

This question is itself a clue to the absence of usable information. Businesses do not themselves know what information is needed to craft a profit pool–driven market strategy. (We address why they are in this position in the section on business configuration which follows.) The easy answer is that market managers need only the sum of the profits generated by all players in the market.

As long as there is no change, such a static view would be very useful in comparing relative profitability (and so attractiveness) across several segments. But time always brings change, and since there is usually much change there is a need for a true understanding of what drives profitability, where it is, and what it is based on. In fact, even the act of discovering segment profitability may cause change, since it makes businesses leaders focus on specific segments—entering or exiting them, changing competitive approaches, or investing/divesting in other ways.

The Southwest Airlines example discussed in Chapter 1 illustrates this phenomenon well. In its early years, Southwest made great profits on its carefully chosen routes. Unfortunately, as often happens with pure plays, the evidence that it was focusing on routes with unusual financial returns became clear to anyone taking the time to look at Southwest's numbers, exposing its segments as being highly attractive. Over time, others jumped into the same routes, bringing down prices and profitability together. Those routes are still much more profitable than the ones maintained by the big airlines, though margins are less than half where they were when Southwest was the only low-cost carrier in town. Oddly, this reduction in profitability is entirely predictable and needs to be factored into market profitability forecasts (using historical precedent and other methods, reviewed in Chapter 5).

Adding or subtracting the number of players in a market is not the only way a market's profitability can change. As we saw in Chapter 2, market profitability is based on the business models at work in that market, and with varying business models, the characteristics of a market's profitability can change substantially (as was vividly demonstrated in the Dell example in Chapter 2). Summing the profit performance of existing business models is too simplistic to be useful. Business leaders need information that will help them develop reasonable views of the impact of the strategies they and others are considering. That information includes the following five types:

1. A profile of existing and potential business models (including their associated economics) generating a market's profits.
2. A characterization of relative customer appeals (and customer economics) of the various offerings.

3. Views of future demand, together with their relationships (elasticity) with price and offering factors.
4. A profile of competitor strengths and weaknesses, likely strategies, and behaviors/responses.
5. A characterization of the impact and power of channels (and their economics).

Thus, market profitability information is much more than existing player economics and must encompass market strategy thinking also, since they are intimately interrelated. Much of this information is highly specific to each market and changes with time.

We have set out here what information is needed and why. So where can we get it? As has already been pointed out, this information is quite difficult to get, such that most businesses don't even bother trying (perhaps not realizing the value it can deliver, nor recognizing its return on investment). In fact, such ambivalence makes the potential value created by this knowledge even greater; the business that accesses this information will be managed with better visibility than its competitors. Businesses don't recognize that information is a critical part of the competitive war: Getting and having it, properly processing it (to economic implications), and leveraging it into high value-add strategies, contingencies, and actions is a key component to shareholder value and financial strength, and therefore market strength also.

The Canned Stuff Isn't Going to Give You What You Need

Most businesses rely very heavily on standardized market information provided by third-party vendors. The information these vendors provide tends to focus on the basics and is addressable to many competitors: unit demand, pricing, and some forecasting of existing markets. It is rarely, if ever, distilled to provide useful economic pictures of markets and their futures. This is not surprising given the rapid change in markets, the uncertainty in information gathered, and the situation- and competitor-specific nature of information needs.

In fact, these three characteristics (change, uncertainty, and situational uniqueness) sound like the sort of risk types investors bear as they place bets in businesses and their management teams. The exposure from uncertainty and continual change (driven by new business models, etc.) is too much for third-party vendors to shoulder. It is up to business leaders to develop their own forward-looking economic information themselves and, as agents of shareholders, to use it as a strategic weapon to create more value than the competition.

To be fair, many (typically larger) businesses do commission their own market research. However, it is research mostly geared around near-term tactical uses—looking to one- to three-year horizons, and limited to understanding why customers made trade-offs between one of their products and the competition's. It is rarely geared around the *solutions* customers may be looking for in the *longer term*, and almost never projected out to future business models and expected economics.

So if packaged and near-term-oriented custom research isn't enough, what should management do? The answer lies in economic-oriented, outward-facing, and long-range-specific, big-picture-building information, outlined next. It takes only a little more effort over what is likely already expended in your business today; it is just a different perspective.

Investing in Competitor Information Pays Off in Spades

Third-party information vendors do provide some of the basics needed to estimate and understand market economics. They are typically grounded in relatively solid fact and serve as powerful foundation points. There are critical gaps, however, that need to be filled in each of the five areas of need set out previously, in order to see existing and likely future market profitability.

For existing markets, and some potentially new expansion markets, many of those gaps can be filled with an insightful view of the competition and their business models (that is, their offerings, their operating models, and their associated economics). Naturally enough, such information is not readily available—though it is easier to find, triangulate, and estimate than it might first appear.

Most business leaders recognize the value of this competitor information, certainly for the tactical time period (1 to 3 years), and less so for the strategic period (5 to 15 years). However, more immediate distractions and a limited focus on it results in almost no organizational capability to gather and process competitive data, and a complete dearth of actual usable information.

Exactly how difficult is it to get the information needed? Let's first look at what the primary sources are:

- Customers.
- Partners (especially channel partners).
- Competitors themselves (investor/public relations, articles, interviews, spec/price sheets, etc.).
- The government (including the SEC, Department of Commerce, Federal Reserve, and others).

- Employees (there is an incredible amount of drift, especially within industries).
- Third parties (market research vendors, investment advisers, and institutions).
- Public sources (including legal surveillance).

This is not a short list. A structured approach to these sources, together with institutional memory, a focus, good processing, and thoughtful tactics, actually delivers very usable and granular information. Obviously, the information is not perfect and, of course, not as good as internal information, though its accuracy improves with time if the business invests even just a little into an ongoing effort. Such information also allows a good assessment of uncertainties and the opportunities to plan around or exploit them.

Analyzing and thinking through this information and its quality gives managers a far deeper insight into their markets—and a solid advantage over the competition. As time goes by, a formal *competitive intelligence* (CI) program becomes incredibly capable at gathering and processing information—improving information coverage and certainties—which dramatically mitigates risk and enhances awareness of strategic options (and so value creation).

Exactly how valuable is this competitive intelligence? Well, it is possible to get answers good enough to judge the worth of investments of all sizes, both high-stakes bets and market redeployments. Let's have a look at the magnitude of value of the decisions it enables and the value of the risks it mitigates (that is, limiting the damage of mistakes).

First is the value of the decisions it impacts, primarily decisions of market targeting and participation—knowing where to invest and/or grow. Actions and decisions resulting from knowledge of market profit pools improve cash flow a nontrivial amount, into tens of percentage points at a minimum. These decisions increase the business's entire value by a similar proportion, likely far in excess of any amount it's possible to spend on a CI program. In terms of risk mitigation, an error in pursuing a market also has the potential of destroying a similar magnitude of value.

Second, as discussed in Chapter 2, in most businesses a large portion of invested capital is in negative return segments. It would not be unreasonable to assume that a CI program would notice such poor results among other market players and lead market managers away from those segments, causing at least half the poorly invested capital to be deployed elsewhere.

The CI investment delivers value in other areas as well, though mostly in areas of near-term concern. For example, knowing how value is created by a competitor's business model can significantly enhance your competitive position, as it reveals their source of economic strength, perhaps in an offering, channel, or elsewhere. It also gives additional insights on the market, relative competitor capabilities, channel and customer behaviors and responses, in addition to a greatly improved understanding of the competitive landscape for ongoing tactical decision making.

Finally, while collecting competitive data is a significant step, it is in its processing that much value is created. Often, a range of different sources delivers data that are quite disparate, and a sensible analysis and integration program is needed to bring it all together to create usable *information*. This includes the right mix of market and economic skills, as well as flexible and capable storage systems. These issues are largely a reflection of having the right skills and processes in the organization, and are examined next.

Businesses Aren't Configured to Get and Process Timely Cash-Based Profitability Information

Getting the sort of visibility outlined in the preceding sections is not impossible, nor even that difficult. Much of the problem is simply related to how the business is configured: First, it is not organized to have a spot for certain key skills, and second, key information systems and processes are not in place.

These issues largely go away as management explicitly focuses on shareholder value creation and a profit pool–driven market strategy. Businesses generally focus on near-term issues, which are difficult enough to get done in the day without sorting out additional information demands. However, without continuously orienting information and decisions around profit pools, the business drifts into using its near-term systems for decisions that ultimately set long-term direction. Without being organized or directed toward understanding the long-term economics of markets, it is no wonder that business leaders end up with such poor visibility.

Needed: A Blend of Finance and Market Strategy Skills

Most businesses are organized in functional groups, usually including a finance group and a separate marketing group. This silo structure is driven by the day-to-day skills needs of each, with the net result that there tend to be few cross-skills in each silo—finance mostly recruits accountants, and marketing mostly recruits product managers.

Now, insightful dissections of markets to find cash-based profitability require a blend of both skills; cutting through GAAP is itself a challenge, to say nothing of properly segmenting a market in an actionable and measurable way. Layered on top of these problems are the other usual inhibitors:

differing motives (GAAP reporting in finance, revenue in marketing), incentives, turf stakes, and others.

The siloing of business understanding gets engrained in the ranks of functional managers and is often reinforced by an ever-specializing job focus and targeted incentive schemes. Indeed, it is that focus that works so well at the tactical level (more sales leads, for example, in marketing). The ability of functional managers to adopt broader, longer-term thinking often becomes impossible following half a career in one of these silos.

Also Needed: Tailored Processes and Information Systems

From this discussion, it is apparent that a profit pool–driven market strategy demands several types of information if it is to help maximize return on invested capital and reduce risk. Much of this information cannot be gleaned from existing GAAP-based information systems, as it is centered on understanding markets and competitors, and it is typically sourced externally.

For example, most businesses do not have much of a CI initiative at all, let alone the necessary supporting process and information repository systems. Competitive information in particular comes in very small fragments, and from a range of places around the business. Without a dedicated process, about 99 percent of the information remains uncollected (from sales, accounts receivable, marketing, new operations employees, and elsewhere), and what is collected is lost due to poor storage facilities (often some individual's memory).

Even within marketing, a great deal of customer market understanding and research that is useful in estimating profit pool attractiveness is not well distributed in most businesses. It often remains undiscovered within the confines of groups or individuals, and so is not shared. This situation is improving, however, particularly with the use of outsourced information vendors who manage content for their clients.

Next, we turn to the last of the four reasons for poor visibility of profit pools: the difficulty in envisioning new markets.

New Markets Are Difficult to Envision

New markets are always difficult to see. In this section, we have a look at the issues preventing business leaders from getting a good picture of what prospective markets will look like. Chapters 5 and 6 outline various approaches to get around these issues, using simple uncertainty-based market assessment and strategy formulation techniques.

At its core, a business's role is to create some sort of value in customer markets, in the form of an offering of products and/or services, and in doing so to port financial value over to the capital markets (owners, debt holders, and others). As a result, it has to address two challenges:

1. What offering will create value for customers?
2. What configuration of business model can create and extract financial value?

Existing businesses have 20/20 hindsight in explaining how this creation and transfer of value takes place. The really entrepreneurial business, however, has to find new answers to these questions, often in markets that are completely new (that is, markets in the "new and uncharted" band of Figure 1.7). In the preceding sections we have seen that, relatively speaking, it is considerably easier to address these two challenges in the lower bands of Figure 1.7, since some level of understanding of the market already exists through established businesses. However, by definition, in new and uncharted markets there is little in the way of established knowledge that can be used to create a viable business.

How can business leaders and investors design a business model that can be invested in with confidence? To answer this we need to first be specific about what is unknown; the first step to understanding uncertainty and mitigating risks.

What Offering Will Create Value for Customers?

To figure out what the offering must look like, business leaders and investors have to address three issues:

1. What customer need will it serve?
2. What form will the offering take (including functionalities and features)?
3. What will customers pay? (Considerable insight can be gained by understanding customer economics.)

Of course, life would be very easy if business leaders and investors could simply ask customers what they want. Unfortunately, it is very rare, particularly in new, uncharted areas, for customers to have any distilled idea of what they want. They do in some cases, but usually either they talk in terms of what they already know, or they are after something that is not economically viable.

This has much to do with customers' lack of familiarity with what is practically possible, whether it be in terms of technology, physical limitations, or other constraints. It also has to do with their not knowing how they would actually respond to a proposition until they are confronted with it—and even then, they may change their position, perhaps needing a direct experience to prompt a change.

These issues are resolved using everyday marketing analysis techniques, though perhaps they need to be oriented to a more long-term time frame (long-term forecasting is explored in Chapter 5). The key steps involve mapping out what is known in the preceding questions, perhaps mapping out customer needs and behaviors through specifically contrived tests, and forcing potential customers to make choices using conjoint tools.

What Business Model Configuration Can Create and Extract Financial Value?

In defining the business model needed to deliver the offerings and returns promised, business leaders and investors have to address the following three internally oriented questions:

1. What operations *can* be deployed to deliver the offering?
2. How will each of those operations options be created?
3. What are the economics of each operations option (initial investment and ongoing operations)?

The first two issues need visibility into the customer solution, in an iterative process with the offering definition challenge mentioned earlier, and a creative understanding of the physical possibilities of the day (such as technologies and the like). Defining the operating model is beyond the scope of this book, but it follows an iterative process similar to the market forecasting described in Chapter 5. Of course, knowledge of the operating model's configuration unlocks the economics, a critical step in the market strategy formulation process addressed in Chapter 6.

Getting It Done

In this chapter we have seen that profit pools go untapped—or improperly navigated—because business has difficulty in seeing them. In the case of internal profit pools, this poor visibility is caused by using GAAP-based systems to manage the business. In the case of market profit pools, it is caused by a market knowledge process that is entirely focused on understanding the market in the near and mid term.

In both cases, most of the information needed to develop useful profit pool views *already exists within the business*! Little incremental information is needed, and little incremental effort is needed to process it. In most businesses it is a short step to adopt the profit pool approach. Given the stakes involved (the amounts of capital invested, the opportunity cost of that capital, and the potential value created), more and more businesses are turning to managing for value. These businesses will inevitably increase their focus on market strategy, incorporating the thoughtful, fact-based approach of finding and exploiting profit pools.

PART II

Your Guide to Early Results

In Part Two we step through a program that puts your business on a cash flow high-growth trajectory, set to maximize value creation. This program has been configured to both position the business for long term value creation, while delivering real, substantive cash flow in the immediate and near terms. This pragmatic approach has three steps, set out in the Figure P2.1.

Each of these three steps is reviewed in the next three chapters:

- Chapter 4 outlines a practical path to getting a clear view of internal profit pools and sets up opportunities for immediate action to boost near term cash flow.
- Chapter 5 takes on the more artful challenge of characterizing market profit pools and creating a strategic view of markets.

Know Your Own ACTUAL PERFORMANCE	Get a STRATEGIC VIEW of Markets	Define a Path That Exploits REAL OPPORTUNITIES
Rapidly get a clear view of **internal profit pools**; immediately boost cash flow by limiting cash drains and boosting cash sources; start process to characterize market profit pools.	Map attractiveness of existing **market profit pools**; immediately start redeployment out of nonstrategic and unattractive markets.	Map attractiveness of new, high-potential market profit pools; **formulate market strategy** options that exploit opportunities; launch market strategy and maximize long-term cash flow.

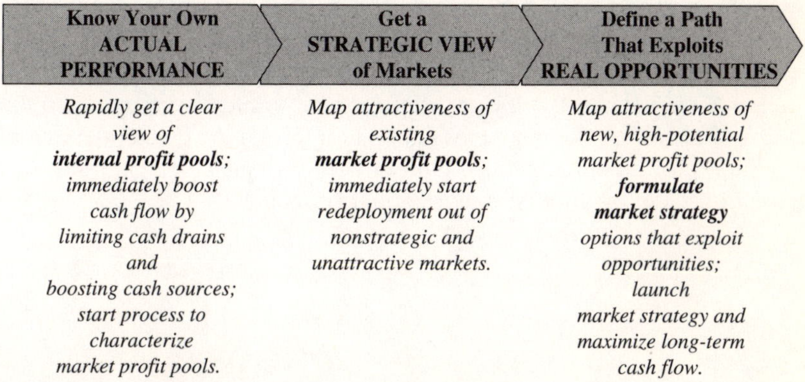

FIGURE P2.1 Getting on the Right Cash Flow Trajectory
Source: Business Intelligence Associates LLC.

- Chapter 6 applies new and traditional market strategy formulation techniques to chart a path forward, balancing the drive to maximize shareholder value with the forces of uncertainty.

How should you tackle this program? Naturally, each business must consider its own unique circumstances and tailor its own path forward. Recognize that there are actually two deliverables: crafting swift value-creating actions and developing an ongoing capability to repeat the process and maintain high rates of value creation. Keep in mind that you will be developing a team and an internal information capability that will become critical to the long-term future of the business. It needs to be staffed by smart, energetic, and, above all, trusted executives, managers, and analysts—all expected to be with the business for some time as much high-value information is going to be revealed. In terms of skills mix, the team needs to comprise primarily marketing- and finance-based resources, though with some operations presence also. No matter the experience to date, these resources need to be fungible and able to rapidly cross-train as the process rolls forward.

It is generally best to bite off only a part of the business to begin with. In this way, a smaller team can take on a less wieldy challenge and be more certain of delivering a win quickly. It will deal with less information and complexity, and it will gain experience and develop cross-functional skills much more rapidly than with a broader exercise. A smaller start also increases speed (targeting a completion in one or two quarters), reduces risks, and gives the organization time to begin the cultural shift that it will inevitably have to navigate over the next few years. This small team can subsequently form the core of a broader initiative, addressing the overall business with confidence, experience, expertise, and, perhaps most important, organizational credibility.

Once the first effort is complete, this new capability delivers far more usable results if it is managed incrementally, with continuous updates rather than annual initiatives. Decisions can then incorporate the input on a rolling basis, as they occur. The resources needed for this are no greater than would be required for an annual effort. Furthermore, the greater organization will not be distracted by another major annual program.

CHAPTER 4

Know Your Own
ACTUAL PERFORMANCE

What is the fastest way to boost cash flow in the near term? Oddly enough, the answer to this Holy Grail of management questions is actually quite simple: Just neutralize losses.

What is the fastest way to boost cash flow in the medium term? Answer: Focus growth investments on the most highly profitable business segments now, and improve the profitability performance of underperforming ones.

While the premise underlying the profit pool approach is that business value is tied to long-term cash flow, driving cash flow in the nearer term has a useful role to play (discussed momentarily). With that in mind, there are three deliverables for this first step in the profit pool approach:

1. Create a snapshot of real, *current* profit performance of business segments, and how operating and economic models are related.
2. Identify opportunities to substantively boost cash flow in the near term and possibly medium term.
3. Develop insights that will be used to develop the longer-term view of markets in Chapter 5, and formulate market strategy in Chapter 6.

With these deliverables, this step builds a platform to drive long-term value creation. The first deliverable, getting visibility of current cash-based profit performance at a granular level, creates the fact base for the second deliverable, as it shows where to act to boost cash flow in the near term. The process of getting that visibility and gauging the impact of actions is all that is needed to create the third deliverable, as the thinking and information reviewed generates keen insights into the sources and drivers of cash flow. Indeed, the steps outlined in the two chapters that follow, including plotting market profit pools and formulating market strategy, have their roots in first crafting a solid picture of the current economic model.

In short, this step comprises only two tasks, each addressed sequentially in this chapter. The first is to develop the snapshot of current profit performance of the business's segments (its internal profit pools), which is largely a challenge of cutting through accounting standards and systems and developing granular profit information. The second task is to act to boost profit performance; opportunities have to be identified and actions must be planned and executed. This second task has to be approached with care; while the enthusiasm to act will be compelling, it must be moderated to avoid actions that will hamstring the current business or limit future opportunities.

For example, it would not be wise to act without understanding the interactions among segments of offerings, customers, channels, and geographies. Take the case of a detergent manufacturer with a dispenser that appears to be a serious profit drain. Management would clearly be foolish if they eliminated it, as such a move would seriously hamper sales of its closely-related and highly profitable detergent. Similar sorts of issues arise in customer portfolio management, where, for example, it would make little sense to abandon a large customer, when the volume of goods sold to that customer is what unlocks a critical reduction in raw material costs (which in turn supports the high cash-based profitability of the entire line). Again, understanding market and other issues is a critical factor in exploiting internal profit pools.

Cut through the GAAP and Other Information Obfuscation

Objective: Create a clear picture of internal profit pools—the sources and drains of profitability within the business.
Problem: The accounting profession and government regulators have created a set of standards and reports over hundreds of years that effectively obfuscate true, cash-based business economics.
Solution: Unwind the tangled mess presented to us in accounting and other systems, and reconstitute the underlying factual information in a way that reflects the business's true economics.

The key to reflecting true economics at a granular level lies in apportioning revenues and expenses using methods that accurately reflect the cash inflows and resource consumption of each segment of the business—each internal profit pool. As previously mentioned, we begin with a focus on current information, typically the latest year, for each of the four types of segments (across the business's offerings, customers, channels, and geographies).

The Unwinding Road

We should start by reiterating that this book is not a how-to manual for finance professionals. In fact, we have gone to great lengths to avoid entering into a litany of finance techno-speak (see the sidebar). Much of what follows is an executive manager's view of what needs to get done and what to watch out for.

> ### Unwinding Accounting Numbers—Quick Caveats
>
> We have adopted a truly managerial approach to the effort/reward trade-off in our discussion on unwinding accounting numbers, carefully circumventing a mutually exclusive, collectively exhaustive approach. There are a great number of works that do unwind today's GAAP-based financial statements in detail, and those professionals looking for tips and standards guides should turn to some of those other works instead. To the contrary, we have oriented this discussion around the needs of business leaders—providing a short review of what the key issues are, where they are to be found, and what needs to be done to develop a useful picture of actual economics:
>
> - *Needed accuracy.* Based on results testing, a 90 percent accuracy rate in internal profit pool cost allocation is sufficient for line items of 1 percent of revenues or less; greater accuracy is only needed for more significant costs. This allows good flexibility to prioritize this effort and focus on what really matters—and get to results quickly. In line with this, the discussions in this chapter specifically highlight approaches, areas, and indicators of where effort to increase accuracy is and is not likely to be worthwhile.
> - *Source information reliability.* Also, in the spirit of judiciously using resources and effort, the words *underlying factual information* in the "Solution" described at the beginning of this section were chosen carefully. Before massaging the information (as required by various standards and regulations), accountants do a considerable amount of footing and ticking of the various flows of money within and between businesses, checking that those flows are well policed. As a result, the core of the historical money flow information is actually tremendously accurate and can be used with a high degree of confidence—provided that the financial analyst is aware of the relevant accounting standards and regulations that need to be unwound.
> - *Properly qualified practitioners.* This brings us to the final caveat. Given the gravity of the impact to business performance, it is very

> important that the sort of work we are advocating, to unwind the accounting, is actually conducted by qualified and competent financial analysts. In fact, to be truly effective, the team addressing these issues should comprise both market and finance resources, which need to be increasingly mixed together as the process rolls forward.

While every business is different, most of the key issues involved in unwinding accounting information to profile internal profit pools are remarkably similar—and, of course, even more similar between businesses in the same industry or sector. Figure 4.1 represents, simplistically, the transformation needed and outlines the key issues in the unwinding process, line by line.

The first thing to notice is that the output doesn't look too dissimilar from the inputs (which are the regular GAAP financial statements, though with granular source information). This is no accident; after all, we are still driving to profit—only in the cash-based philosophy we have removed artificially injected numbers and other distortions. Notice also that the various line items remain mostly the same, which seems natural, since we are dealing with the same business functions.

At a high level, there are two tasks that need to get done. In addition to cleaning up (removing) the number manipulation within each of the GAAP statement's line items, line-item dollar amounts must be parsed out to each internal profit pool in an apportioning process.

It is in this second, parsing-out task where things get a little tricky. Most businesses do not think in terms of internal profit pools today, and there is certainly no common approach in information systems to defining what those business segments are at a granular level within each functional area (such as sales, marketing, and others), let alone a common approach to apportioning the dollars. Part of the reason for this incongruence between business functions is that each one has considerable control over the information systems it uses, and prioritizes its systems solutions from the perspective of managing that function over other possible motives (such as conforming with a high-level business view of what the segments should be). In sales, for example, *salesforce.com* may be the system of choice, and they may have parsed the business out by customer type. In manufacturing, however, they may be using *MAPICS* and look at the business by product type, with a particular orientation around the bill of materials.

Each line item needs to be unwound separately and individually, though concurrently to make sure the time periods in the review are the same. Appendix A sets out, for each line item, a brief outline of what the typical

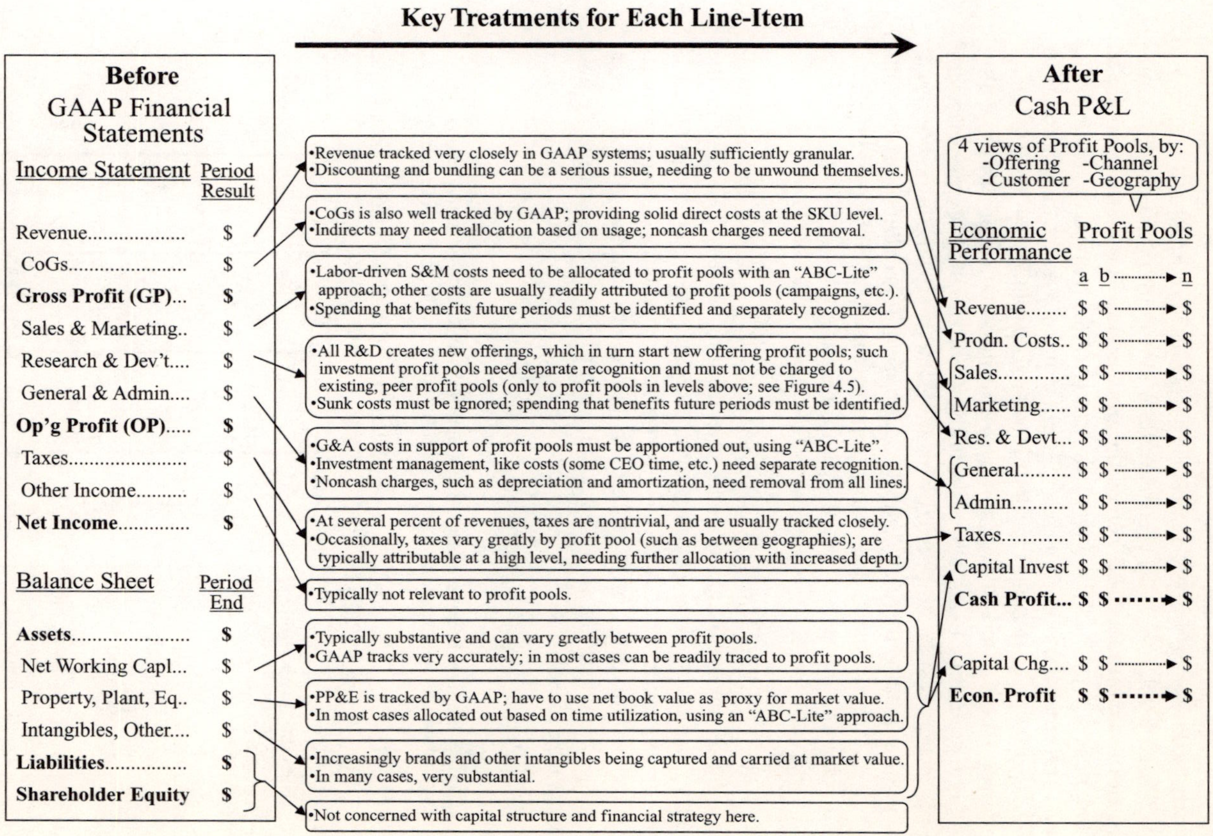

Key Treatments for Each Line-Item

Before
GAAP Financial Statements

Income Statement — Period Result

Line Item	Amount	Key Treatments
Revenue	$	• Revenue tracked very closely in GAAP systems; usually sufficiently granular. • Discounting and bundling can be a serious issue, needing to be unwound themselves
CoGs	$	• CoGs is also well tracked by GAAP; providing solid direct costs at the SKU level. • Indirects may need reallocation based on usage; noncash charges need removal.
Gross Profit (GP)	**$**	
Sales & Marketing	$	• Labor-driven S&M costs need to be allocated to profit pools with an "ABC-Lite" approach; other costs are usually readily attributed to profit pools (campaigns, etc.). • Spending that benefits future periods must be identified and separately recognized.
Research & Dev't	$	• All R&D creates new offerings, which in turn start new offering profit pools; such investment profit pools need separate recognition and must not be charged to existing, peer profit pools (only to profit pools in levels above; see Figure 4.5). • Sunk costs must be ignored; spending that benefits future periods must be identified
General & Admin	$	• G&A costs in support of profit pools must be apportioned out, using "ABC-Lite". • Investment management, like costs (some CEO time, etc.) need separate recognition. • Noncash charges, such as depreciation and amortization, need removal from all lines.
Op'g Profit (OP)	**$**	
Taxes	$	• At several percent of revenues, taxes are nontrivial, and are usually tracked closely. • Occasionally, taxes vary greatly by profit pool (such as between geographies); are typically attributable at a high level, needing further allocation with increased depth.
Other Income	$	• Typically not relevant to profit pools.
Net Income	**$**	

Balance Sheet — Period End

Line Item	Amount	Key Treatments
Assets	**$**	
Net Working Capl	$	• Typically substantive and can vary greatly between profit pools. • GAAP tracks very accurately; in most cases can be readily traced to profit pools.
Property, Plant, Eq.	$	• PP&E is tracked by GAAP; have to use net book value as proxy for market value. • In most cases allocated out based on time utilization, using an "ABC-Lite" approach.
Intangibles, Other	$	• Increasingly brands and other intangibles being captured and carried at market value.
Liabilities	**$**	• In many cases, very substantial.
Shareholder Equity	**$**	• Not concerned with capital structure and financial strategy here.

After
Cash P&L

4 views of Profit Pools, by:
- Offering
- Channel
- Customer
- Geography

Economic Performance — Profit Pools

	a	b	...	n
Revenue	$	$		$
Prodn. Costs	$	$		$
Sales	$	$		$
Marketing	$	$		$
Res. & Dev't	$	$		$
General	$	$		$
Admin	$	$		$
Taxes	$	$		$
Capital Invest	**$**	**$**		**$**
Cash Profit	**$**	**$**		**$**
Capital Chg	$	$		$
Econ. Profit	**$**	**$**		**$**

FIGURE 4.1 Key Elements to Unwinding Accounting Obfuscation

Source: Business Intelligence Associates LLC.

information situation is, the typical dollar magnitude of the line item (to help in prioritization), and what approaches are needed; much of it is illustrated with examples. The discussion in Appendix A uses Figure 4.1 as a sort of road map, addressing the key issues for each line item in turn.

At a high level, however, there are three important prerequisite notions that must be well understood before the unwinding. The first is granularity and the need to properly navigate the trade-offs involved in assembling granular information, both in terms of depth or *fineness* of the data and in how to segment the business to define internal profit pools and delineate boundaries. The second notion concerns the importance of distinguishing investment spending from other spending—and treating it properly (for example, when is spending actually an investment creating a new internal profit pool?). Finally there is timing, when spending occurs and benefits are reaped; current results inevitably benefit from previous spending, and current spending inevitably benefits future results.

GETTING GRANULAR PROFITABILITY INFORMATION As a rule, the finer the granularity of the information, the better the insights, and so the greater the potential for improved results. However, in some cases the information is simply not available, while in others great effort is needed to get it—perhaps a prohibitive amount—and a prioritized approach enables greater, faster management impact. Figure 4.2 sets out example levels of granularity and the types of issues that will be encountered.

As a rule, the finer the granularity, the better the insights and potential results; however, fineness requires high levels of effort and runs into practical constraints.

Granularity/Fineness
- The finer the granularity, the better the insights and results.
- The finest levels of granularity are usually achievable; key barriers are:
  - Special queries of several systems.
  - Special analysis to measure *tailored* allocation metrics.

Approach Process
- The finest levels of data granularity should be sought first:
  - Problem areas are found quickly.
  - Sources are tapped only once.
- Conversely, the actual *analysis* should be at high levels to identify issue areas (for example, ongoing high losses or profits, quick opportunities) and prioritize efforts.

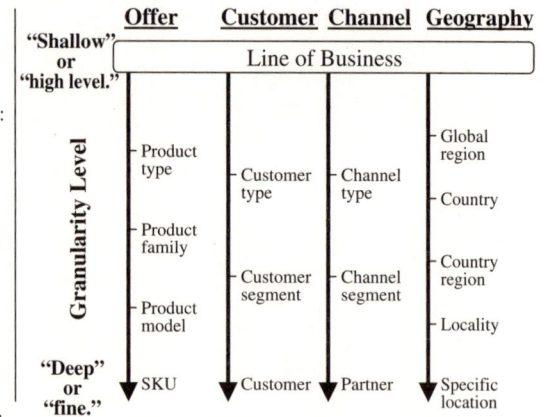

Granularity Level	Offer	Customer	Channel	Geography
"Shallow" or "high level."	Line of Business			
	Product type	Customer type	Channel type	Global region / Country
	Product family	Customer segment	Channel segment	Country region
	Product model			Locality
"Deep" or "fine."	SKU	Customer	Partner	Specific location

FIGURE 4.2 Getting Granular

Source: Business Intelligence Associates LLC.

The best approach is to start by attempting to get the finest information, passing over issue areas where the effort is likely significant, and moving to the next area so that a broad picture is gained. In this way it becomes clear where the gaps are and what level of effort is needed to fill them, and most of the organization will be tapped with data requests only once. Obviously, granular information can be consolidated to create higher-level information, and not so in the reverse. Once the information has been acquired, the analysis should start at the shallower levels of granularity, assessing internal profit pools at the lines-of-business level, and then going down to deeper levels as information availability and acquisition effort allows. Naturally, in line with the philosophy of getting to results quickly, this has to be prioritized; areas with substantive losses or good positive-profit growth potential should receive the bulk of initial attention.

Table 4.1 looks at how a printer company like Hewlett-Packard might structure its internal profit pools. In addition to data fineness, the question of what schemes to use in segmenting the business and defining boundaries between profit pools must be addressed. Offerings, customers, channels, and geographies need to be grouped in ways that will provide insights as to sources and drains of profitability. The value of the profit pool approach hinges on the segmentation schemes used; groupings must give insight into market and customer behavior, allow measurement of activities and results, and facilitate targeted actions. And perhaps just as critical, the definition of each profit pool must be exactly the same for all line items in Figure 4.1 (to be internally consistent and mutually exclusive).

The first time around, it is best to start using whatever segment scheme is currently most prevalent in the business, and using its existing information sources. For example, offerings may already be segmented in many of the business's systems by product family, with perhaps only minor differences in definition between the functions. This existing segmentation should be adopted initially and used to generate initial profit pool views. However, segmentation schemes must be adjusted over time so that the business can focus on segments in a way that promotes business value creation. Typically, changes in segmentation schemes are needed at each step in this program as it proceeds from internal profit pool assessments to market profit pool assessments and on to market strategy formulation.

IS THAT SPENDING OR INVESTING? In most people's vocabulary, *investing* is associated with deploying capital in an acquisition that, it is hoped, will deliver a financial return. Within a business, however, such an understanding cannot hold, since any spending by a business is in some sense intended to deliver a financial return (and the business is itself the investment vehicle). A new robot that paints cars on a production line is a business investment, since it is intended to reduce operating costs and increase unit profitability, thus creating incremental cash flow and delivering a financial return.

TABLE 4.1 Example Profit Pools for Hewlett-Packard

	Offering		Customer		Channel		Geography	
Level	Level	Example	Level	Example	Level	Example	Level	Example
1	Lines of business include printers, computers, technology services, etc.							
2	Product type	Office printers	Customer type	Fortune 500, industrials	Channel type	Value-add resellers (VARs)	International region	North America
3	Product family	Laser printers	Customer subtype	Auto manufacturer	Channel subtype	National VARs	Country	United States
4	Product model	1200 dpm printer	Customer	Ford	Channel partner	Micron	National region	Great Lakes
5	SKU	Gray, 120v, etc.					Locality	Detroit vicinity

An advertising campaign that will grow brand awareness and boost share and profits is also commonly thought of by business managers as an investment. In fact, the same principle can be applied to almost any cost in business—labor, machinery, even business partners, since they all help the business deliver.

However, for our purposes of characterizing internal profit pools and using them to understand the sources and drains in businesses, we limit the meaning of *investment* by business to spending that is intended to create a *new* area of value creation. While this may seem to be something of a minor word game, the implications to how profit pools are defined and their economics are compiled are hugely significant. This is because spending to develop a *new* business area has no place being charged to existing business areas, since it is akin to seeding a start-up with venture capital and is expected to have its own revenue and ultimately profit streams down the road. It may substitute out existing businesses at some point, but that does not mean that it should be considered as an expense for that business.

Profit pools can be defined in terms of offerings, customers, channels, or geographies, and so spending that creates a new element to any of these is, for profit pool purposes, investing. Figure 4.3 illustrates how such

A clear view of where spending will benefit the business is required; that spending must only be incorporated into profit pools it benefits; new profit pools must be created as needed.

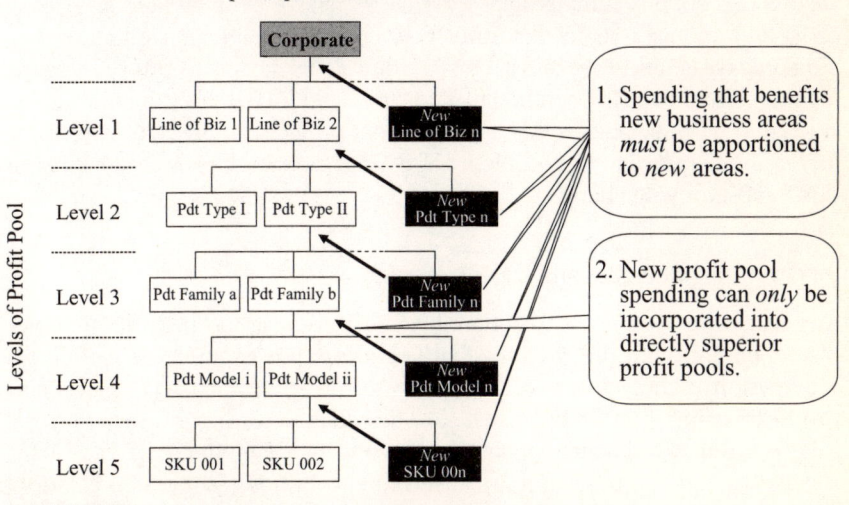

FIGURE 4.3 Investment Spending Creates New Profit Pools
Source: Business Intelligence Associates LLC.

spending needs to be incorporated into a hierarchy of profit pools—in this case, oriented around offerings.

A clear understanding of *where* spending benefits the business is paramount. More often than not, spending benefits several areas and needs to be apportioned out, including to new businesses areas as necessary. Sales campaigns illustrate this well. Take the case of a campaign that covers a family of laptops, including a new laptop expected out at some point in the future. In the process of apportioning out the cost of the campaign, some amount needs to be charged to a new internal profit pool, representing the new laptop. Naturally, it would be misleading for the cost of the campaign to be entirely charged to the existing set of offerings in that family of laptops to the exclusion of the new launch.

However, when looking at a higher level of profit pools—perhaps, say, across all laptop families—the entire cost of that sales campaign would be fully captured, along with all of the economics of that laptop family—its existing offerings and the expected new launch. Profit pools incorporate the economics of all subordinate profit pools, both existing and expected. This principle extends all the way up to the corporate level, where business lines are profit pools and spending in new business lines must be regarded as the investments it undoubtedly represents.

Finally, there is the notion of *sunk costs*, a very real management principle that must be adhered to (though is brazenly violated in the noncash charges GAAP applies with depreciation and other amortizations). Historical investment spending, as previously defined, is of no further concern to investors (except any remaining assets that may have been created as a result of it) and should not be of further concern to management either. These are sunk costs, and they must be regarded as irrelevant to future decision making—no matter how difficult that is to accept! An interesting and useful side effect of sunk costs is that as investment projects progress, they become increasingly attractive to complete (of course, provided projected estimates don't substantively change).

Synchronizing Revenues and Expenses

Any single-period view of profitability must address the need to synchronize spending with the fruits of that spending. For example, is it right for a television manufacturer to assess the current performance of one of its products, using a profitability measure that includes a down payment for a sales event that will actually take place two years down the road? Curiously, it was this sort of question that caused the accounting profession to adopt its entire scheme of noncash charges—depreciating capital investments over arbitrary time periods, and even amortizing intangible assets where it was not clear that their value actually depleted with time. They never extended the scheme to account for time mismatches between noncapital spending and their expected results, possibly recognizing how thorny the issue can become, and how unsuitable it all is for standardized amortization schedules.

So how should business reporting deal with these timing mismatches? After all, there are many areas where spending in one period is to the benefit of future periods—for example, in marketing, where advertising has a lasting impact on brand recognition; in sales, where a long sales cycle benefits a subsequent period; in operations, with long-lead time purchasing efforts; and of course, in R&D. Figure 4.4 illustrates such spend/return timing mismatches, noting that even revenue is subject to timing ambiguity depending on how it is defined, in addition to the issues of synchronizing it with spending that created it.

The good news is that the problem is not very significant in most situations, given that most business enterprises are in a steady state or something relatively close to it. The objective of single-period profitability measurements is to get a snapshot of current performance, preferably one that characterizes steady-state profitability, perhaps also showing the impact of non-steady-state conditions, if applicable. A business in steady state (neither it nor its market is substantially growing or shrinking) may have expenses shifted in time; however, those expenses are *likely to be the same in magnitude over a repeating period*, such as a year. As a result, the snapshot of profitability will be the same, whether it contained a straightforward slice

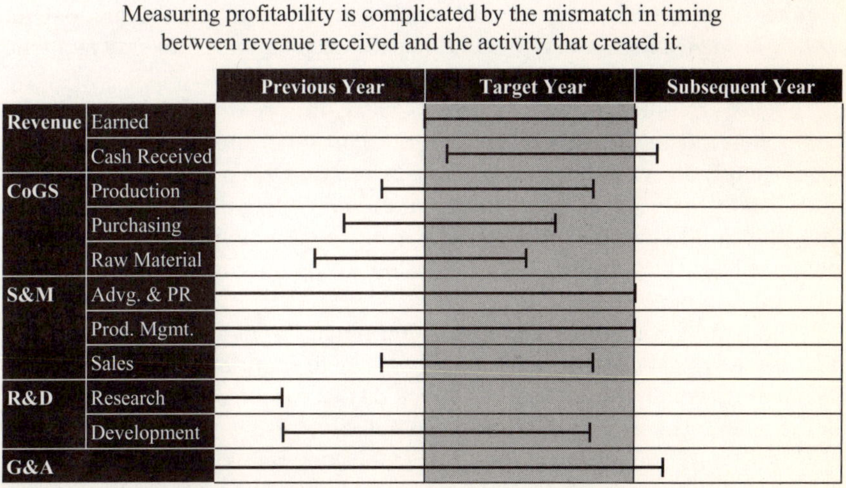

Measuring profitability is complicated by the mismatch in timing between revenue received and the activity that created it.

		Previous Year	Target Year	Subsequent Year
Revenue	Earned		⊢─────────┤	
	Cash Received		⊢────────────┤	
CoGS	Production	⊢─────────────┤		
	Purchasing	⊢──────────┤		
	Raw Material	⊢───────┤		
S&M	Advg. & PR	⊢────────────────┤		
	Prod. Mgmt.	⊢────────────────┤		
	Sales	⊢─────────┤		
R&D	Research	⊢──┤		
	Development	⊢──────────┤		
G&A				⊢┤

FIGURE 4.4 Timing—An Illustration of the Spending and Returns Mismatch
Source: Business Intelligence Associates LLC.

of revenue and expenses over the target period (such as the shaded year in Figure 4.4), or whether each expense was found, isolated, and directly matched to the revenue earned. The former approach delivers a result that accurately reflects actual profitability, while avoiding a great deal of complication that would probably lead to errors, disagreement, and delay.

The problems arise in situations where a business is not in steady state—such as where growth spending is succeeding in driving growth and causing differences in other spending between the beginning and end of the period. In fact, simple market growth or decline also causes similar differences in spending between the beginning and end of periods. In these circumstances, steady state profitability is still the primary measurement need; adjustments are needed for the fact that growth or shrinkage is distorting performance results. Of course, in the case of growth, distortion comes as a result of higher expenses (to drive that growth), and the reverse is true for shrinkage.

Now we see how complex the issue can be, but it turns out that there is a very pragmatic approach to dealing with it. The solution lies in finding economic profit (EP) for all internal profit pools, and then in those internal profit pools where the investment problem is believed to exist, an additional steady-state EP is estimated at a very crude level of accuracy.

In this way, the effort expended is limited (focused on just the issue areas) and the estimate is only sufficient to see if there is a substantive issue to account for. In most cases, the issue areas are few—though it is worth finding where they are, since growth is critical to value creation (as explored in Chapter 6). When the small number of issue areas is identified, a more in-depth, accurate calculation of steady-state EP can be made—but *only if needed*; often, it is not needed as it doesn't alter the overall strategic picture.

Figure 4.5 illustrates this process, using the offering portfolio of the technology business assessed throughout Part One. In the chart, "Normal" EP is simply EP calculated including *all* relevant spending in the period, and "Steady State" EP is as calculated in the preceding discussion. The third line, the "Milk Line" EP, is reserved for those cases where the business is being milked; it is usually only compiled in circumstances where an exit strategy is underway.

In Figure 4.5, all three EPs were determined for all internal profit pools. This is rarely needed, since the impact of growth spending is often relatively small, and overall insights are not affected (this can be seen in the example in the chart). The more pragmatic approach of focusing on likely issue areas is well tested. The alternative, to accurately determine steady-state EP for all internal profit pools from the start, quickly becomes mired in questions over subjective judgments (for example, exactly which expenses constitute growth spending) and becomes bogged down in political agendas and

Economic Profit Margin (EP/Invested Capital)
(Percent)

Solid: Normal — EP with all current period expenses

Thick: Steady-State — EP with expenses that maintain zero growth, or declines that match any market declines

Dotted: Milk Line — EP excluding all expenses that do not deliver current-period benefits

Invested Capital ($ Millions)

Issue Areas:
Where steady-state spending is estimated to be significantly at variance with current spending.

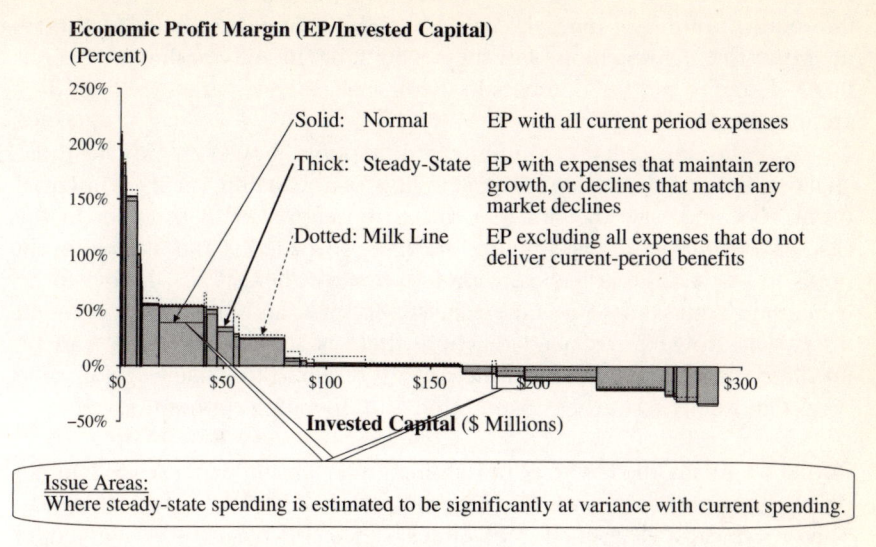

FIGURE 4.5 Calculating Single Period Profit, and Adjusting for Steady State
Source: Company reports, Business Intelligence Associates LLC.

roadblocks. By having normal EP set a solid, fact-based stake, and using focus to limit the number of issue areas, decision making is able to move forward relatively unimpeded.

Cleaning Up Accounting Adjustments and Parsing Out Profits

With the issues of granularity, investment spending, and time synchronization in mind, the process to unwind financial reports can begin: cleaning up accounting manipulations and apportioning the dollar amounts in the line items of Figure 4.1 to each internal profit pool. The following discussion takes a high-level look at what needs to get done, starting with revenues, then moving on to expenses and capital. A more detailed review, by line item, is in Appendix A.

Overall, the cleaning up task is simple in concept, just to remove non-cash charges, though it takes some investigative persistence to get done. Noncash charges are primarily depreciation and amortization, and the problem is driven by the great variety of ways that GAAP-based systems book them. Depreciation can be found in cost of goods, where plant and machinery depreciation charges are calculated and somehow allocated out in standard costs. It can also be found in sales and marketing and in R&D, where it may have been allocated; or it is consolidated and entirely charged to general and administrative (G&A) expenses. There is little more to say on the removal of those noncash charges, except to reiterate that it is primarily a quest of investigation, and the accountants in your business who put these elements into the numbers in the first place know exactly where they are hidden.

Apportioning dollars to internal profit pools, however, can be more challenging; it requires an understanding of the nature of each internal profit pool and how the dollars came to be earned or consumed. In the case of *attribution*, dollar amounts are directly related to the internal profit pools in question; this is clearly preferred since there is no sharing to be concerned with, and so it is the easiest and most accurate apportionment. *Allocation*, however, is needed where there is sharing and there can be no direct attribution; allocation metrics are required to parse out dollars in ways that reflect resource consumption and operating economics.

REVENUE   Again, the key to apportioning revenues and expenses to internal profit pools is to *make sure that they are matched* in time and in relevance. This is typically clear-cut for revenues, since the business is segmented into internal profit pools using market viewpoints (offerings, customers, channels, and geographies), and revenue information is tracked by GAAP-based systems closely, and at a very granular level. Nevertheless, some issues arise in cases of bundled sales and pricing; Appendix A reviews some of the intricacies involved.

EXPENSES   The bulk of what needs to be apportioned lies in costs; most of the issues that arise, and effort expended, will be in dealing with costs. Of course, the tool that best apportions costs to the part of the business that consumed them is activity-based costing (ABC). Formally introduced in the mid-1980s, this is a technique with which most of today's managers are quite familiar. Interestingly, however, only a very small number of businesses actually use it. Several studies say that ABC is used to some degree by approximately one-fifth of major companies, though all acknowledge it is extremely rare to find it used systemically, rather than in support of seeing costs within a few operational functions. Those and other studies report that just about all other businesses use their GAAP-based reporting systems for managerial reporting—together with their inherent use of inaccurate apportioning and amortizing methods.

Consistent with the pragmatic approach of this book, and the consequential need to use focus, prioritization, and appropriate accuracy, we strongly advocate a method that we call *ABC-lite*. In this approach, the intention is to get expenses apportioned to a 90 percent accuracy rate, though using only a fraction of the effort of a full-blown ABC initiative. Prioritization is the key—focusing on substantive line items and expending little or no effort on trivial ones (indeed, without prioritization, analysts get mired in the detail and freeze the process). In tests, it turns out that *for a typical business*, wrongly apportioned line items of 1 percent or more of total revenues could cause a substantive shift in the EP margin of an average internal profit pool *relative* to other profit pools (in the order of +/−5 percent of the full range of the EP margin across all internal profit pools). Of course, this result is situation-specific to the company, the line item, and the profit pool. While 1 percent of total revenues may not seem much, it actually provides a huge amount of flexibility to the apportioning process.

So how does ABC-lite work? How is it different from regular ABC? Both intend to apportion expenses in proportion to the consumption of resources. In the case of ABC-lite, however, an exhaustive list of cost allocation metrics is not developed—just a few (say, five to ten) that deliver the sufficient 90 percent accuracy. However, they are much more thoughtfully selected than the two (revenue and unit sales) typically used in GAAP-based reporting.

The following example illustrates the application of ABC-lite to apportion the marketing expenses of a printer manufacturer. The charts in Figure 4.6 profile two different and relatively high-level views of how marketing expenses were apportioned. One view looks across the four different

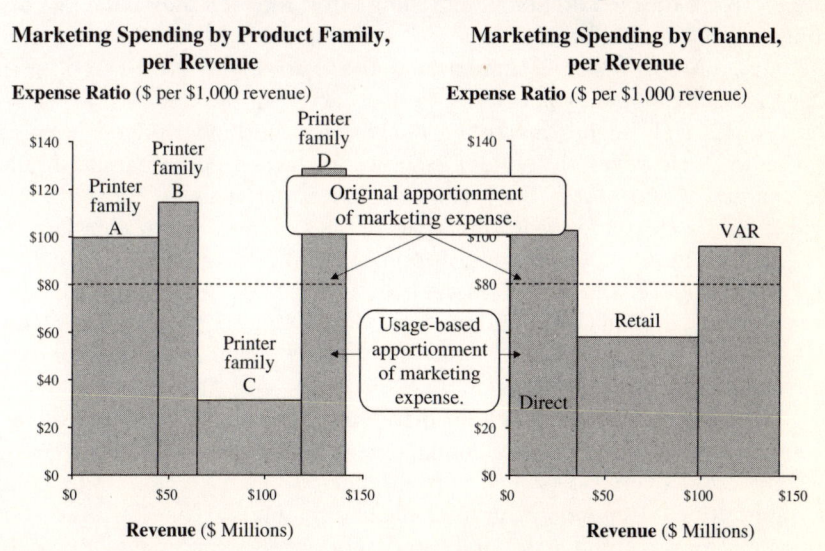

FIGURE 4.6 Example of Seriously Inaccurate Expense Apportionment—Part 1
Source: Company cost accounting reports, Business Intelligence Associates LLC.

families of in-office digital printers, "A" being the low-cost printer family, rising to "D," the top-end offerings. The other view looks across the three types of channel: printers sold through the direct sales force, through retailers, and through value-added resellers (VARs).

Historically, this business used revenue as the allocation driver for all marketing expenses. The amount apportioned to each internal profit pool under this original scheme is shown by the dotted line: $81 for each $1,000 of printer sold. The same approach and metric was also used to allocate marketing expenses across channel types. The solid line shows the apportionment of marketing expenses based on actual consumption.

We will briefly look at how actual consumption charges were determined in a moment. Focusing on the results for now, it is clear that printer family C actually consumes marketing resources far less than other printer families (around $31 per $1,000 sold) and is probably considerably more profitable than today's reports indicate as a result. Conversely, the other printer families, A, B, and D, are probably perceived to be significantly more profitable than they actually are, since they have been undercharged at $81 per $1,000 of sales versus their actual consumption rates of $100, $115, and $129 respectively.

One of the most interesting aspects of this situation was that the accountants chose revenues as the allocation metric because it was simple to implement, gave an acceptable result in compliance with GAAP, and *they felt it was more accurate* for large-ticket items to have a proportionately larger charge for the additional marketing effort they felt they must be consuming. With this in mind, Figure 4.7 sets out the same information from the more intuitive costs per unit basis. In the chart on the left, it can be seen that they actually got what they set out to achieve; the dotted line shows the progressively higher marketing charges for the higher-priced printers, B, C, and D. However, the solid line shows what each printer family should be charged based on the marketing resources they actually consume and reflecting the clear and misleading inaccuracies of the original approach.

As with most expense types, apportioning these expenses was a story of both attribution and allocation. As may be expected, in this case ABC-lite was adopted, minimizing the number of cost allocation drivers and applying them as widely as possible, with the intent of achieving an accuracy rate of at least 90 percent.

The main subfunctions within marketing in this example were advertising, public relations, channel management, product management, market research, and overhead (which is predominately management and shared administration). Depending on their relative magnitude, one or more subfunctions may warrant a separate and unique apportionment approach, though there is usually a significant amount of similarity in how they need

High-price printers were simplistically and erroneously charged
with larger share of marketing expenses.

Marketing Spending by Product Family, per Unit

Expense Ratio ($ per 1,000 units sold)

Marketing Spending by Channel, per Unit

Expense Ratio ($ per 1,000 units sold)

Original apportionment of marketing expense.

Usage-based apportionment of marketing expense.

Printer family A, Printer family B, Printer family C, Printer family D

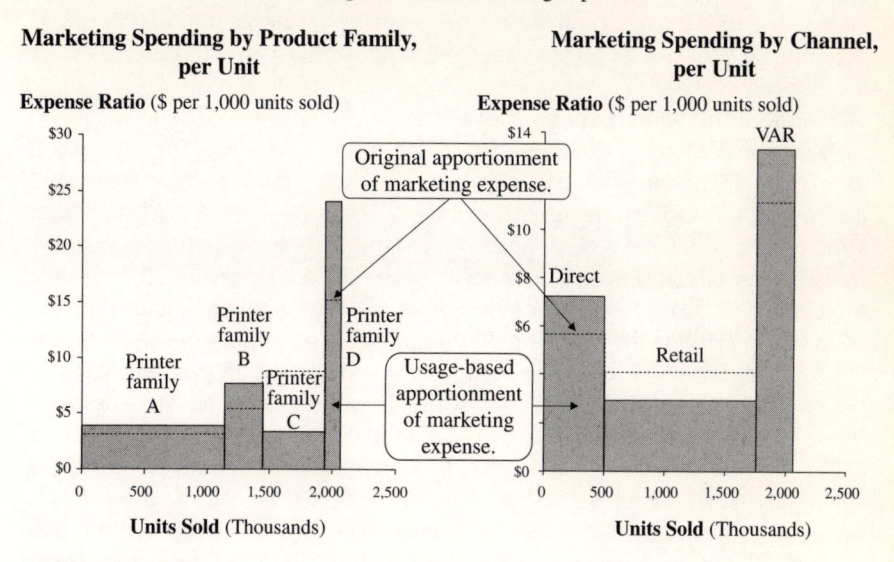

Direct, Retail, VAR

Units Sold (Thousands)

FIGURE 4.7 Example of Seriously Inaccurate Expense Apportionment—Part 2
Source: Company cost accounting reports, Business Intelligence Associates LLC.

to be treated. In nearly every business, such subfunctions are accounted for separately, for departmental budget tracking purposes, and are further subcategorized into items such as labor, travel, and the like. Furthermore, significant initiatives, such as campaigns to launch products, boost sales, and others, are also tracked separately; as a result, they are readily attributed directly, requiring little allocation.

Many expenses are often readily classifiable into either labor-based costs or a finite number of specific initiatives. Of course, labor-based expenses are allocated out in proportion with how individuals or teams spend time on each internal profit pool (which is one of the most used metrics in the ABC-lite approach). Expenses that are *attributable* to one or more internal profit pools need to be directly applied to them, perhaps needing some subsequent allocation if there is some subsequent sharing.

In terms of labor-based expenses, tracking of each marketing subfunction by GAAP-based systems is typically quite detailed, as is its expense categorization, such as salaries, bonuses, travel, and the like, and some allocated services, such as utilities, which are typically trivial. Under the 90 percent accuracy regime, many expense types simply need to be summed together and allocated out to internal profit pools based on where the entire department spends its time. While an in-depth time sheet analysis could be used, the ABC-lite philosophy urges using a simple high-level assertion by relevant mid-level managers of where time is being devoted over the period.

Some attributable expenses can pose a challenge and drive the need for additional metrics. Charges that are attributable to only one area, such as a mail campaign to boost sales of a specific printer to certain retail customers, are not an issue, while others, such as a mail campaign that aims to boost a family of printers to a range of customer types, need to be subsequently apportioned. This is where educated managerial judgment is needed; in most cases, the sums involved are relatively small, and the spending managers are sufficiently well trained and familiar with the issues to arbitrarily make allocations (keeping a key metric in their minds, such as the number of mail pieces that are relevant to printer X and/or customer type Y). In cases where the amounts are substantive, and where there is a lack of clarity, additional metrics will have to be carefully thought out and measured accurately (mail pieces or design time are perfectly acceptable approaches in the case just mentioned). These circumstances are not common, though in marketing there are two areas where it is often needed: in advertising and in PR. These types of spending are often substantive, paid to outside entities, and benefit many internal profit pools. Metrics that might be considered include brand impressions, quotes, web page views, and others.

Finally, there are allocations of allocations. For example, the utilities expenses in this illustration are typically relatively equal among similar workers, such as office workers, and are usually allocated to subfunctions using head count; this is sometimes already done by the GAAP-based reporting systems. They are then subsequently allocated, as described in the preceding paragraph. Overhead, such as the VP of marketing and associated staff, will also need to be allocated out, though again, specific inquiry is needed to determine where these individuals spend their time.

Keeping in mind the trade-offs of accuracy and significance in line item apportionment, it is worth looking across industries to see where allocations issues are likely to be. Figure 3.1 from Chapter 3 gives high-level income statement information for representative companies in 12 industries. As we saw earlier, cost of goods is a relatively less challenging cost to apportion (once noncash charges are removed), limiting the effort needed in defense, construction, and other industries. Conversely, those industries with significant marketing, sales, and G&A expenses will have more of a challenge; including entertainment, pharmaceuticals, retailing, and others. Research and development tends to be in the middle in terms of the challenge posed; most projects are tightly defined and readily allocated—though, of course, as an investment the relevant internal profit pools are separated out (and best treated as a multiperiod, long-term investment opportunity, addressed in Chapter 6).

CAPITAL As we saw in Chapter 3, the cost of capital is a critical consideration in assessing performance, as is capital investment spending made in the period. Naturally, both are charged against economic profit, and our task here is to get a clear view of both capital spending and capital employed by each internal profit pool.

So what qualifies as capital? At a high level there are three types of capital, with some subcomponents:

1. Net working capital.
    + Cash
    + Accounts receivable.
    + Inventory.
    − Accounts payable.
    ? Others.
2. Fixed assets (property, plant, and equipment).
3. Intangibles.

The first type, net working capital, comprises elements that tend to have a direct relationship with specific transactions and offerings, making it relatively easier to assign to internal profit pools (in contrast to expenses). Specifically, cash and accounts receivable are closely related to transactions and associated revenues, whereas inventory and accounts payable are more related to the cost of goods profile across internal profit pools; each of these is a good starting point for use as a capital allocation metric. Other items, typically less substantive, occasionally qualify as *current assets* and may warrant inclusion as working capital, such as payroll payables, and will need allocation using similar or new metrics.

Beyond net working capital the two other nontrivial types of capital investment are property, plant, and equipment (PP&E) and intangibles, which are different by virtue of the fact that it is more likely there will be divergence between their current value and their cost. Why is this important? Simply because we are interested in capital opportunity costs, and capital charges need to be based on what someone else is prepared to pay in exchange for the asset—its current market value.

Unfortunately, fixed assets (PP&E) are not tracked at market values under GAAP. Instead, GAAP initially records assets at acquisition cost and, except for land, depreciates them over a preset timeline. In many industries, these depreciated values are reasonably close to market values, and can be used to determine PP&E capital charges *on an exceptions basis*; but a high-level scan of significant value assets is warranted to detect substantive discrepancies. Generally, market values exceed book values, and so capital charges may tend to be underestimated. In situations where alternatives are being considered, liquidation costs need to be factored in where the asset cannot be readily redeployed internally.

In terms of apportioning PP&E assets to internal profit pools, the basic driver is time utilization; that is, the asset is apportioned to internal profit pools based on the proportion of time it serves in support of each. Of course, in non-capital-intensive industries PP&E is primarily property-related and significantly aligned with the labor in sales and marketing, R&D, and G&A, and is quite accurately allocated out based on staff time and head count within each of the these separate areas. Conversely, in capital-intensive industries an ABC-lite type effort may be needed to understand what the time utilization is of production machines and the like, by each internal profit pool. More considered time studies may be warranted for particularly high-value capital assets.

In many industries, intangible assets have represented a substantive capital investment, though in the past they have mostly been expensed when purchased or created within a business, or they were capitalized and amortized over 40 years or less by GAAP when acquired in a *business combination*. As a result, it has been very difficult to track and charge for these capital investments. That all changed in 2001 under the FASB's Statement of Financial Accounting Standards (SFAS) 141 and 142; suddenly, these assets acquired a value recognized in the accounting, but only in limited circumstances! If acquired externally, such as in an ordinary purchasing transaction or a business combination, they are assigned a fair value and booked as assets. The asset is then assigned a lifespan and amortized over that period (in the case of an indefinite lifespan, their value is tested annually for impairment, providing for downward changes in value only). This is all good news, as we now have useful information with which to understand the cost of these investments, and they can be charged to economic profit in a way similar to PP&E. Unfortunately, *similar intangibles created internally continue to be expensed* at cost under GAAP, and a specific effort is needed to get an understanding of what their values are.

For the most part, the accuracy needed in apportioning capital investments to internal profit pools is not as great as that needed for the expense line items. There are two reasons for this. First, the charges that are actually made to internal profit pools are usually relatively much smaller than those other line items, since only a fraction of the asset is charged (remember, the average opportunity cost for equity capital is 10 to 14 percent annually, and debt interest is approximately 4 to 8 percent). Second, the differences in assets apportioned to one internal profit pool versus another are usually much less than the differences in apportioning expenses, and so the impact of a more accurate apportioning scheme is reduced considerably.

Reconstitute the Numbers and See the Internal Profit Pools Emerge

At this point, when your business's financials are reassembled around granular internal profit pools, real insights start pouring out on how the business works and how its various segments are performing. The march to collect and analyze the required information is mundane and time consuming, but when it's done, you and other business leaders have an immensely powerful tool with which to manage the business.

Again, the reconstitution of the financials must be done by qualified finance professionals; a fair amount of book work is needed. The output depicted in Figure 4.1 may seem simple, but from there the business's economics will be reflected in a range of supporting and commonly structured spreadsheets that fan out from that simple output sheet. Two sorts of supporting sheets will be needed, both interacting with each other: those that represent outputs for each internal profit pool and subordinate internal profit pools (feeding into and being cumulated by the final output), and those that capture the raw data and apportioning information, and feed into one or several of the internal profit pool sheets.

The task of reassembling the financials needs to be taken very seriously, since the output is actually a model of your business and is extremely useful for decision making well beyond this initial exercise. The individuals tasked with building it need to be trusted, experienced with modeling, and expected to be with the business for some time; the knowledge they will develop on how and where the business is generating cash flow is a competitive asset. Further, the model itself must be *dynamic* in that all supporting spreadsheets should easily and accurately pass on changes, such that they report a correct and updated output following any change. There will be changes, as decisions are considered and outcomes weighed, both in this cycle and in future years.

Finally, information integrity is the critical concern. Thankfully, some of the principal checks of quality, of both the information collected and the economic model, are relatively straightforward and easy to implement. In its simplest form, does it all add up (or, in accountant speak, does it "foot")? Executives need to satisfy themselves that the output totals match the information from source data—such as the original GAAP financial statements. This is easily done by having the model deliver two additional views that specifically deliver two comparisons: one matching output information with the GAAP financial statements; and one matching preapportioned, departmental line item information with the GAAP financial statements (this second view is extremely useful for finding errors).

Now It's Time to Act: Neutralize Your Drains and Boost Your Sources

The time has come to make decisions and get some early results. And at this point there is a fork in the road; there are decisions that can be made now as a result of the information that is newly available (and are likely to seem obvious and nagging), and there are more subtle issues and opportunities that need to be gelled, and warrant further thought and research.

We go down the first path in the remainder of this chapter, highlighting the issues and opportunities that can be acted on immediately, leaving the second path for the next two chapters—though there is little to prevent simultaneous progress down the second path if there are sufficient resources at hand.

What *Can* We Do?

So what sorts of performance-improving opportunities become available at this (still relatively early) point? The short answer is that they can be both significant in impact and readily executable.

Three types of near-term performance-improving actions become possible with the availability of this single-period profit information (first listed in Chapter 2): neutralize profit drains, grow good profit sources, and improve the returns of poorly producing assets. Figure 4.8 repeats a chart from Chapter 2, setting forth these potential actions as applied to the example technology business studied throughout Part One.

NEUTRALIZATION CANDIDATES "Okay, so let's just stop doing that stuff on the right." In some quarters, there is an ever-present temptation to simply discontinue profit drains—internal profit pools with negative economic profit performance (on the right of Figure 4.8). That would surely leave a pile of cash in the business, right?

Not so fast. There are, of course, always market consequences associated with a withdrawal, both in terms of not having any further presence in the market, and in the act of withdrawal itself. In addition, Figure 4.8 reflects only the performance of offering-type internal profit pools; a similar situation and set of market-related issues need to be investigated and assessed for the other cuts of performance, primarily customers and channels, though also geographic internal profit pools.

Economic Profit Margin (EP/Invested Capital)
(Percent)

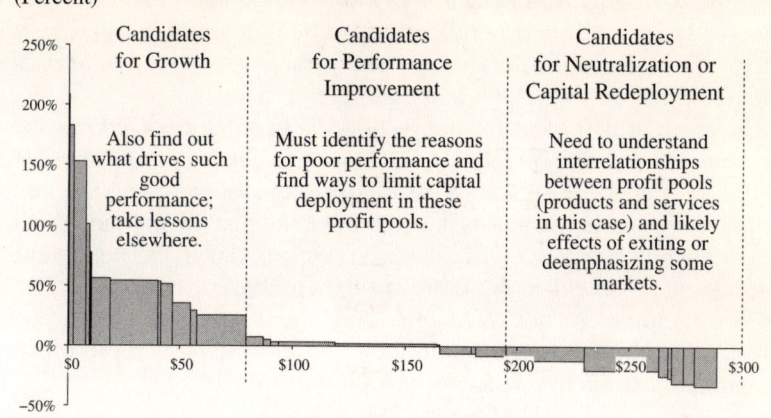

Candidates for Growth	Candidates for Performance Improvement	Candidates for Neutralization or Capital Redeployment
Also find out what drives such good performance; take lessons elsewhere.	Must identify the reasons for poor performance and find ways to limit capital deployment in these profit pools.	Need to understand interrelationships between profit pools (products and services in this case) and likely effects of exiting or deemphasizing some markets.

Invested Capital ($ Millions)

FIGURE 4.8 Actions Deserving Immediate Consideration
Source: Company reports, Business Intelligence Associates LLC.

The use of the word *neutralization* is deliberate. The discontinuation of internal profit pools is not the only option for profit drains. In fact, given the transition costs that are always involved in discontinuations, the first choice is always to simply stop losses with the minimum in change, now that we have a visibility of performance at a granular level.

Visibility and information are the places to start. There are two information-related issues that need to be dealt with. The first is to make sure that the key blocks of cost that are responsible for the negative results are accurate. If one of the offerings that is a major profit drain has a relatively large share of, say, distribution costs, management would be remiss if they do not follow up to make sure that the report is valid, or that there is not some unintended factor that can be easily remedied. For example, in the apparel industry, one vendor routinely used expensive one-day shipping services for core supply chain transport, when far more reasonable cost alternatives took *just a few hours more* (in a program that lasted months!). Following the money trail like this often delivers results quickly, and the situations where they exist are surprisingly prevalent.

The second information-related issue is to assess the broader context of negatively performing internal profit pools, to explain their performance in strategic, market, and operational terms. One source of explanation, as we discussed in the unwinding process, is whether the internal profit pool is in steady state. A business in growth mode must be understood from the viewpoint of its expected long- and medium-term returns, whereas a business in a withdrawal mode should be delivering attractive, harvestlike returns now. Alternatively, a negatively performing internal profit pool that is involved in some sort of bundle needs to be thought of holistically: What is the result of the bundle of internal profit pools? How would the package or bundle perform with a different component makeup?

However, if it is clear the profit drain is genuine and reflects steady-state performance, then obviously, management needs to move rapidly and proactively rectify the situation. Again, short of discontinuing the internal profit pool in question, options that will meet the goal of stopping the hemorrhaging while avoiding transition costs (associated with closing operations or shrinking a market footprint) are strongly preferred.

So what are those options? Generically, there are five for internal profit pools that need near-term neutralization, the idea being that profit is hemorrhaging and corrective action is needed quickly:

1. *Raise the price enough to move the business into positive profit.* As a direct result, market share will be ceded in line with the prevailing price elasticity; of course, share losses need to be considered in conjunction with the market impact on other parts of the business.
2. *Reduce the cost to make the offering.* This may reduce customer appeal, resulting in reduced share in line with demand elasticity, bringing with it its own set of market issues.
3. *Reduce the cost of the operating model.* This is also likely to reduce share, similar to option 2.
4. *Terminate part of the internal profit pool.* A look deeper into the internal profit pool may identify particular problem areas—perhaps particular customers, offering features, or the like.
5. *Terminate the internal profit pool entirely.*

Any change will have an impact on other parts of the market, and interrelationships with other internal profit pools must be understood and weighed with care. Of course, the objective is to deliver an overall positive profit result without jeopardizing any desirable strategic market positioning. When in doubt, it is a good idea to limit changes until the strategy formulation work of the next two steps in the program have been completed.

It is also obvious from the preceding list of options that there is a very limited number of relatively standard market unknowns that need to be answered to decide on the optimal path forward:

- What is the price/share elasticity of that internal profit pool?
- What is the nature of interrelationships with other internal profit pools?
- What changes in market dynamics (price, volume, competition) are likely or expected?

One interesting consideration is the recognition that withdrawing from a profit pool can also have benefits. A buyer may be willing to pay for the business or its assets, reducing or perhaps even reversing transition costs, such that capital redeployment is a readily available option. Or a reduced market footprint can have a positive effect on the brand (and on other internal profit pools), showing a focus and a specialty, which can have a very positive impact on pricing and returns elsewhere, depending on the market.

Although these options are rational and well tested, decisions involving withdrawals or shrinkage are unusual and often feel like a leap of faith, and so can take some time to get agreement. This is one of the principal reasons for getting started as early as possible—to bolster the fact base, allaying market concerns in particular, and getting the buy-in process under way.

Typically, most negatively performing internal profit pools can be neutralized in the long run—say 80 percent of total profit drainage is halted. In the process, perhaps only 20 to 40 percent of the negative-profit internal profit pools concerned are actually discontinued. In the immediate term, pending the decisions of upcoming strategy formulation steps, businesses are often comfortable with starting the neutralization of 10 percent of negatively performing invested capital, delivering a very powerful near-term boost to cash flow.

Of course, whatever the remedy devised, it is clear that management *must stop growth investments* in negatively performing internal profit pools—unless there is a very compelling strategic reason.

NULL INTERNAL PROFIT POOLS Internal profit pools that are just earning their expected rates of return are not as urgent an issue as the other two types. In addition, the action needed for them to improve performance is typically something of a medium-term proposition. There are exceptions to this, particularly in the light of newly gained insights from the internal profit pool review; that review always identifies several easy-to-fix opportunities (such as the use of costly transportation in the apparel example earlier).

In terms of the medium-term improvement opportunities, it is obviously preferable to get them under way sooner, rather than later. Of course, a chicken-or-egg issue arises: Which internal profit pools will be eliminated in the strategy formulation of the last step (since it would be pointless to devote considerable effort into an area that is ultimately discontinued)? As each situation is unique, the guidance on which improvement initiative is worth investing in is just as unique; it is generally better to postpone investing effort in internal profit pools that have relationships with negative-profit internal profit pools, pending decisions over their own futures.

Funds redirected away from growing negatively performing internal profit pools are now available to help improve the performance of these null-contribution internal profit pools. The principal measure is the *marginal* return from such spending. In other words, would better results be achieved from improving the performance of these internal profit pools (note that we are always interested in long-term results), or from some of the opportunities likely to be available from the high-return growth candidates discussed next?

INTERNAL PROFIT POOLS FOR GROWTH   "Let's just grow the hell out of those guys on the left." It always seems much easier to invest for growth in high-return internal profit pools, and to some extent that's true in near-term decision making. Although the goal may remain the same—that is, to promote growth—there are crucial differences among high-return internal profit pools. Business leaders have a duty to use investment resources effectively and must fully understand the differences in potential between opportunities. Simply spreading growth investment funds like butter, equally among internal profit pools, is not sufficient and is reminiscent of pre-value-maximizing management philosophies.

The path forward must strike a balance between three factors. The first and most obvious factor is the relative rate of return between internal profit pools; naturally, higher-return investments are preferred. But it is not a simple case of investing in the internal profit pools at the extreme left of Figure 4.8; for one thing, there may not be any scope for growth left in them.

What is needed is an understanding of the likely returns on marginal capital investments—we need to get under the hood of each internal profit pool to see *where* additional investments will deliver the most return. Each internal profit pool has a set of characteristics, and a change in the formula is likely to change those characteristics. Growth spending may not be possible, or it may intensify competition or drive other profit-reducing effects.

The second factor that must be considered is the need to act consistently with whatever strategy is crafted later in the program. To some degree this needs some crystal ball reading, and acting for near-term results before knowing long-term strategic directions always carries the risk of having to reverse course. However, there are usually obvious indicators for most internal profit pools. It would probably be a solid bet, for example, to increase growth investing on something that is a high positive performer and core to the business (as high-end servers are to Dell, or even its direct-to-consumer Internet channel), or an offering that the brand is commonly associated with (as Classic Coke is to Coca-Cola).

The last factor needing consideration is portfolio balance. Simply put, the interrelationships between the internal profit pools are such that changes (such as attempts to grow a specific internal profit pool) invariably have further effects both internally in operations and externally in the market. Accelerating the growth of a line of detergents, for example, will invariably drive a need for greater capacity and raw material demand, potentially impacting other lines of detergents with increased costs, or perhaps reducing their available shelf space in retail partners.

More likely than not, however, a growth investment in a high-return internal profit pool is going to be a net gain for the business, no matter where it goes. The three issues just discussed are generally nice ones to have and must not deter rapid actions to focus growth on high-return internal profit pools.

Indeed, in all of the three types of possible near-term action—grow, improve, and neutralize—the economics have to be reworked with the new expected conditions and outcomes. Naturally, no action should proceed without economic simulation of the new, post-action environment. Decision makers must ensure that the new, changed business model and internal profit pool economics are substantively more favorable than the original configuration. Within the business, proposed changes will cause capacity to be redistributed and reshaped, such that costs and assets must be reapportioned across internal profit pools. Market conditions will also alter in response to changes, driving changes in pricing, demand, competition, and other factors. The following discussion reviews these market issues at a high level, identifying what the key factors are and how they can be addressed quickly and forthrightly.

Get Market Input Before Taking Action

What the market will do, with or without any changes from your business, is a vital input in all of these decisions. The goal is to get to the end of this first step with enough market information to decide the high-potential opportunities to boost near-term cash-based profitability. This market information will also be invaluable in developing insights that shape the next step (developing a strategic view of markets). With timing in mind, market reaction assessments must get under way *in parallel* with the development of the economic profile outlined in the first half of this chapter.

WHAT DO WE NEED TO KNOW?   At this point in the process, where we are limited to finding obvious, quick wins to boost performance, we are relatively focused in the market information we need. The more in-depth market assessments and strategy formulation of the next two steps demands its own set of market information, more extensive than what is needed here, though the insights found here significantly help in setting up those efforts.

In fact, the information we need for immediate decision making is largely focused on the needs of neutralizing negative internal profit pools and growing highly positive internal profit pools. Null internal profit pools are candidates for performance improvements, and have their own unique, typically lengthier paths forward. Further, the likely remedial action for both negative and highly positive internal profit pools has similar information needs, including:

- Market dynamics (elasticity—price and demand, competitive responsiveness, etc.).
- Future prospects (expected pricing, demand—including substitutes and competitive offers, etc.).
- Interrelationships between internal profit pools of all types (offering, customer, channel, geographic).

Fortunately, it is likely that much of the information needed for this near-term decision making is already present in the business. Unfortunately, in most businesses it exists unprocessed, and work is needed to find and synthesize it.

UNDERSTAND MARKET DYNAMICS Among the most important things to understand when considering change is market dynamics: How will customers, competitors, and suppliers respond? The surprise is that very few businesses have *synthesized* elasticity measurements. In many cases, a rational observer of market behaviors would be forgiven for thinking that most companies operate believing elasticity is infinite—that is, a change, such as a relative price hike, will result in a complete collapse in share.

Assessments that are more thoughtful reveal that elasticity is not infinite, and that there are actually several elasticities. For a particular offering, there is an elasticity for each customer group, and there is an elasticity for each time horizon (near-, mid-, and long-term). Without a quantitative understanding of elasticity, market managers just guess—which almost always degrades in an overly cautious approach and a default to protecting revenue and share.

There are many very good works on the topic of elasticity, and we won't add to them here, though it is worth considering the following example. In the 1990s, an alcoholic beverages brand relied on monthly special sales in stores to drive volume. A review of customers' behavior showed that they were very loyal to the brand, but they had learned to wait for the first weekend of the month before buying at 50 percent off (at a loss to the vendor). In elasticity tests, it was found that customers could be weaned off this monthly purchasing behavior with a trivial loss in volume. On one hand, the impact of recovering 30 percent of sales back to a more reasonable price drove product-line profitability up over 120 percent. On the other hand, only a little extra advertising spending was needed to recover volume lost.

Stopping the monthly sales brought the market back to a more stiffened price elasticity, even though the prevailing wisdom had been that without such sales, volume would plummet and the brand would ebb, driving down profits across the entire month. The business subsequently studied price elasticities across the portfolio; when they had finished improving their targeting of customer types and adjusting incentives and the merchandizing/advertising mix, profitability for the business as a whole had increased two-fold.

Competitive behavior is clearly another critical consideration to factor into a change in market management. Take the case of a technology vendor competing globally with two other players; all competitors were making a positive return in the American market, and none at all in Europe and Asia. In fact, this vendor had pulled out of Japan some years before, where there was a fierce market and net negative profitability, draining the two players that remained there. Later, the opportunity arose to capture a key U.S. customer and deal a death blow to one of the remaining competitors—and the vendor rejected it. Why? That death blow would probably have given the one remaining competitor a profitable base in Japan, strengthened its hand around the world, and led to intensified competition in the United States. Better to let the other two competitors continue to slug it out in Japan, than give one of them the financial power to compete more intensely in the United States.

Again, there are many solid published works on competitive behavior, and it is not our intent to repeat them—though mapping likely reactions is another essential input to market change decisions. Notably, competitive insights are frequently built on looking at historical behaviors (both at the company level, and at the individual executive level) as well as the specific situation at hand.

CHARACTERIZE FUTURE PROSPECTS When will the internal profit pool end? This is a question not asked often enough with sincere intellectual honesty. A closely related question, "What are the future profit prospects over that time period?" is almost always passed over without much second thought at all.

Both questions can demand a great deal to get answered, and are addressed in greater depth in Chapter 5. However, at this step in the program, we are interested in the obvious: What internal profit pools can we act on now? To that end, we can turn to simply finding the strong indicators of what is in store for the markets in which action is being considered.

Those indicators of change are *market inflexion events* (MIEs) and are discussed extensively in Chapter 5, though they are useful at a very simple, high level here: Is there an upcoming market event that indicates, with a high degree of probability, that the market is in for accelerated growth or decline? We can see such events that have occurred in the past: the shift of many markets from direct mail to the Internet (computer parts, certain book types, even political donations); the slow evolution of cars, a highly predictable event itself (the SUV emerged as the station wagon diminished); and others. There are many indicators of change that are obvious now, such as the hybrid car and hybrid SUV, cell phones that do it all (with extendable, flexible screens, door keys, money transfers, and much more), and others. What is expected in your market, what will the impact be, and how inevitable is it?

Profitability is a little more difficult to forecast, though it, too, can be estimated with a level of predictability that is relevant in near-term internal profit pools decisions. Again, future events need to be plotted, though with a slant to acknowledging more competitive intensity types of event: What will happen to market prices? How will raw material and production costs change? The answers to these questions are oriented more around competitor and supplier-driven events.

Again, both demand and profitability MIEs and expectations are addressed in Chapter 5; several aspects of those more in-depth frameworks are readily applicable at this earlier stage in the process.

MAP OUT MARKET INTERRELATIONSHIPS The term *interrelationships* refers to the effect that a change in one internal profit pool has on another. In this context we are focused on market interrelationships—changes conducted through the market, rather than through internal operations and economics.

The most common form of interrelationship is in a bundling of offerings; for example, some printers offered for sale also need installation, maintenance, and supplies. In these circumstances, the economic assessment by internal profit pools must be evaluated in terms of the bundle, as well as individually. The loss of a printer sale results in the loss of all related sales. Other interrelationships include geographic coverage issues, such as the insurer that recognized it needed to have a national offering if it was to win many Fortune 500 accounts, on account of their broad employee footprint. Interrelationships also exist across channels, as in the case of the computer manufacturer growing its Internet channel and incurring the wrath of its value-added reseller (VAR) channel, which was upset at the direct competition.

Some years ago, a major pharmaceuticals manufacturer in North America was in a position where it had a portfolio of 18 product types, serving 13 different markets. Since the products were relatively small in market scale, the size of the sales force the business could maintain was also relatively small, able to serve only a few of the 13 markets optimally. In this position, the business found itself spreading its sales resources very thinly and underserving all of its products. This led to substantial underperformance in all internal profit pools. Its business leaders then made a bold move, dramatically reducing the portfolio of offerings and focusing on just those that best leveraged the existing sales capacity. This one move resulted in both a huge cash influx from selling several product lines (selling them to players that were willing to pay far more than they were worth to the seller, because they had large sales forces), while dramatically improving the market and profit performance of the remaining offerings.

Sometimes, it is too easy to think only in terms of the negative interaction effects of changes in internal profit pools. In many cases, the reverse is true, as this case illustrates, where narrowing the offering portfolio resulted in hugely improved performance for continuing offerings and a substantial influx of capital. In fact, interrelationships between internal profit pools come in all types and cross many boundaries. In this case, a channel issue was driving a less-than-optimal performance in several offering internal profit pools, and by eliminating conflicting channel demands the issue was resolved; performance was enhanced, and capital was released to invest in remaining offerings.

In most cases, the important interrelationships are easily identified at an early stage, though it is not uncommon for the economic analysis to run its course before hypotheses can be developed on potential actions—such as whether a particular internal profit pool should be discontinued. Whatever the timing, the market impact of a proposed change is paramount in deciding whether the change should be made at all, even in determining the path forward itself, to the point that specific market research might be required to get the answer.

Recast the Numbers and Make Your Move

We started this chapter by setting out the principal deliverables for this step. The first two were to get good visibility of internal profit pools and to take actions that will boost profit performance in the very near term (without damaging longer-term opportunities). The third deliverable was to generate insights on performance and the market to use as a foundation for the next two steps of the program—getting a strategic view of markets and formulating market strategy. As it turns out, simply taking the journey to achieve the first two deliverables puts us through a fact-finding and decision making process that gives what's needed to achieve the last deliverable.

Further, the preceding discussion on understanding the market was tightly focused on assuring that the actions taken in this step do not limit future options. Before actions are taken, however, it is critical to characterize the changes that decisions are expected to have on the business and map out their economic impact. Again, no action should proceed without a solid economic simulation of impact; decision makers need to be confident that changes deliver much more favorable results than the status-quo. Within the business, proposed changes will cause capacity to be redistributed and reshaped, such that costs and assets must be reapportioned across internal profit pools. Market conditions will also alter in response to changes, driving changed pricing, demand, competition, and other factors and behaviors.

So how should the new economics be compiled? At a high level, three tasks need to get done; for every change, and across all internal profit pools, decision makers need to:

1. *Define the action.* Stipulate exactly what the action is (such as eliminating a channel in a certain geography), together with its associated timing and costs. The resulting changes also need to be characterized, both in the market (such as modeling potential customer losses, reflecting the likelihood that they would switch to competitors following the closure of a channel) and in operations (such as a reduction in costs as that channel goes).
2. *Run the simulation.* Given the uncertainty in some market changes, it makes sense to define ranges of likely outcomes, setting extreme boundaries and most likely expectations. If the proposition remains a net positive even in extremes, then it is probably a solid opportunity—provided it doesn't close off any potentially attractive future opportunities.
3. *Make the call.* Coming out of this step, there are usually three types of near-term action:
   a. Defined and immediate actions.
   b. Defined near-term actions, needing fine-tuning and planning.
   c. Undecided potential actions, needing further work (possibly in the next step or later in the strategy formulation step).

The first type, defined and immediate actions, includes such things as a price hike, perhaps pulling sales or marketing activities from a certain channel or customer type. Given the relatively low effort needed, these should be implemented rapidly, though some delay may be warranted if there is some question over the potential impact to possible future strategies.

The second type of near-term action, those needing further fine-tuning, will likely have to wait for a time, depending on their expected distraction to upcoming strategy formulation efforts (they may require the same staff to do the work, for example). In addition, they, too, may have strategic implications, such that it would be prudent to wait to ensure consistency with future strategies. A market withdrawal is a good example of this; market exits take planning to minimize disruption while maximizing returns, and need to be carefully considered. Generally, it makes sense to ignore the principle of critical path management you were taught in Project Management

101, and try to postpone activities that have lasting effect, such that you keep options open until strategy formulation is at or near completion (minimizing commitments and transition costs). In these cases, the value of the option to postpone exceeds the marginal benefit that may be gained by getting ahead a couple of months.

The last type of near-term action—those where the answer is not immediately clear, and more work is needed—are usually best left until strategy formulation is complete. It may make sense to get ahead with some specific market research or similar, though the work itself is usually a distraction to other activities and deserves delay.

Got It, What's Next?

In this chapter, we have characterized internal profit pools and studied how they can dramatically boost near-term profitability. We have also seen that the decisions to achieve these boosts must be carefully considered, and must address market and operational issues before they are acted on. Going forward, we now turn to Chapter 5 and market profit pools, finding value opportunities in markets, and to Chapter 6 and market strategy formulation, exploiting the opportunities we find to boost business value.

CHAPTER 5

Get a STRATEGIC VIEW of Markets

Any investor would pay handsomely to know today where pools of market profit will be over the next 20 years, and what capabilities will be needed to compete effectively in those areas. In fact, investors try hard to create such insights to drive investment strategies, but have limited information and connections with markets.

Business leaders should create these insights too—at least those who want to prosper! After all, they are in direct contact with customer markets and have a much greater view of information. Yet few actually do this effectively. Why? Because many factors have to be taken into consideration, and it's easy to lose sight of the big picture, get bogged down in a swamp of detail, and never produce high-confidence, strategically significant, and actionable answers.

Our goal in this chapter is to show how a relatively simple market opportunity valuation framework can help you build a strategic view of markets, one based on a simple estimation of where the pools of market value are. Here are the basic components you will need to create your own strategic view:

- A crisp definition of industry and markets.
- A 10-year historical summary of market demand volumes, prices, and unit costs.
- A view of upcoming key events in your industry (including technology).
- Basic macroeconomic forecast assumptions (population growth, etc.).

In this chapter we use the U.S. printing press industry as an underlying example to show *how* to do this simple strategic market assessment, *where* to add depth to add value, and *why* it's a matter of strategic life or death to get it right, and to have the courage to act. In the process, we focus on examples in submarkets to illustrate points, while stepping through four sections:

1. Outline what is meant by a *strategic view*.
2. Show how to estimate the value of market profit pools.
3. Show an approach to assessing the strategic fit of market profit pools.
4. Synthesize these inputs into an action-oriented strategic view

Note that the illustrative examples used in this chapter are from the perspective of an in-office digital printer vendor, such as Hewlett-Packard (HP), considering the potential for digital printing in traditional printing press markets (such as newspaper, fabric, book, and other printing presses).

What's in a Strategic View?

How is it Amazon.com, which didn't exist before 1995 and has become one of today's dominating book retailers, is not part of a long-standing business like Borders, Waldenbooks, or Waterstone's? These were dominating forces in books in the 1990s, and yet they ceded most of the Internet book market to Amazon.com.

What about Kodak, which always derived much of its profits from photographic film, but now faces losing the entire cash flow stream? Why? The digital camera—a product *it* developed in 1975! Digital cameras don't need film; Kodak knew that 30 years ago, and it also saw digital cameras becoming mainstream back in 1996. Only when financial events started to overtake it did Kodak respond, shifting to a market that was obvious many years ago: printers.

In both cases, the source of future profitability moved, yet incumbent market leaders didn't follow the shift, despite colossal advantages. Not taking advantage is one thing, but losing a cash flow stream without having a replacement in time, as with Kodak and others, is simply embarrassing.

The Traditional Strategic View

Too often, thinking *strategically* is taken to mean thinking in terms of what is going on adjacent to the business in the three-month to three-year time frame. This tends to point attention to a concern for existing market size and ongoing growth, and the position the business is in relative to competitors. When asked for a strategic view of their market, many business leaders respond with something like, "We almost matched competitor X's share this year. It was our investment into widget a couple of years ago when it became clear widgets would continue to grow at that colossal rate, and we'd need a lot of features."

So what information does a typical business traditionally have in its strategic view? Example 5.1 illustrates a perspective many would recognize; it is reminiscent of images found in strategy sessions and annual reports. In this case it is based on the perspective of an in-office digital printer vendor.

Example 5.1 A Traditional Strategic View

For an In-Office Digital Printer Vendor

The traditional view inevitably focuses on monumental changes in the existing market, such as those in the accompanying figure: huge growth, new multiple-use devices (printer, copier, fax, and scan), and leaps in performance (e.g., today, printers priced at a few hundred dollars put out 20 pages per minute, something that would have cost several thousand dollars just a few years ago!). The story with this view includes an observation that some market area is large and will be larger in three years, and the business must go after it before competitors. In fact, that becomes the market strategy and its rationale. Since a powerful manager is accountable for that area, he then seeks to consolidate power with that growth.

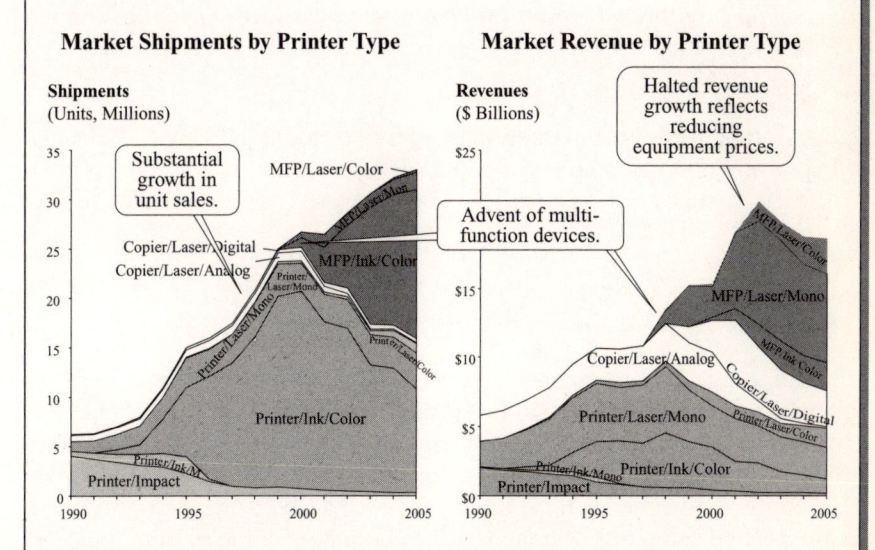

Market Shipments by Printer Type   **Market Revenue by Printer Type**

Source: IDC 2007; Business Intelligence Associates LLC.

Further, vendors then focus on a few strategic issues. The market is getting fully penetrated—sales are increasingly just replacements (a

> growing problem as print speeds increase and printer demand reduces). Also, as supplies drive profits, there are efforts to grow consumption (black covers 5 percent of a sheet, color covers 20 percent; making home-print photos a priority). Last, supplies substitution by third parties is cutting profits.

What's wrong with the strategic viewpoints in Example 5.1? Surely these are all high-impact opportunities and issues? True, and they must be addressed. However, there is a larger picture of long-range opportunities of much greater value. While vendors focus on predominantly near-term issues, such as the latest printer evolution or promoting color adoption, a maverick can move in and, for example, apply digital printing to whole new areas—and lock in swathes of business value.

The Value-Oriented Strategic View

In contrast to the traditional view, businesses focused on value creation proactively manage long-term cash flow and keep an intellectually honest eye on where it will come from in the market. For them, a strategic view of markets is defined as follows:

> *A map profiling where and how economically attractive market profit pools are, and what the requirements are to succeed in each one*

A value-oriented strategic view is really a map of opportunity, with the relative attractiveness of markets marked out, in addition to areas of danger. Of course, market attractiveness is not only a question of economic potential; each market profit pool needs to be assessed along two dimensions:

1. Magnitude of potential business value creation.
2. Strategic fit of capabilities that market players need for success.

Unfortunately, the second of these is often easier to see and estimates often have greater certainty, and so many businesses unconsciously fall into the trap of allowing it to be the primary guide forward. Using the market's capability requirements as a guide to market strategy is absolutely the right thing to do—however, it *must not be allowed to be the primary criterion*. If a prospective value opportunity is large enough, or if the existing business is not attractive enough, it is likely to be worth stretching the organization a little out of its comfort zone to make a new area work.

A market profit pool's value summarizes its economic potential. The future evolution, demand, competitive environment and other factors influencing that market are distilled into a single measure: its total future profit potential (with an uncertainty profile). This provides a new and important input for prioritizing market opportunities and is essential for value-oriented market strategy formulation, addressed in Chapter 6. The power of this understanding is visually apparent in Example 5.2, where market profit pools in the U.S. printing press industry are compared. One market stands out as immensely attractive, in-office printers, while four others also offer substantive value creation opportunities.

Example 5.2 Market Profit Pool Values

U.S. Printing Press Industry Example

In the U.S. printing press industry, the in-office printer market offers the most attractive value-creation opportunity, followed by four other markets: packaging, advertising, magazines, and catalogs. Just about all the value in these markets is driven by future digital printer supplies profits. The value opportunity in equipment manufacturing for digital or traditional presses is relatively negligible.

Profit Pools by Industry Application

Present Value of Future Market Cash Flows ($ Billions)

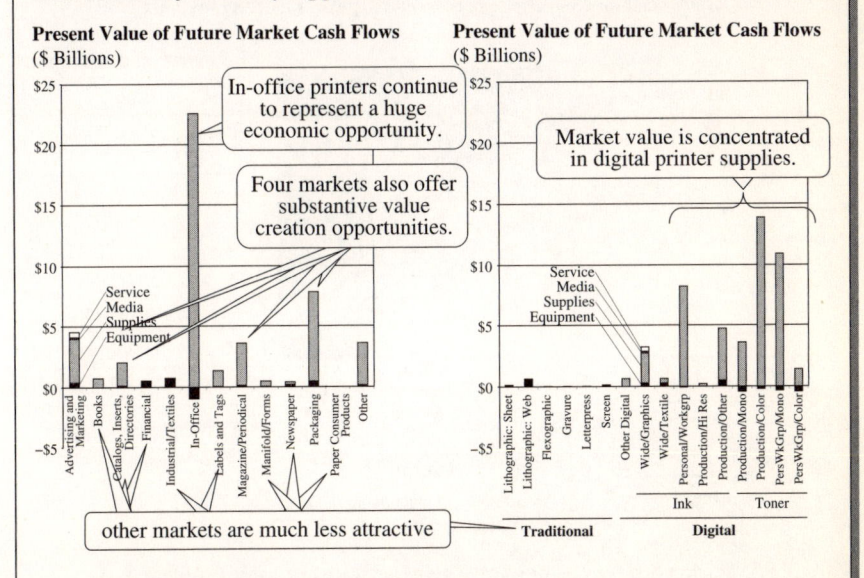

In-office printers continue to represent a huge economic opportunity.

Four markets also offer substantive value creation opportunities.

other markets are much less attractive

Profit Pools by Printing Process Type

Present Value of Future Market Cash Flows ($ Billions)

Market value is concentrated in digital printer supplies.

Traditional | Digital
Ink | Toner

Source: Business Intelligence Associates LLC.

What Is the Scope of Market Assessments?

In Chapter 1 we saw that there are three levels of market strategy, each with its own risk/reward profile. Figure 5.1 provides a more complete version of that strategy level framework. The traditional strategic view tends to focus on the first two levels, which often become very familiar—remaining in the existing market/game, and moving into market/game spaces charted by others. Because of the poor visibility into the third, uncharted level, many businesses are hesitant to fully explore those options; when they do, it is often with very limited exploration experience.

The value-oriented strategic view, however, requires a *proactive effort to search out and consider all areas* of market opportunity—especially those in the third level. If ignored, disproportionate amounts of value will be left on the table. There are two types of market strategy in this third level: *disruptor* strategies, which are moves into completely new games (a topic examined well in *Blue Ocean Strategy* by W. Chan Kim and Renee Mauborgne, Harvard Business School Press, 2005); and *pioneer* strategies, which are moves into completely new customer sets.

While this level typically presents some of the greatest value creation opportunities, it is usually also one of the most challenging to forecast. For

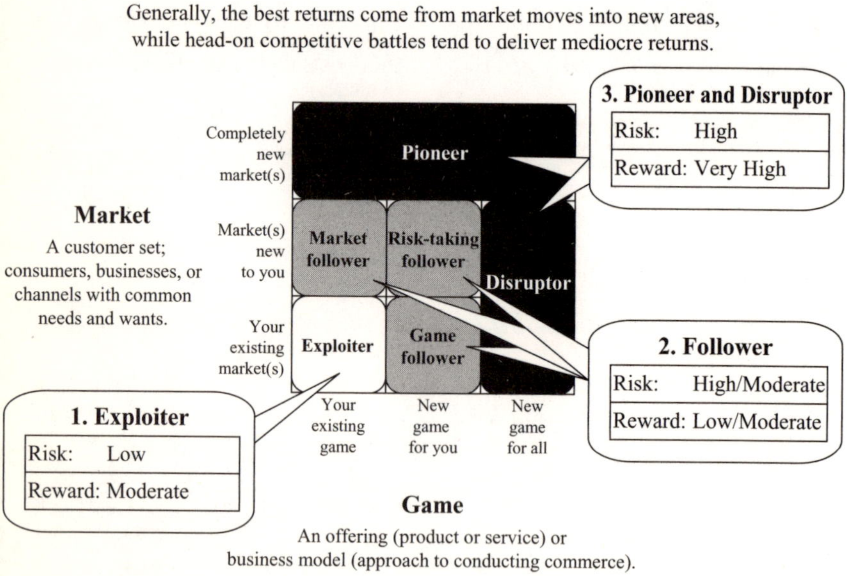

Generally, the best returns come from market moves into new areas, while head-on competitive battles tend to deliver mediocre returns.

Market
A customer set; consumers, businesses, or channels with common needs and wants.

	Your existing game	New game for you	New game for all
Completely new market(s)		Pioneer	
Market(s) new to you	Market follower	Risk-taking follower	Disruptor
Your existing market(s)	Exploiter	Game follower	

Game
An offering (product or service) or business model (approach to conducting commerce).

1. Exploiter
Risk: Low
Reward: Moderate

2. Follower
Risk: High/Moderate
Reward: Low/Moderate

3. Pioneer and Disruptor
Risk: High
Reward: Very High

FIGURE 5.1 Market Strategy Types and Their Usual Risk/Return Profiles
Source: Business Intelligence Associates LLC.

this reason, we have used it in the following examples in this chapter to illustrate how to characterize market profit pools; specifically, we have focused on pioneer opportunities. Note that this focus is only for convenience; other levels of opportunity can and should be characterized using the same approaches and tools.

Example 5.3 outlines the range of pioneer opportunities likely to be available to in-office digital printer vendors. Strictly speaking, these are pioneer markets because they are new customers to digital printer vendors. However, as they are markets already served by traditional printing press vendors, there is some existing market structure; so they are really in a gray area between market follower and pioneer strategy types.

In this section we have outlined the meaning of a value-oriented strategic view of markets, contrasting it with a traditional view and recognizing the need for it to have a broad scope. The next two sections review how to create the two sets of information called for by that strategic view: valuing market profit pools and assessing their strategic fit.

Example 5.3 Pioneer Market Opportunities

For In-Office Digital Printer Vendors

From a digital printer vendor's perspective, the classic disruptor strategy would be a competitor starting to compete with a total cost of ownership message: selling ink at a low price and so destroying the market's supplies-based profit model. There was a threat of this when Dell entered the in-office digital printing market in 2004; the fear was Dell would use its operations capabilities to do something others couldn't—make profits only from the printers themselves.

In contrast, a pioneer strategy for a digital printer vendor would refer to taking digital printing into new customer markets. There are many potential customer markets, including businesses that print wallpaper, books, product packaging, newspapers, even carpets and much more. They are currently served by traditional press manufacturers, mostly with lithographic offset presses (though other press types exist, such as flexographic, screen, and others).

To begin the assessment of these market opportunities (the subject of the rest of this chapter), the question that must first be asked is, "What is the universe of potential?" Following is a list of all the substantive printed matter markets exhaustively, each one deserving assessment for value creation potential:

Structure of the U.S. Printing Press Industry

Category	Market	Submarkets
Publishing	Books	Education, religious, university, professional, trade, mail order, book club, mass market, other
	Magazines and periodicals	Consumer: special interest; consumer: mass, business
	Newspapers	Morning, evening, weekend, other
Marketing and Sales	Advertising and marketing	Direct mail, displays/posters, inserts, other
	Catalogs and directories	Consumer, business, hybrid, telephone, other
Business Operations	Financial	SEC and related, bank and related, other
	In-office	Corporate, small office/home office (SOHO), other
	Forms	Unit set carbonless, unit set with carbon, other
Product	Labels and tags	Paper, pressure-sensitive, other paper, nonpaper
	Packaging	Paper-based, other
	Industrial/textiles	Apparel, furnishings, wallpaper, other
	Paper consumer products	Toiletries, utility, other
Other		

Source: Business Intelligence Associates LLC.

Estimating Market Profit Pool Values

Businesses inherently predict the future each time they make an investment, and even in not making an investment (whether by choice or due to ignorance of the opportunity). Unfortunately, few businesses explicitly develop their own long-range understanding of markets or their economics. We intend to change that with this review. Only with *specific and quantitative forecasts* will your business gain a superior understanding of strategic opportunities and threats, and become proficient at characterizing market profit pools and driving after value.

In this section, we review how to identify and use expected market events (called *market inflexion events*, or MIEs) to forecast the market's evolution and volume demand. The same techniques are then extended and used to forecast the other, more economic factors needed to estimate market profit pool values.

Forecasting Market Evolution and Demand Volume

The first task is to plot out each market's evolutionary path, in terms of expected MIEs. With this, a draft forecast of volume demand can be compiled, using existing demand levels as a starting point. This draft acts as a baseline for the next task, where other factors are forecast (such as price, margins, and the like); these are then all iteratively adjusted as additional information is learned and factors are drafted. First we must see what time horizon the forecast has to cover.

WHAT IS THE FORECAST HORIZON? How far ahead must businesses forecast markets and plan their actions? This question is far from an intellectual curiosity; event certainties, the value of money, and many other factors diminish over time. Conversely, the cash flow your business will generate in the near term accounts for only a fraction of its business value. An unscientific, experientially based survey (a guesstimate based on past client work) indicates most businesses look at, and manage to, three-year time horizons. This might extend to five years in exceptional circumstances or markets. This is shockingly shortsighted! Just 15 percent of the value of the business (typically) is covered by the next three years' cash flow. Figure 5.2 sets out a simple and easily calculated phenomenon: the proportion of business value captured in the next few years of cash flow.

It shouldn't be controversial to assert that the key to maximizing business value is to manage to a time horizon where most of the value is! And that, in a typical business, means 15 to 20 years ahead. In this range, both the majority of value is captured *and* the accuracy of forecasts and predictable behaviors can be readily managed. Contrary to popular myth, it is *not* true that everything beyond three years is unpredictable and there should be no attempt to forecast it. As we will see, much is known today that will help deliver robust estimates (perhaps more for some industries than others). To the extent there is uncertainty, simple probability-based tools readily help with decision making; as we see shortly and in Chapter 6.

Long-range forecasting should be looked at in terms of executive responsibility: What are business leaders doing now as they make decisions that impact the long term? Are they really managing to a three-year time horizon, and trusting luck for the remaining 85 percent of their business's value?

Proportion of a Business's Intrinsic Value
(Percent)

Cash Flow Growth	Discount Rate
0%	12%
5%	14%
5%	12%
5%	10%
10%	12%

The next three years' cash flow represents only 15% of a business's value.

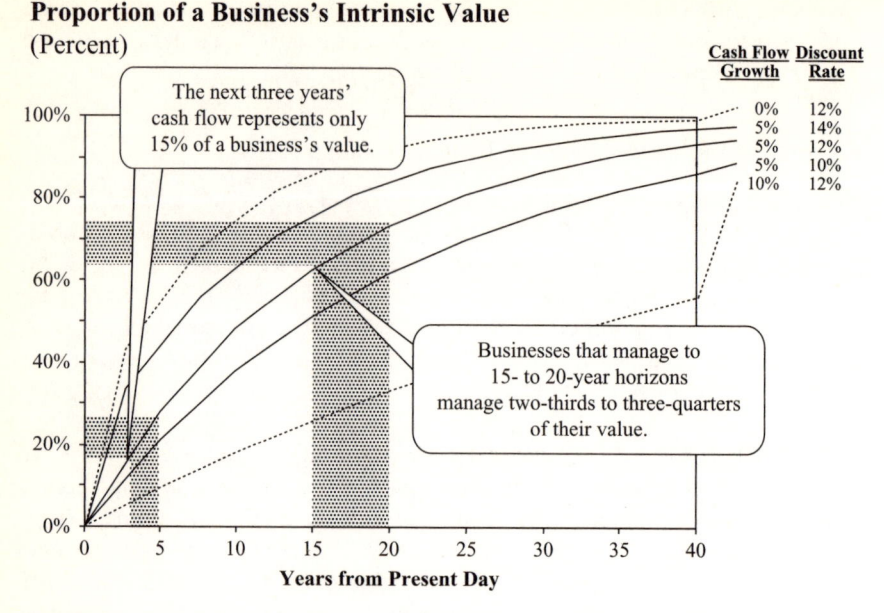

Businesses that manage to 15- to 20-year horizons manage two-thirds to three-quarters of their value.

Years from Present Day

FIGURE 5.2 Proportion of Intrinsic Business Value in Near-Term Cash Flows
Source: Business Intelligence Associates LLC.

PLOTTING A MARKET'S FUTURE DEMAND Now we plot out the market's key future events, its MIEs, and use them to draft a demand forecast. We start by studying historical events and characterizing how the market has responded in the past. From there, expected events are scanned to identify those that will shape the future; these are put together with estimates of current demand and used to project out a quantitative volume forecast.

Get to Know Market Behavior The best place to start to plot a market's future demand is to understand current and past demand behavior. Given the preceding discussion on scope, this understanding is needed for all markets of interest—beyond existing markets and including the second and third levels of strategic opportunity.

Moreover, a true understanding of demand is in terms of customer need and not supplier output. This directly contradicts the traditional understanding of what constitutes a strategic view, which often addresses only the existing market and is based on the supplier's perspective of demand. In Example 5.1 the focus was on printers sold, while from the customer's perspective it's about printed matter; only an *understanding of the underlying demand*, in that case printed matter in the office and elsewhere, will give useful insights into the demand for printers themselves.

The key to understanding market behavior is to see what happens to market demand following a relevant event of some kind, an MIE. These can be sudden, such as an introduction of a substitute product, or they can be a slow change that evolves over time, such as a change in consumer tastes. Either way, they substantively alter the market's long-term momentum, primarily in terms of quantity demanded but also competitive intensity, profitability, and other factors.

Market inflexion events of varying types and impact magnitudes hit every market regularly. Turning to our U.S. printing press industry illustration, and focusing on newspaper presses, we see that two MIEs had a profound impact over the years, described in Example 5.4.

Example 5.4 Historical Market Inflexion Events

U.S. Printing Press Market: Newspaper Market Example

The U.S. newspaper printing press market gives a clear view of the impact of MIEs. Two major ones have struck—the first in the 1950s, the second in the 1970s.

First, the lithographic offset ("litho") press changed the situation behind the scenes. Actually developed at the end of the 1800s, it wasn't until the 1950s when the unlocking MIE took effect. Then it penetrated newspapers widely, from under 5 percent in the 1940s to well over 95 percent in the 1990s, a result of its much lower set-up and operating costs. The unlocking MIE? Litho printing plate quality was not good enough for newspapers before the 1950s. While the right plate technologies were developed in the 1930s and deployed in the 1940s, it took 20 years to adopt them due to the longevity of press equipment and the large capital investment each represented.

The second MIE began with the introduction of television in the 1930s, a new source of entertainment that included immediate news. However, it wasn't until the 1960s when TVs penetrated homes en masse, driving declines in newspaper circulation. First, evening papers suffered from the new use of after-work hours in the 1970s. Increasingly, morning papers also suffered as ever more time was devoted to other entertainment. In the 1940s, 80 percent of adults read papers daily; that fell to a little over 50 percent by 2000.

Circulation by Type of Newspaper

Annual Circulation (Billions)

- First TV broadcasts.
- TV penetration accelerates, programming appeal broadens.
- cable TV multiplies channels, color accelerates.
- Weekly
- Evening
- Morning

Circulation by Printing Process

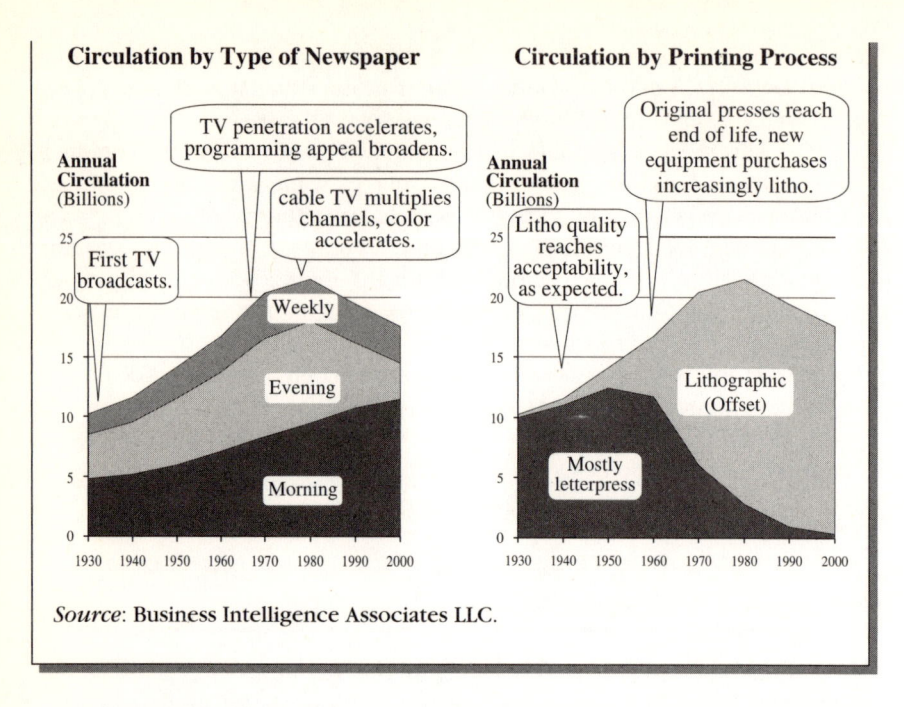

Annual Circulation (Billions)

- Original presses reach end of life, new equipment purchases increasingly litho.
- Litho quality reaches acceptability, as expected.
- Lithographic (Offset)
- Mostly letterpress

Source: Business Intelligence Associates LLC.

Often, MIEs do not have a sudden, massive impact when they first occur. Usually there is a series of related events that unlock the impact to various applications. In the example, it wasn't the development of the litho itself that drove the switch in newspaper presses—it was the new press plate technology; and it wasn't the development of the TV that drove circulation declines, but its wide adoption as TV prices lowered. Interestingly, both *root* and *unlocking* MIEs were very visible to market observers for decades. Indeed, it is clear that business leaders watched the initial MIE pass without much impact and developed an inappropriate sense of security.

Similar events can be observed across all markets. In our U.S. printing press illustration, substantive events continuously impact each component market, even in just the last couple of decades. The Internet turned growth in financial printing from a solid 2 percent annual growth into a 3 percent decline after 1995, as users shifted away from printed financial information like annual reports and analyst reviews. Indeed, subsequent unlocking by ever more internet technologies continue to drive change; advertising's shift to the Web slowed magazine growth from 3 percent annually to zero after 2000, and Internet-based financial trading has pushed more pages online, accelerating declines in financial printing to 6 percent since 2000. Other events include a shift of manufacturing to China, taking with it a lot of packaging printing (declining 1 percent annually since 1998), changes in entertainment preferences halting growth in book sales, and many others.

Each of these provides a critical starting point to identify future root or unlocking MIEs, put them into context, and then to scale current demand volumes into their likely future.

So understanding past market behavior is a fundamental part of forecasting—painting a picture of past MIEs and market responses, and profiling current market conditions. This is where third-party research firms have a key role to play: providing the facts and data that directly limit room for qualitative misinterpretations and are independent of internal agendas. Firms such as those used here—IDC and PRIMIR/NPES in the technology and printing industries, respectively—independently deliver extensive and accurate baseline facts that are directly applicable to characterizing historical market behavior.

Plot Out Future MIEs to Guide Demand Forecasts With 20/20 hindsight it is easy to be glib about the obviousness of how a market unfolded. How inevitable was it that litho would dominate newspaper printing, or newspapers would succumb to TV's visual entertainment and news? The truth is, there was a lot pointing to both inflexions in terms of both facts and predictions by executives and technologists.

So far, we have assembled a quantitative view of history, including units sold, their underlying demand drivers (such as prices and the like), and MIEs that altered market momentum. While these reveal a lot about market responsiveness and existing demand magnitudes, the last and most critical input to forecasting is in identifying and understanding *future* MIEs. In most if not all markets, most (if not all) key future MIEs are already visible; it is their impact that is less certain. With this final ingredient, it is a subjective task to translate the inputs into a quantitative plot of future demand.

Again, we turn to the U.S. printing press industry for our illustration, this time focusing on the book market. Example 5.5 identifies the key MIEs in the U.S. book printing press market—past, ongoing, and expected—and outlines the impact they are expected to have on each of the market's segments.

Example 5.5 Future Market Inflexion Events

U.S. Printing Press Industry: Book Market Example

Five MIEs have a continuing influence on the various book market segments:

1. *Internet*. At critical mass from the mid-1990s, the Internet boosted demand slightly as a low-cost retail channel with search capability.

But it also substitutes reference books; it put mail order in decline and is impacting professional and college segments of the book market.
2. *E-books*. An e-book was launched in 1999, but it was in 2005 when Sony launched a serious offering with marketing (though expensive, at $250). Prices will be near $15 by 2010, and book functionality will be standard on PDAs by then, too. One unlock event will be e-paper, increasing PDA display sizes by unrolling larger screens out of the side of PDAs. Another unlock will be copyright protection—see item 4.
3. *Digital Book Press*. The first digital press was launched in 2004, but one with attractive costs and through-puts isn't expected until 2010. It will allow while-you-wait, in-store printing (reducing distribution costs) and chapter cherry-picking by customers (reducing the total area printed and supplies used). It will also eliminate today's waste (print-to-order, rather than a minimum of 5,000 books in every run and wastage) and will speed the publishing process.
4. *Digital rights management*. Digital rights management (DRM) laws are expected by 2010 or 2012, encouraging more texts to be available digitally.
5. *Writable flexscreens*. None have been developed yet. They will allow writing to be stored on a screen with an image (just like paper). This unlock event may reduce elementary school book sales.

In short, adult trade and mass market books will be greatly substituted by e-books. Professional, university, and college books are very susceptible to retail printing which, together with consumer editing, will reduce total print areas. Keepsake books will be little impacted by digital, most notably religious and law books.

In the next illustration, Example 5.6, we see how these MIEs are used to guide today's demand trends into the future to create a forecast. For simplicity, the narrative is focused only on the adult/trade and mass market segments. It sets out the baseline demand drivers and applies them, with MIEs from Example 5.5 and judgment guides, to extend current demand numbers into the future.

The output is an unequivocal forecast chart, depicted graphically in the example, setting out total demand for printed matter by each segment over time. At a high level, we see it makes intuitive sense. The most substantive inflexion expected in the market is in adult/trade and mass market, judged by forecasters to be almost a complete loss of that printed area over the next 20 years. Other segments have also been impacted by these same MIEs;

although growth in those segments continues, it is short of its underlying drivers, such as national or high school population growth. For example, trade/juvenile is also likely to see a shift from print to e-books, but the shift will be limited (not a complete substitution) since many parts of the children's book market are better suited for paper books. Similar forces are at work in the education/elementary/high school segment.

Example 5.6 Making Quantitative Forecasts

U.S. Printing Press Industry: Book Market Example

Each segment's demand was forecast using (1) today's demand level, (2) trends in underlying demand drivers, and (3) the estimated impact of expected MIEs, as shown here:

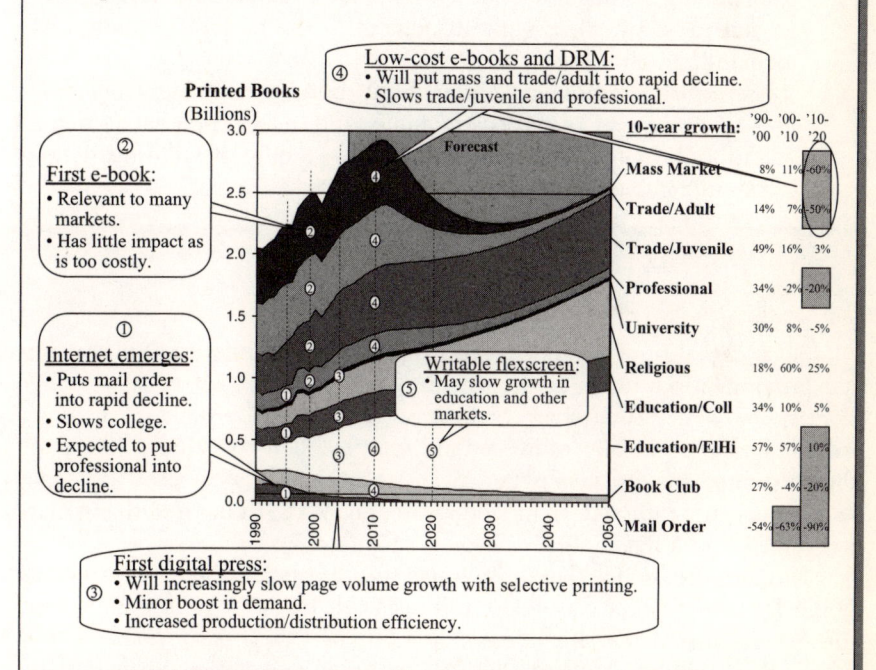

④ **Low-cost e-books and DRM:**
- Will put mass and trade/adult into rapid decline.
- Slows trade/juvenile and professional.

② **First e-book:**
- Relevant to many markets.
- Has little impact as is too costly.

① **Internet emerges:**
- Puts mail order into rapid decline.
- Slows college.
- Expected to put professional into decline.

⑤ **Writable flexscreen:**
- May slow growth in education and other markets.

③ **First digital press:**
- Will increasingly slow page volume growth with selective printing.
- Minor boost in demand.
- Increased production/distribution efficiency.

Segment	'90–'00	'00–'10	'10–'20
Mass Market	8%	11%	-60%
Trade/Adult	14%	7%	-50%
Trade/Juvenile	49%	16%	3%
Professional	34%	-2%	-20%
University	30%	8%	-5%
Religious	18%	60%	25%
Education/Coll	34%	10%	5%
Education/ElHi	57%	57%	10%
Book Club	27%	-4%	-20%
Mail Order	-54%	-63%	-90%

Source: PRIMIR/NPES; Business Intelligence Associates LLC.

For trade/adult and mass market segments, the underlying demand drivers are as follows:

- *Population estimates and literacy rates.* These are key underlying drivers of demand (different demographics for each segment). Both have stable growth rates.

- *Market penetration and consumer preferences.* Individual reading times in the United States are declining.
- *Overall.* Historical underlying market momentum has been a simple 2 percent annual growth.

Combining these with MIEs and precedents, a forecast can be asserted:

- *Previous market evolutions.* Videos, records, CDs, and the like trace a likely switchover for e-books (similar economic, entertainment, functional issues).
- *Asserted forecast.* Modeled on these previous evolutions, printed adult and mass book demand will reduce 50 percent in 10 years, later falling to negligible. Also, 70 percent of volume will be by digital press by 2010, with 10 percent in the form of printing on demand.
- *Uncertainty.* Confidence is high; the 95 percent confidence interval is +/−20 percent of forecast volume, and +/−30 percent of digital adoption rates. The uncertainty of the timing of DRM has little economic impact.

Since digital printer vendors are likely to be most interested in the digital printing opportunity, forecasts must deliver both total printed matter demand as well as that share of it to be substituted by digital over time. Although not specifically addressed in Example 5.6, forecasting volumes for digital printed matter, versus that from traditional presses, uses the same techniques and approaches, indeed also many of the same underlying market drivers and MIEs.

Furthermore, notice that these forecasts are *expected* demand estimates going forward in time. As these forecasts are made, it is important that forecasters also make an assessment of *upper and lower limits* within which they believe demand will lie, capturing what they believe is 95 percent of most likely outcomes. This probability range is extremely important, since uncertainty is a very real part of decision making. Uncertainty can, and must, be addressed head-on, as we will see shortly and in the next chapter. Technically, the 95 percent range represents confidence to approximately two standard deviations in a normal probability distribution.

Finally, the forecasts in the chart in Example 5.6 go out to 2050. In fact, this extensive range is not needed. As we will see later, cash flow beyond 20 years (approximately 2030 in this case) is almost valueless. Indeed, the MIEs we plotted out were only identified for the next 20 years; the forecasts in the chart beyond 2030 are simply a continuation of the market's momentum (other, new MIEs will pop up later and impact that momentum down the road!).

Stepping back, the overall deliverable is to develop demand forecasts for all pioneer-type market profit pool opportunities, and to that end the same demand forecasting approach needs to be applied to all U.S. printing press markets. That has been done off-line, and we can see expected demand for all printed matter in Example 5.7. Again, this is an initial forecast that will be iterated as the market is studied more closely to characterize its economics in the next task. In that task, demand forecasts are used as a foundation, upon which economic outlooks are built and market profit pools are valued. For our U.S. printing press example illustration, where the opportunity is being considered by digital printer vendors, it is the *digitally* printed volume forecasts for each market that are needed most.

Example 5.7 Completed Demand Forecast

U.S. Printing Press Industry Example

With forecasts of all printing press markets drafted, a complete picture of expected demand can be assembled (see the accompanying figure). A lot of change is expected, much of it specific to end-use markets and the expected viability of digital in large-scale printing.

Overall, demand will decline as new technologies substitute print media, exemplified by dramatic declines in publishing, particularly magazines, catalogs, and newspapers. Little reduction in print per office worker is expected for in-office; technology is not likely to change paper-based work styles much. Depending on the future of off-shoring, packaging printing may return to GDP growth levels, but it is not in the "expected" category. Nevertheless, that and other outcomes are incorporated in each market's uncertainty estimate (not illustrated in the chart).

Further, each market has volume forecasts both for the total and for digital and other print processes. These have been summed in the chart on the right, reflecting digital's increasing dominance as its speeds increase and costs lower.

Market	ⒶInternet emerges (circa '95)	ⒹE-paper introduced (circa '05)	ⒼFast variable printing (circa '13)
Inflexion	ⒷOff-shore critical-mass (circa '00)	ⒺDRM technology (circa '10)	ⒽWritable flexscreens (circa '20)
Events	ⒸInternet critical-mass (circa '00)	ⒻPDA/e-books (circa '10)	ⒾNew display technologies (circa '30)

Demand by End Use

Printed Area (LSEs[1], Trillions)

Packaging and in-office grow to dominate. — Forecast

Books impacted less than other traditional print media markets.

Paper Consumer Industrial / Other Products / Textiles

Packaging

Forms

Financial

Labels & Tags

Catalogs, Inserts, Directories

Advertising and Marketing

In-Office

Newspapers

Magazines

Books

Demand by Printing Process

Printed Area (LSEs[1], Trillions)

Forecast — Overall printed matter declines.

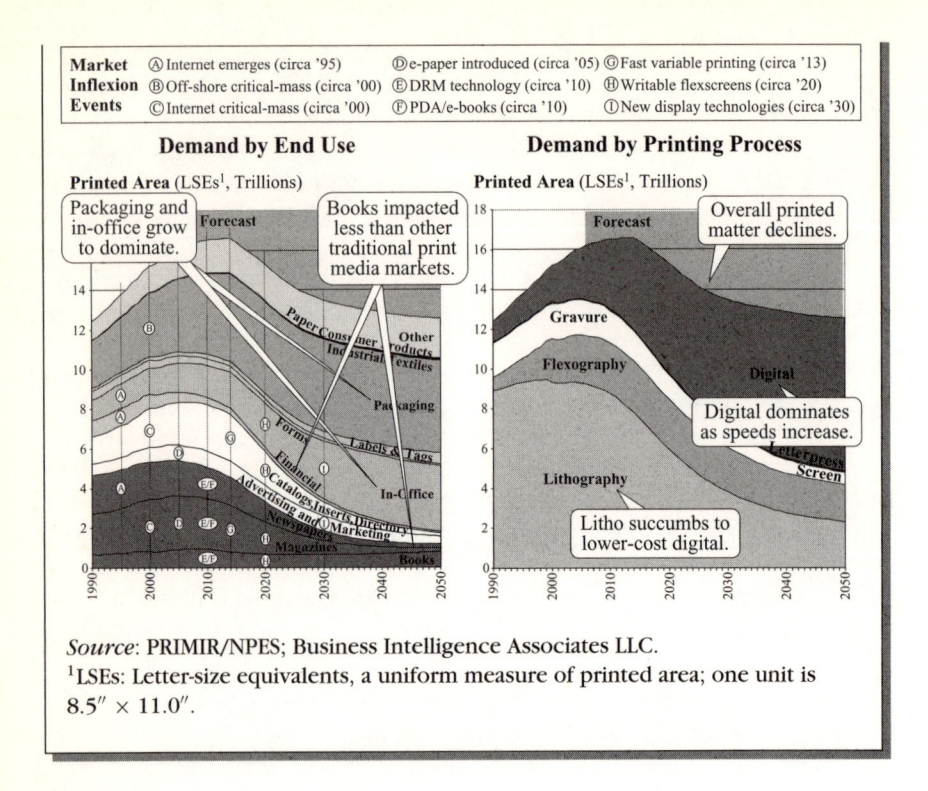

Gravure

Flexography

Digital — Digital dominates as speeds increase.

Lithography — Litho succumbs to lower-cost digital.

Letterpress

Screen

Source: PRIMIR/NPES; Business Intelligence Associates LLC.
[1]LSEs: Letter-size equivalents, a uniform measure of printed area; one unit is 8.5″ × 11.0″.

Characterizing the Economics of Market Profit Pools

It's well and fine to have an understanding of the magnitude and nature of future demand—but what of the market's prospects to deliver value? In this task, we build on demand forecasts to characterize each market's ability to deliver cash profits over time; this is distilled in the second part of this section to create an estimate of each market's present value, together with an uncertainty assessment.

As we start, it is worth pointing out that each market's economics are determined based exclusively on expected market conditions. Consequently, a good amount of relevant market understanding is acquired in the process, which is the true value of the profit pool approach. In this process, events and outcomes are defined, uncertainties are characterized, and insights into market dynamics are captured—critical issues in strategy formulation:

- What markets are truly suitable for us? What skills and capabilities will a successful play in each require, and how does that fit with our skills?
- What are the critical waypoints and indicators that the market will evolve as expected? What should we do if it doesn't?

In this section, we review what is needed to characterize each market, identifying specific factors that will be used to develop the second deliverable, a forecast of each market's future cash flow generation. Again, the U.S. printing press industry example is used to illustrate key points and approaches.

UNDERSTAND THE MARKET'S KEY FORCES Market forecasting is somewhat circular. On one hand, without knowing price, how is it possible to determine future volume demand? But on the other hand, without an understanding of future demand, how can price be predicted? A start is needed somewhere, and the best place is almost always a forecast of demand, as we conducted in the preceding task. However, as we now step through additional forces to characterize market economics, such as competitive intensity and others, there will be a need to circle back to adjust initial forecasts iteratively.

A simple framework for identifying and quantifying key market forces and issues, needed to estimate cash flow streams, is set out in the market forecast framework of Figure 5.3. Based on Michael Porter's "Five Forces" model (from his book *Competitive Strategy*, Free Press, 1998), the framework calls for four market forces to be characterized over time: customers and (volume) demand, the competitive environment, offerings and value propositions, and suppliers and (business) economics.

In the end, these forces and the factors that make them up are used to create forecasts for four sets of economic performance numbers that will define future market cash flow. They are (1) the volume of units sold over time, (2) the market price over time, (3) the cash profit margin (which addresses costs) over time, and (4) capital investment over time.

The technique to using the market forecast framework is as simple as it is intuitive. First, the factors underlying each of the four forces in the framework are identified, such as the impact of a changing number of market competitors in driving competitive intensity. Each of these factors is quantitatively forecasted out; again, MIEs are used to guide estimates. Finally, these factor forecasts are then applied to the market's current economic performance numbers (units sold, price, margin, and capital) to create forecasts. This last step is subjective and needs some judgment to gauge impact and create a quantitative output.

Again, the best place to start is with customers and demand, since it is typically the easiest force for which a quantitative baseline can be created—for volume demanded. It is also a core influence on the other forces; for example, a solid assessment of future demand volume helps in characterizing future competitive intensity (which, for example, tends to get fiercer with a shrinking market). Since volume forecasts were already addressed in the previous task, we can move directly to the remaining factors, dealing first with the competitive environment.

Four forces need to be characterized and applied to existing market conditions to develop a forecast of future market profitability and volume.

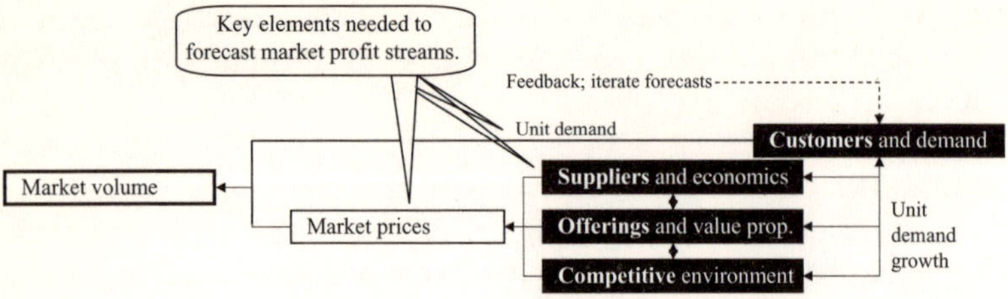

Force		Considerations	Key Outputs for Forecasting
Customers and demand	Characterization of customer demand.	• Customer needs • Viable customer solutions	• Market unit demand
Suppliers and economics	Characterization of input supplies and market economics.	• Supplier markets • Operating economics • Unit demand growth	• Operating costs • Capital investment needs
Offerings and value prop.	Characterization of the value of the offering to customers.	• Substitutes • Customer economics • Unit demand growth	• Market price elasticity
Competitive environment	Characterization of the intensity of competition.	• Entry/exit barriers • Competitor orderliness • Unit demand growth	• Competitive price pressures

FIGURE 5.3 The Market Forecast Framework

Source: Business Intelligence Associates LLC.

Competitive Environment Three high-level factors have a dominating influence over competitive intensity, and so have great impact on a market's future profit generation potential:

1. A market's *entry/exit barriers* (around all or part of the market, and the defensibility of spaces) and the number of players in it. Competition increases with low entry barriers, high exit barriers, and the number of players in that market.
2. *Competitive orderliness*. Competition increases with disruptive behavior, such as continual attempts to change the share lineup and the propensity to use price competitively.
3. Volume *demand growth*. Competition increases with stagnant or shrinking market size, as players struggle to retain benefits of scale; in market growth, more are interested in land grabs than share fights.

Some factors are measured directly. For competitive environment assessments, a simple review of historical share positions is very informative for many factors. These tell the current number of players in each segment, the frequency of market entries and exits, dominating and leading share positions, and many of the other measures listed alongside the three factors just listed. For an assessment of current competitive orderliness, qualitative insights are needed, including signs of the leader imposing discipline, market margin stability, and the depth of nonprice competition.

With an understanding of the current situation and of historical behaviors and patterns, future MIEs need to be identified as done previously to forecast demand volumes in the preceding task. Again, these MIEs are used to guide forecasts of each competitive factor into the forecast horizon, using some amount of judgment. A sample competitive environment assessment is given in Example 5.8, this time focusing on the in-office printer market. In it, the table shows an example assessment of specific competitive behaviors and trends in the market, much of the information coming from the share chart underneath it. Further, specific competitive MIEs expected in the future are cited, including their expected timing and probabilities.

Example 5.8 Competitive Environment Assessment

U.S. Printing Press Industry: In-Office Market Example

Competitive observations and potential changes are shown in the accompanying table.

Observation		History/Events	Likely Future Events	Prob.
Entry/Exit Barriers	Few new players can overcome market positioning and technical entry barriers	–Universe of major players is small and stable (HP, Lexmark (Xerox in high-volume), Epson, Canon, others) –Entrants need *great* market strength (technical strength in PCs + direct channel); Samsung latest entrant (great printer presence delivered little; similar for others)	–Several major technology players have ability (Lenovo, Fujitsu, others?) –Market offers much value to pursue	50% one new major player by 2012
	Competitor positions often change at market inflexions	–Inflexions mostly driven by new offering/technology (ink displaces impact, multi- displaces single-function) –HP was not leader in impact, but captured lead in toner; used that and technology advantages to lead in ink	–Periodic inflexions expected; dual home photo/printers, color prevalence, rewritable paper, others	Every 5 yrs? 20% HP dislodged by 2020
Competitive 'Orderliness'	Competitors avoid focus/sales messages on supplies pricing	–Consumer messaging historically focused on printer price –Focus on supplies pricing and total cost of ownership minimal; only 3% cited TCO as the most important factor, 62% price, 23% for resolution, 12% for speed, etc.	–Potential for player with alternate profit stream to disrupt market order (though expected, Dell not disrupted market economics to date)	90% not disrupted before 2020
	Competitors tend to follow leaders	–Tendency to follow share leader, HP, in price/performance of offerings –HP's market leadership has been responsible and effective, keeping order while maximizing cash flow for all –Leader exits markets first (HP from mono ink, HP from ink single functions)	–Technology progressions tend to make market players mostly act at once –Leaders tend to have financial advantage	95% will follow leader to 2020
	Leader tends to lose share over time	–HP seems to capture much share after inflexions, but share ebbs over time	–Market inflexions will continue; leaders will cede share rather than intensify competition (equipment or price-based)	100% leaders continue to choose order
Demand Growth	Rapid growth in printers to date has limited share fights	–PCs penetration (office and home) opened the opportunity with widespread desktop publishing –New offerings unlocked new customer sets (such as ink's lower prices, unlocking SOHO/consumers in '90s) –Some models now sold at loss; overall equipment profit is breakeven	–Full penetration appears to have been reached; future limited to equipment replacement and economic growth	80% printers sold at loss by 2020
	Analog copier decline has pushed copier players to printers	–Xerox and Kodak increasingly solely focused as digital equipment / printer players	–Competitors from traditional print press market may target in-office market also	5% traditional players to join market by 2020

(Callouts: "Specific expected events identified.", "Specific behavioral traits identified.", "Probability and timing estimates included.")

Source: IDC 2007; Business Intelligence Associates LLC.

U.S. in-office printing market competitor positions from 1995 to 2005 are depicted in the accompanying share chart.

- Market dominated by leader.
- Orderly competition (little share change).

Printer Sales
(Units, Millions)

- MFP/Toner/Color
- MFP/Toner/Mono
- MFP/Ink
- Copier
- Printer/Toner/Color
- Printer/Toner/Mono
- Printer/Ink
- Printer/Impact

- Leader cedes share over time.
- Leader recaptures leading share on market product inflexions.

Lexmark, HP, Epson, Dell, Canon, Brother, Samsung, Lexmark, Brother

Other, IBM, Compaq, Panasonic, Oki, Lexmark, Epson, HP

- Few market entrants
- Dell was successful (thanks to channel strength).

Source: IDC 2007; Business Intelligence Associates LLC.

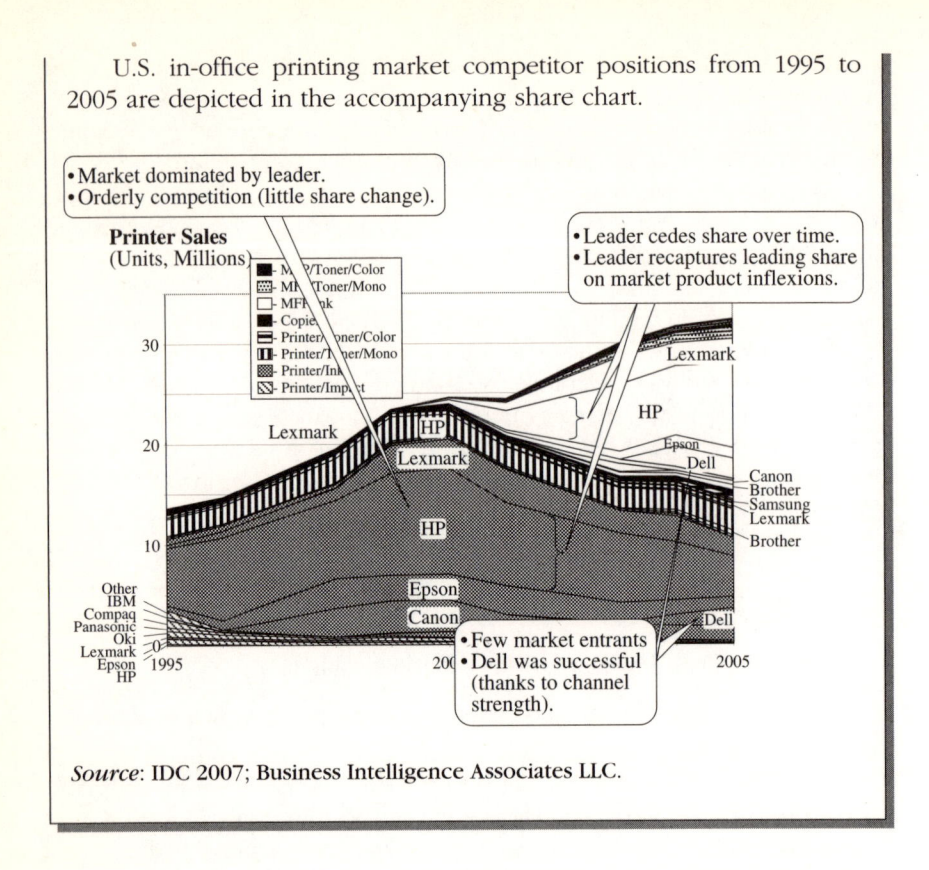

Offerings and Value Proposition The offering itself and the value proposition it presents to the customer have a powerful influence over the future of every market. Three high-level factors are particularly influential on market profitability:

1. *Substitutes* to the existing solution. If a better mousetrap comes along, the customer will switch; rudimentary economics dictate that volumes for the existing solution then fall, as do prices—both bad for profits.
2. *Customer economics.* Of course, the greater the ratio of value created for the customer versus the vendors' cost, the better vendor profits can be.
3. Volume *demand growth*. Market economics also dictate that the greater the demand, the higher the profits can be for the vendor.

Again, many of these are measured directly in markets, and can be forecast based on expected events—such as upcoming substitute offerings, changes to customer costs or benefits, and the like. The approach to identifying relevant MIEs and quantifying their impact is very similar to that outlined for the competitive environment in Example 5.8.

Suppliers and Economics Naturally, supplies costs and operating economics also drive market profitability. There are also three high-level factors influencing outcomes here:

1. *Supplier market dynamics.* Supply restrictions, from raw materials to components, have a substantive impact on market profits; issues arise with limited sources, or when major buyers alter buying patterns.
2. *Operating economics.* Of course, the higher the cost to produce, the lower are unit profits, reflecting the reality that prices are set by the market while costs are a function of the operating model.
3. *Volume demand growth.* Scale economies accompany demand growth; as supplies consumption increases, unit fixed costs decline—usually for both suppliers and buyers; capital investments also increase with scale.

Using the same approaches adopted in the two previous forces, many of these are measured directly and can be forecast using expected events.

The importance of the interaction between each of the market's forces and factors cannot be understated, leading to a certain amount of iteration and adjustment. One tool that helps in the process to ensure internal consistency is a time-based chart, setting out the key MIEs and showing how they evolve. This is demonstrated in Example 5.9, which also relates to the U.S. in-office printer market. It charts out MIEs by their area of impact, and captures their timing and estimated probabilities. This simple tool also helps crystallize the understanding of a market's future and push the forecasting buy-in process along.

Example 5.9 MIE Sequencing and Timing Summary

U.S. Printing Press Industry: In-Office Market Example

The key MIEs impacting the in-office printer market are set out graphically here. Dependencies and sequencing are captured in the use of arrows, such as the evolution of supplies substitution by third-party manufacturers. Third-party manufacturers first appear substantively in the mid-1990s, and supplies substitution rises steadily to 35 percent in the mid-2000s; it is expected to stabilize by 2020 at 40 percent.

Note that the chart groups MIEs by their primary influence force: offerings, customers, competitive, and suppliers.

	1990	2000	2010	2020
Offerings and value prop.	Quality color ink printers introduced	MFPs introduced / Third party manufacturers launch / Affordable digital cameras	MFP volumes supercede printers; copiers collapse / Supplies substitution reaches 35% / Digital camera printers	Major technology introduction (85%)	Supplies substitution stable at 40% (70%)
Customers and demand		SOHO printer market opens up / Internet critical mass	Consumer base beyond PC printers / SOHO penetration nears limit; switch to replacements / Local printing mainstream	Office installed base starts decline as printer page capacity rises (100%)	Paper consumption reaches double 1995 rate (95%)
Competitive environment		On-line direct channel critical mass; led by Dell	Dell enters printer market / Copier players intensify focus on printer market / Profit on printer equipment drops to breakeven	One major player enters market; Lenovo, China? (50%) / Average loss on printer sales up to 20% (80%)	
Suppliers and economics		Supplies-based market profit model inherited from 1980s		Supplies-based market profit model not disrupted	Supplies margins reduced by half (95%) / Supplies-based market profit model not disrupted (90%)

Annotations on figure: "Progression of root and unlocking MIE stracked." · "Timing and probabilities captured." · "All four forces summarized." · "Now"

Source: Business Intelligence Associates LLC.

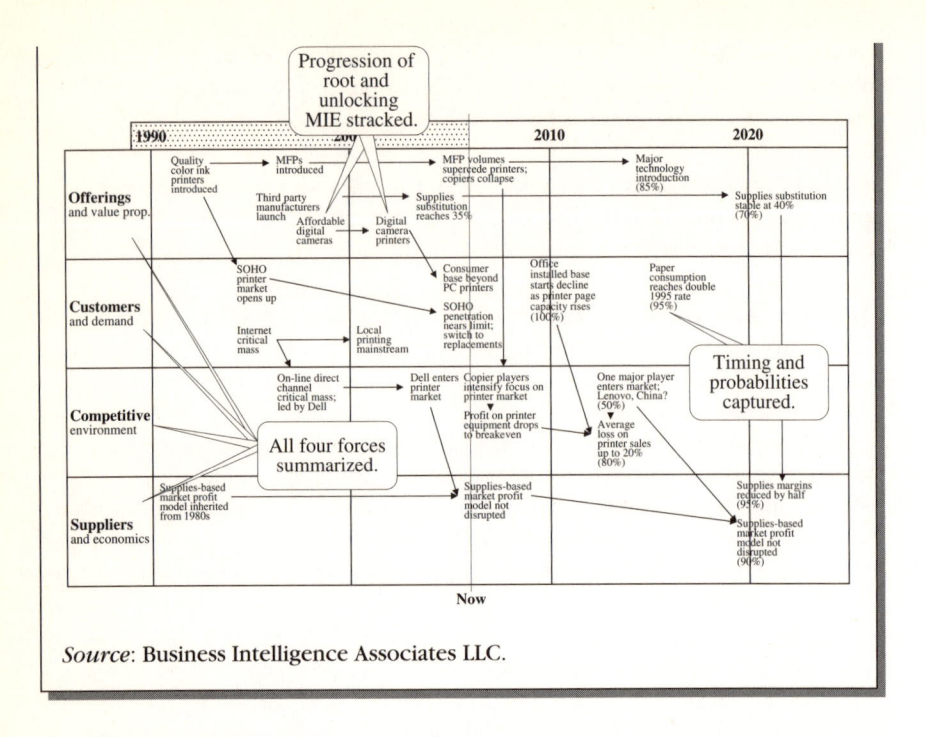

While it is important to get accuracy, there is a real trade-off between increasing it on one hand, and the potential loss of insights on the other. As a general rule, the bias should be to limiting accuracy—certainly when characterizing profit pools for the first time. The insights acquired the first time around far outweigh the benefits of diving deep into the information. The entire exercise is a marathon, with the big picture being the most important deliverable at all times.

With forecasts for each of the market's key factors in hand, its expected economic performance (in units sold, market price, profit margin, and capital investments) can now be plotted out into the forecast horizon.

QUANTIFYING MARKET PROFIT POOLS The transition to a long-range estimate of market cash flow needs only some basic math, and an analyst with a spreadsheet for a short while. Thus far, we have used MIEs to forecast each market factor. Each of these, in turn, has played a role in determining the market's economics by driving one or more of units sold, market price, profit margin, and capital investments. For all markets, the estimation of future cash flow always eventually boils down to simply multiplying the first three together and subtracting out capital investments. Of course, the factors used, the values they assume, and how they influence market economics, are all highly unique to each market. Example 5.10 briefly describes the factors and their use to estimate cash flow for the in-office printer market.

Market profit pool cash flow forecasts are then discounted to today's values using the prevailing discount rate for each market in question and reflecting that market's expected aggregate capital structure—a weighted average of equity and debt capital. In the case of new markets, or a unique situation, discount rates may need to be generated using a standard and widely recognized technique called the capital asset pricing model (CAPM), which is a practitioner's tool and outside the scope of this book.

Example 5.10 Estimating Future Cash Flow

U.S. Printing Press Industry: In-Office Market Example

There are primarily two streams of cash flow that need to be estimated for the in-office printer market: that from printer sales and that from supplies sales. The principal elements of the economics are characterized in the accompanying chart.

The key factors underlying market forces (defined and forecasted in the previous task, and partially captured in Examples 5.8 and 5.9) are explicitly used to drive forecasts of one or more of the market's economic measures: units sold, price, margin, and capital investments. For the in-office market, the key ones are future substitution rates of ink and toner cartridge sales by third parties, supplies prices, customer supplies consumption per page (such as photos using a lot of ink), and printer life span and throughputs.

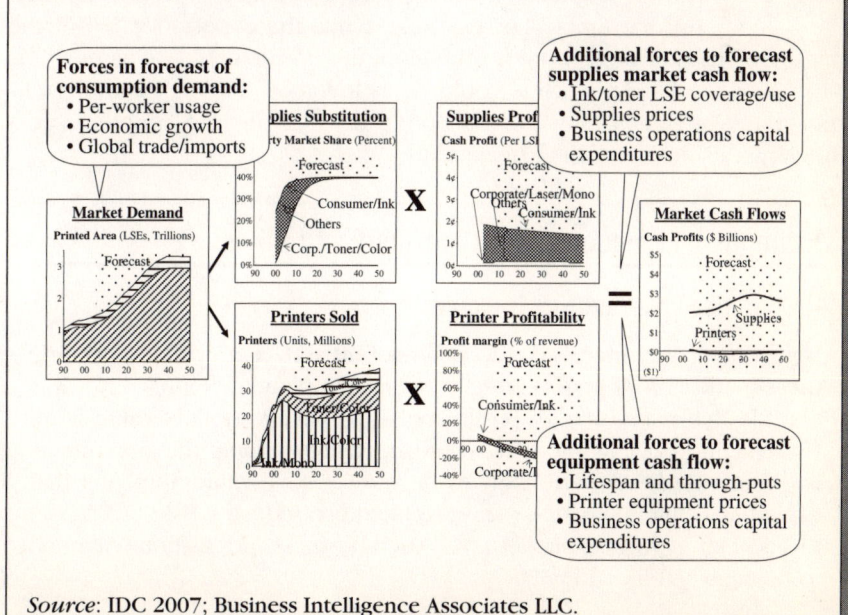

Forces in forecast of consumption demand:
- Per-worker usage
- Economic growth
- Global trade/imports

Additional forces to forecast supplies market cash flow:
- Ink/toner LSE coverage/use
- Supplies prices
- Business operations capital expenditures

Additional forces to forecast equipment cash flow:
- Lifespan and through-puts
- Printer equipment prices
- Business operations capital expenditures

Source: IDC 2007; Business Intelligence Associates LLC.

In this task, we have seen how to use MIEs to guide forecasts of the forces that drive cash flow (including competitive, offering-based, and supplies forces) over a 15- to 20-year horizon. We also saw how to transform those forecasts into cash flow estimates for each market, and derive a value for each market profit pool. Next, we examine the role and challenge of estimating uncertainty.

Capturing Market Profit Pool Uncertainty

At the beginning of this chapter we saw the values of market profit pool opportunities in the U.S. printing press industry set out in Example 5.2. From that information it was apparent that the in-office, packaging, advertising and marketing, magazines, and catalogs markets offer substantive value-creation opportunities for any digital printer vendor. Economic comparisons of market profit pools can and should include a simple comparison of the relative magnitudes of expected value creation. That, however, is not enough; real insights come from understanding a market's issues and the alternative paths its evolution might take (and what the signals will be of such changes). The uncertainties associated with these are critical, and in some cases pivotal, considerations in Market Strategy formulation, since they directly impact decision making and help reduce risk.

With that in mind, market profit pools must be considered not just in terms of their expected value, but also accompanied by their range of uncertainty. In most situations, this range is set such that 95 percent of most likely outcomes are captured—that is, we're pretty sure we've captured the outcome in that range. For example, while the expected value of the packaging market profit pool is $8 billion; the upside could be as much as $16 billion, and the downside could be as low as $1 billion. Example 5.11 recasts the original view of market profit pools in the U.S. printing press industry, this time including uncertainty.

Example 5.11 Uncertainty in Market Profit Pools

U.S. Printing Press Industry Example

With uncertainty included, the potential attractiveness of U.S. printing press market profit pools changes (see accompanying figure). First, it is feasible that many market profit pools will have very little value at all (except in-office). While that would be disappointing, the good news is that none of them are likely to have a negative value, implying that capital investments will be recoverable and so reducing risk. Of course, this is at an aggregate market level; each business proposition will need to be analyzed individually.

Furthermore, upsides appear very attractive. The packaging opportunity upside is comparable to the expected in-office market profit pool. The causes of these less probable outcomes are examined later. We know from the market review that the in-office market profit pool has an existing set of digital printer vendors serving it, making it likely a challenging market to enter. However, the other market profit pools have few, if any, digital printer vendors serving them today.

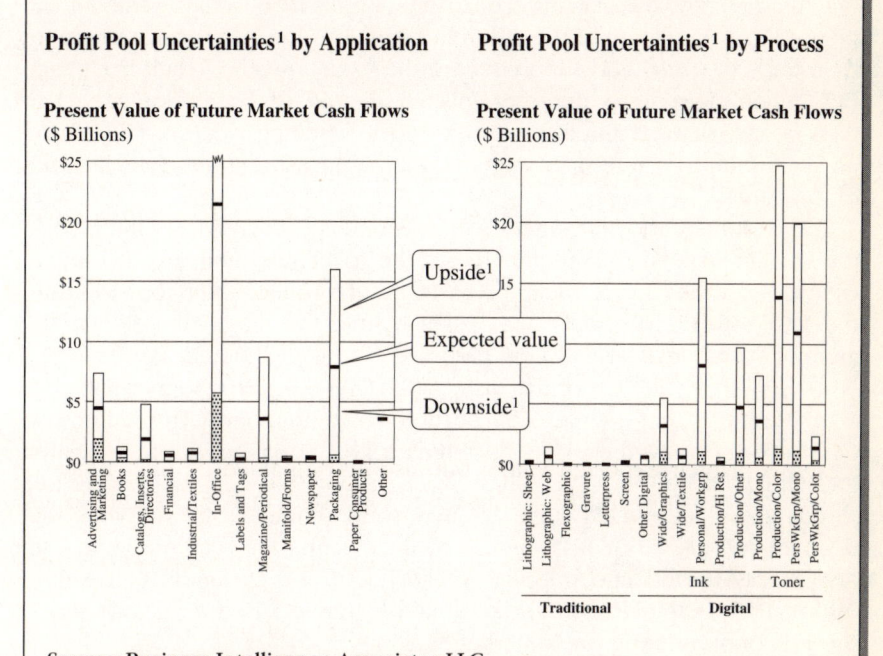

Profit Pool Uncertainties[1] by Application

Present Value of Future Market Cash Flows
($ Billions)

Profit Pool Uncertainties[1] by Process

Present Value of Future Market Cash Flows
($ Billions)

Upside[1]

Expected value

Downside[1]

Source: Business Intelligence Associates LLC.
[1] The short, thick horizontal lines are *expected* values; the white columns show the estimated range of each value to a 95 percent uncertainty limit.

So how are the uncertainties in market profit pool values figured out? Surprisingly, the technique is very simple, and is based on a tool called the *Monte Carlo simulation*. This tool conducts a very simple task, though it takes a huge amount of mundane number crunching to get there. In simple terms, it takes your uncertainty estimates for each of your inputs to a valuation, and runs them through your spreadsheet-based discounted cash flow (DCF) model of the market to figure out the uncertainty in the valuation itself.

It works like this. Despite our best forecasting, we know there is uncertainty in our forecaster's estimates of the inputs used in DCF valuations, inputs such as price, raw material costs, share, and others. That input uncertainty translates through to uncertainty in the output, cash flow (which itself results in uncertainty in value). Now, there are two ways to estimate that output uncertainty. One way is to build an enormous mathematical formula describing the business model and the uncertainties of its inputs, and solve for a mathematical function that describes the expected value and its probability distribution. That's the tough approach.

Alternatively, the existing spreadsheet-based DCF valuation model can be used in a simulation of the different conditions the inputs can assume (in thousands of *trials*) and simply record the valuations that result from each trial. When the series of trials are finished, a standard distribution curve can then be retroactively fitted by any PC to the resulting value profile, giving an assessment of value uncertainty by simply measuring the characteristics of the curve.

The Monte Carlo simulation is that second approach. Most Monte Carlo tools available today only require forecasters to include summary uncertainty estimates as they make their forecasts. As they enter their forecasts into the DCF valuation models, they also include the range of how far the amount could deviate, and how that deviation is distributed. For example, is it spread out like a normal distribution curve, or is it lognormal, or a simple triangle shape either side of the expected amount? They must also define correlation—the extent to which a change in one input is related to changes in one or more others, such as price changes being sensitive to quantity changes. Although this may sound complex, the software that does it (Crystal Ball or Risk Simulator, for example) is very simple to use, and simple to add into popular spreadsheets. See Appendix C for more information on the Monte Carlo tool, and Example 5.12 to see it applied to the U.S. book printing press market example.

Example 5.12 Profiling Market Value Uncertainty

U.S. Printing Press Industry: Book Market Example

The accompanying figure shows how easy it is to use the Monte Carlo tool to figure out market profit pool value uncertainty. In this case, just two variables are forecast, profitability and volume; to get cash flow, these are simply multiplied together in a spreadsheet model.

To figure out the uncertainty in value, the forecaster includes his estimate of the uncertainty of each of the two forecasts, profitability and volume. As profit forecast estimates are typed into each spreadsheet cell, the tool asks for uncertainty: What uncertainty distribution curve does that profit estimate have (lognormal, normal, other)? What does the forecaster believe is the lower 95 percent uncertainty limit? What correlations exist? The uncertainty profile for volume is input in a similar way. When complete, the tool runs a series of trials (usually 1,000 is enough) and the market value's uncertainty is output (a distribution curve and standard deviation).

There are two rows in the chart. The top one shows nominal dollars, the lower one shows present value dollars. When next to each other, the time value of money is very clear; only cash flow in the 20 years really matters.

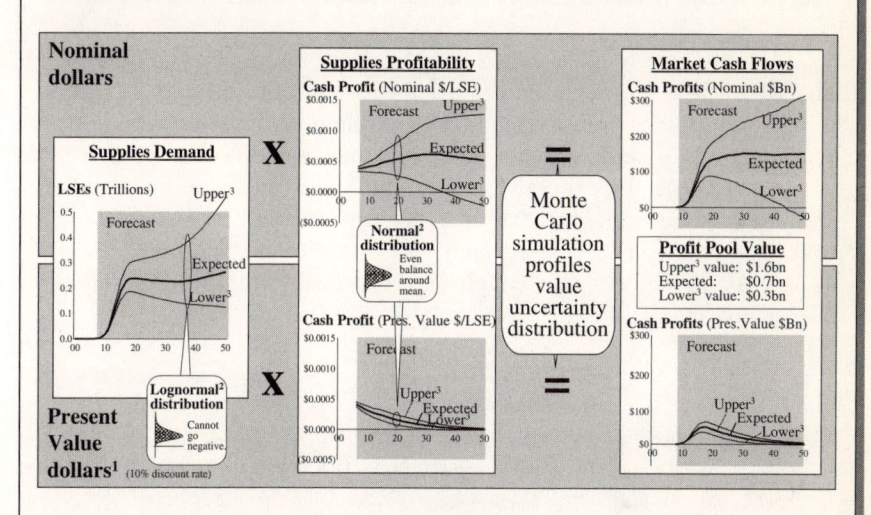

[Figure: Monte Carlo simulation diagram showing Supplies Demand × Supplies Profitability = Market Cash Flows, in both Nominal dollars and Present Value dollars[1] (10% discount rate) rows. Profit Pool Value: Upper[3] value: $1.6bn, Expected: $0.7bn, Lower[3] value: $0.3bn. Notes on Normal[2] distribution (even balance around mean) and Lognormal[2] distribution (cannot go negative).]

Source: Business Intelligence Associates LLC.
[1] Market weighted average cost of capital 10 percent over forecast period.
[2] Many estimates are normally distributed, some are not (such as volume demand, which cannot be negative and is likely lognormal).
[3] Estimates given to 95 percent certainty (statistically, within two standard deviations).

What accounts for the uncertainty in market profit pool values? On the upside, there is a real chance that forecaster estimates of expected inputs (for example, prices or volume demand) were too low. These upside potentials are worth capturing and including in market strategy formulation, since we do not want to leave large amounts of value on the table. On the downside, the primary hitch that could hit all of these markets is they may not properly adopt the attractive supplies-based profit model that digital printers enjoy in the in-office market. And even if that profit model is adopted, there is a nontrivial chance that those supplies could be mostly provided by third-party manufacturers, as we see them trying to do in the in-office market. Indeed, there is a chance that the in-office market's own value could also be hit by similar breakdowns in its own economics.

These and other alternate outcomes were flushed out in the preceding task. Another useful tool to capture the major MIEs and their alternative outcomes, which are driving the uncertainty extremes, is depicted in Example 5.13. This kind of summary has proven very useful for discussion and consensus building within the organization.

Example 5.13 Forecast Events Summary

U.S. Printing Press Industry

This figure lists the major outcomes across each of the markets in the U.S. printing press industry, including baseline assumptions and corresponding values, and alternate outcomes that shape the extremes.

For example, the expected substitution of 50 percent of mass market and adult trade books by 2020 is cited in the first line of the "Books" row; however, the forecasters believed that the substitution could be as low as 20 percent or as high as 80 percent, within a 95 percent uncertainty interval in 2020 (normally distributed).

	Expected Market Outcome		Alternate Market Outcomes	
	Value	By 2020 …	Increase value …	Reduce value …
Advertising and Marketing	$4.1bn	…digital share rises to 50% of display/posters …digital captures 20% of Direct Mail …content targeting reduces DM print volumes 10% …supplies cash margins 25%; 20% substitution	–Digital rises to 75% –Captures 40% of DM –Doesn't reduce vols. –Margin 35%; 10% sub	–Captures 10% of DM –Reduces volume 20% –Margin 15%; 50% sub
Books	$0.7bn	…Mass/Adult volume 50% supplanted by e-books …internet reference supplants 50% of '00 Prof/Un …Religious continues at almost population growth …digital captures 70% of non-long-run prints …selective printing lowers certain mkt vols by 10% …local printing increases certain mkt vols by 4% …supplies cash margins 25%; 20% substitution	–Only 20% supplanted –Margin 35%; 10% sub	–Vol. 80% supplanted –Lowers vol. 20% –Doesn't increase vols. –Margin 15%; 50% sub
Catalogs, Inserts, Directory	$2.0bn	…digital captures 40% …targeted content red… …internet supplants 10… …supplies cash margi… …internet/local print s… …digital captures 70%… …supplies cash margins 25%; 20% substitution	…% of vol. s. by 30% ; 10% sub upplanted % of vol. –Margin 30%; 10% sub	–Captures 10% of vol. –Reduces volume 90% –Margin 15%; 50% sub –Vol. 90% supplanted –Captures 50% of vol. –Margin 15%; 50% sub
Industrial/Textiles	$0.7bn	…30% of today's printed fabric switches to digital …digital increases printed fabric market 5% …supplies cash margins 20%; 20% substitution	 –Increases market 10% –Margin 30%; 10% sub	–Only 10% switches –Market not increased –Margin 10%; 50% sub
In-Office	$22bn	…print per worker consumption increases 20% …worker population growth continues at av. GDP …increased printer pdty reduces installed base 20% …supplies cash margins 20%; 40% substitution	–Cnptn. increases 30% –Margin 25%; 20% sub	–Cnptn. doesn't change –Installed base stable –Margin 15%; 60% sub
Magazines/Periodicals	$3.5bn	…digital… …targ… …intern… …suppli…	–Captures 75% of vol. –Only 10% supplanted –Margin 40%; 10% sub	–Captures 20% of vol. –Reduces volume 40% –Margin 20%; 50% sub
Newspapers	$0.4bn	…intern… …digital captures 70% of newspaper print volumes …supplies cash margins 30%; 20% substitution	 –Margin 40%; 10% sub	 –Margin 20%; 50% sub
Packaging, Labels, and Tags	$8.0bn	…manufg. drift to Asia halts US Packaging growth …digital captures 20% of Packaging print volumes …supplies cash margins 25%; 20% substitution	–Pkg. growth half GDP –Captures 30% of vol. –Margin 35%; 10% sub	 –Captures 10% of vol. –Margin 15%; 50% sub
Paper Consumer Products	$0.0bn	…10% of today's printed cons pdts switch to digital …digital increases printed cons products market 5% …supplies cash margins 30%; 20% substitution	 –Margin 40%; 10% sub	 –Margin 15%; 50% sub

Callouts: Key baseline market assumptions identified. Possible deviations from expectations explicitly recognized. Expected values use baseline assumptions.

Source: Business Intelligence Associates LLC.

In this section, we walked through the process to forecast and value market profit pools, and to incorporate uncertainties in those valuations. In the next section we turn to the second aspect of a strategic view, that of the fit between the existing business and the markets under consideration.

Strategic Fit: What It Takes to Play

It goes without saying that what's needed for success in one market can differ markedly from what's needed in another, and for that reason the key attributes of a successful business model must be profiled for each market profit pool. Most business leaders are quite at home with the topic of market capability requirements, possibly because day-to-day experiences paint a very vivid picture of what works and what doesn't. When taking an extended view into the future, these almost intuitive understandings of what's required are especially useful—and readily available when considering markets related to existing businesses. Knowing that, it is no surprise that there are many ways to characterize what business models need to succeed.

The business model assessment framework is one such approach; it calls for a characterization of six aspects of a business model—three relate to customer markets, two relate to internal operations, and one relates to supplies markets and other business model inputs. In this section, we use this framework to assess the fit of a generic in-office digital printer player into a generic traditional printing press market (and assume they all require approximately the same attributes). Since there are so many ways of doing this fit assessment, and the understanding of what's needed is so widespread, it is not a primary thrust of this book and is addressed briefly, and in this section only.

The business model assessment framework is depicted in Figure 5.4. Each of its six business model aspects are examined next, including high-level looks at how they apply to our printing press industry illustration. Each of the six need to be characterized in two ways: in terms of what customers demand from a successful play, and also what the competitive environment will require.

Customer Markets

The most obvious requirements for success relate to the business model's capabilities in customer markets, including the offering, brand, and distribution/sales characteristics.

OFFERING The word *offering*, in this framework, refers to the product or service itself and not other elements of the customer experience, such

Six aspects of the business model must be characterized to assess potential for success; for each, an understanding is needed for:

- The right *level* of strength to simply deliver to customer markets.
- *Relative* strength to thrive competitively.

Supplier Markets

Access
- Reach
- Relationships
- Power/scale

Internal Operations

Capabilities
- Management
- Functional (production/operations, sales/marketing, technical, etc.)

Economics
- Operating costs
- Investment scale

Customer Markets

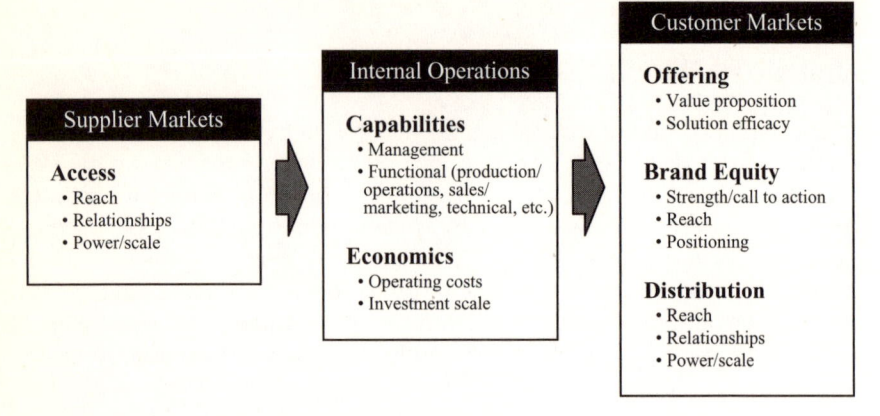

Offering
- Value proposition
- Solution efficacy

Brand Equity
- Strength/call to action
- Reach
- Positioning

Distribution
- Reach
- Relationships
- Power/scale

FIGURE 5.4 Business Model Assessment Framework
Source: Business Intelligence Associates LLC.

as brand and sales/after-sales. At the most basic level, a successful business model needs to offer the market something it can use, something that delivers value to customers that is equivalent to or above the current market offerings, if any exist. This is intuitive and there isn't any need to dwell here on what a value proposition is or why a suitable one is needed. It is, however, worth looking at what has to be considered in assessing the fit between the proposed offering and the needs of the target market:

- Will the proposed offering *deliver incremental benefit* or functionality?
- To what degree will that incremental benefit matter, particularly in terms of *customer economics*?
- Will *transition costs* pose a substantive switching barrier to the customer?

For an example consideration of these issues, we again turn to the U.S. printing press industry in Example 5.14. While the discussion there stops at a qualitative review, subsequent steps should include quantitative assessments of the efficacy of the offering, relative to what customers will expect and the competition will deliver. Investment amounts must also be estimated.

Example 5.14 Success Requirements: Offering

For a Digital Vendor Targeting Traditional Markets

There is a good fit between a digital offer and what printers/customers demand; preparation times can be reduced from weeks to days (no image printing plates needed in digital printers), and waste is eliminated (Litho wastes 40 percent of runs, digital wastes little), greatly reducing fixed costs. However, digital's variable costs (ink and *run-time* labor) are relatively high. Litho printing has high fixed costs, but variable costs are very low. As a result, digital is relatively less expensive for runs below 2,000 to 20,000, depending on specifics. This threshold increases as digital gets faster; its speeds are expected to increase tenfold in the next 10 years. Digital also opens new markets for customers, like variable printing (where each image is unique/user-specific).

However, there are large gaps in today's digital solution, which vary by market (see accompanying figure). Digital vendors will need to expand their offer in paper handling and finishing equipment (binding and the like). While it's not necessary to make the entire solution, digital vendors will need to know it intimately, and partnerships will be needed with others (who, notably, have current relationships with traditional manufacturers). It may be necessary to find new approaches to pre- and post-press, given how digital alters workflows; a potential source for additional differentiation.

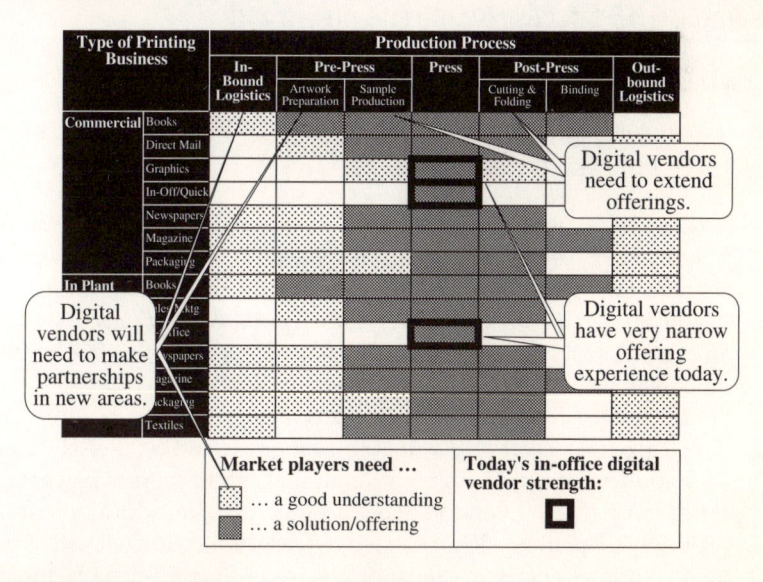

Type of Printing Business		In-Bound Logistics	Pre-Press		Press	Post-Press		Out-bound Logistics
			Artwork Preparation	Sample Production		Cutting & Folding	Binding	
Commercial	Books							
	Direct Mail							
	Graphics							
	In-Off/Quick							
	Newspapers							
	Magazine							
	Packaging							
In Plant	Books							
	Mktg							
	Office							
	Newspapers							
	Magazine							
	Packaging							
	Textiles							

Digital vendors need to extend offerings.

Digital vendors will need to make partnerships in new areas.

Digital vendors have very narrow offering experience today.

Market players need ...
- ... a good understanding
- ... a solution/offering

Today's in-office digital vendor strength: ■

Source: Business Intelligence Associates LLC.

BRAND EQUITY Any player thinking about a move into a new market must consider whether their brand will be an asset, or a drag. A brand's reach, its strength, and its positioning come together to play one of the most influential roles in determining whether a market strategy succeeds.

Reach refers to the geographic coverage and customer awareness a brand enjoys. At the most basic level, is the brand there to be seen? If so, will the people that matter understand it? A brand's *strength* refers to the power the brand has to make customers comfortable with the solution on offer, independent of the solution itself, and also to motivate customers to be associated with the brand. Familiarity and scale play significant roles in driving comfort levels, and are good measures to investigate to assess brand strength. Image and exclusivity are powerful drivers motivating customers to the brand. Finally, brand *positioning* is a factor that determines which market segments the offering can be applied to, and as a result has tremendous influence over the volume and profit potential of customers that can be captured. Positioning is also an integral component of differentiation, which has a direct impact on prospects of competitive success. For example, in a market where most sales are to a segment that most values uptime and is adverse to downtime, a brand that represents low running costs at the potential expense of uptime is not likely to have great appeal, likely losing out to a brand representing uptime. Example 5.15 assesses these, qualitatively, for the ongoing U.S. printing press example.

Example 5.15 Success Requirements: Brand

For a Digital Vendor Targeting Traditional Markets

The accompanying figure summarizes the brand issues for digital entrants into printing press markets.

> *Reach*. Digital printer vendors have solid brand advantages; they are a relevant presence in offices and homes and are as recognizable as traditional printing press vendors. It is also likely that production digital printers are already in customer photocopy rooms.
> *Strength*. Digital vendors are advantaged here also. Office equipment has passed a purchasing process; transactions have closed, brands are trusted, and business relationships exist. In brand scale, digital players have very valuable brands (HP, IBM, Xerox; lately Dell and Samsung), outshining traditional printing press players.
> *Positioning*. Digital vendors have a range of brand positions, from reliability to quality to low cost. High-value brands fit well with commercial printer needs; in digital production printers, most prominent are Canon, HP, IBM, and Xerox. In desktops there are HP, Lexmark,

and Epson (focused on ink-jet). Some may have difficulty—Brother (known for low equipment costs), Dell (known to subcontract printer production), and Samsung (predominantly a consumer positioning).

Recent moves suggest digital players are testing waters with subbrands. Hewlett-Packard acquired and maintains the Indigo line, and moved into production ink printers with a new low-cost, high-speed subbranded Edgeline. Kodak has a subbranded NexPress, targeting exactly those markets held by traditional players.

	Reach		Strength		Positioning	
	Geographic	Awareness	Familiarity	Scale	Focus	Reputation
Digital Players	Digital printer brands cover the United States uniformly.	Most individuals recognize digital printer brands; in most offices and homes.	Commercial /industrial printers likely already doing business with leading[1] digital printer brands; purchasing them for homes and offices use.	Many digital printer manufacturers[1] have dominating scale, far outweighing traditional press manufacturers.	Some digital printer brands known for desktop versus production printing, others known for toner versus ink.	Full range of quality, capability and price/cost combinations exists.
Traditional Players	Little coverage variation or focus.	Awareness very high to existing customer markets thanks to existing business.	Key players have close business relationships with commercial /industrial printers.	Traditional players have relatively small brands; cannot brag "no one ever got fired for buying an IBM."	Digital seen as very different from traditional presses; limited credibility afforded to traditional players for digital.	Full range of quality, capability and price/cost combinations exists.

☐ Critical importance entering markets with existing competitor lineup
☐ Relative weakness
☐ Some strengths
☐ Relative strength

Source: Business Intelligence Associates LLC.
[1] Canon, HP, IBM, Lexmark, Xerox; lately Dell, Brother, Samsung; perhaps Konica Minolta, OKI, Kyocera, Toshiba, Sharp.

DISTRIBUTION *Distribution* refers to the business's sales and channel capabilities. A sales force, and the relationships that come with it, is incredibly difficult to build from scratch, though pivotal for market success; the same applies to a productive channel partner network. The mechanics of developing the right relationships can by itself make market entry prohibitive, to say nothing of building new sales and marketing organizations, and all the necessary distribution logistics. These are often formidable barriers, and sometimes only overcome by leveraging a third party's existing capabilities—whether through acquisition, partnership, or otherwise. Again, these are qualitatively assessed in Example 5.16.

> ### Example 5.16 Success Requirements: Distribution
>
> #### For a Digital Vendor Targeting Traditional Markets
>
> None of the U.S. digital printer manufacturers have much in the way of sales or marketing, distribution logistics, or preexisting relationships in traditional printing press markets. Entry into these markets by any digital player will be difficult, best executed by an investment in a third party with an established infrastructure.
>
> An acquisition of, or partnership with, a traditional printing press market player appears to be in the offing, though there are other avenues, such as partnership with other solution providers (installers, related equipment vendors, others). Such partners are probably motivated to offer digital solutions.
>
> This lack of existing distribution assets is the primary area of weakness for digital vendors.

Internal Operations

Success in new markets also depends on the suitability and likely performance of the business model's internal operations, including operational capabilities and economics.

CAPABILITIES Whether the organization can actually deliver is typically what mid-level managers think of first when significant market moves are in play. While organizational capabilities are important, and are potentially very significant barriers to market entry, there is a range of viable remedies similar to those discussed under "Distribution," including acquisitions, partnerships, contract relationships, and many others.

In fact, these approaches are proven and relatively quick to achieve, and can be highly value creating. In the case of acquisitions, the price paid is often closer to the value of the existing business being acquired than it is to the value of that same business with a wider profitable stream running through it—leaving open the door to substantive value creation. Note, however, that over time most businesses tend to forget the original reasons for making an acquisition and the initiative fails as a result, not capitalizing on the original market strategy intention (some reports suggest two-thirds of all acquisitions do not meet the expectations laid out at the outset).

ECONOMICS Can the solution be delivered at a price sufficiently attractive to both investors and customers in the new market? And if so, does the business have the wherewithal to raise the financing needed for a successful market entry? This topic is within the purview of many other books modeling economic performance, and is not addressed here.

Supplier Access

The lack of access to supplies can be a factor that throws a market into the "unattractive" category. For one reason or another, in some markets a few players hold a great deal of share and market power, and have the power to restrict raw materials and inputs to subsequent markets—a structure that, naturally, leads to relatively higher prices and may even limit supplies. At a minimum, new market players need relationships with key suppliers, together with supplies guarantees and something to bargain with, as those suppliers are likely to value their existing and larger customers more.

Example 5.17 summarizes the prospects of digital printer manufacturers as they evaluate the traditional printing press markets, relating to internal operations and supplier market access.

Example 5.17 Success Requirements: Operations/Suppliers

For a Digital Vendor Targeting Traditional Markets

OPERATIONS

- *Internal capabilities.* In production, existing capabilities can be easily redirected, as can supplemental sales and marketing organization resources.
- *Internal economics.* Commercial and in-plant printers will likely adopt digital printing; reports indicate the economics are attractive for both ends of the deal.

SUPPLIERS ACCESS Component sources are almost entirely highly liquid and transparent markets, not subject to constraints or likely to be. A few components, primarily printer engines, are specific to digital printers; even here, there are several suppliers, each with its own technology. However, these new printers will lead technology (speed, print area, reliability, operating costs) and the supplier field is a little narrower.

Synthesizing Your Strategic View

As described at the outset of this chapter, a value-oriented strategic view of markets is a profile of market opportunities, synthesized for business leaders interested in maximizing business value. This strategic view is oriented around two assessments: the value each market profit pool is expected to deliver, and what is required from a business model to succeed in each.

1. *Market profit pool value assessment.* This is a view of the present values of future cash flows of each part of an industry or market of interest. That industry or market needs to be delineated into segments in a way that promotes value-oriented market management: which markets to enter and exit, and how to compete in each. In addition to expected market profit pool values, the *range* of likely values, to a 95 percent confidence level, is also needed for use in market strategy formulation.
2. *Business model assessment.* This is a view of how easy or difficult it would be for your business to enter or participate in each market profit pool. That view comprises an assessment of what the target market requires, and addresses how that fits with your business model and other assets.

This strategic view is a cornerstone starting point for market strategy formulation, addressed in Chapter 6. It helps to draft specific opportunities for consideration in strategy formulation; the insights—and the information itself—are core inputs to the evaluation of business propositions, strategic options, and strategies as a whole.

Your Summarized Strategic View

To wrap up, a highly summarized strategic view for the U.S. printing press industry is set out in Example 5.18. Several traditional press markets offer the same order-of-magnitude value as the in-office market (from where digital printer vendors originate): packaging, advertising, magazine, and catalog applications. Digital printer vendors now must choose whether and how to invest in these market opportunities. That may mean targeting a dominating position in small market profit pools, or it may mean focusing on the large ones (for some players, that's the only way to add nontrivial value). Further, if a technology focus is needed, toner-based production printing presses offer the greatest value creation opportunity.

In terms of requirements for success, there are both similarities and substantial differences between the strengths in-office vendors have and what is needed for success in traditional printing press markets. The greatest challenges are in distribution (getting a properly targeted sales channel) and in crafting an integrated offering/solution (including binding, in-bound media handling, and the like). There are several strategic options that may help overcome these challenges, making them expensive problems rather than prohibitive issues. A partnership with a traditional printing press vendor is in the cards, as they have existing sales capabilities and relevant brands. An acquisition would bring the most control, and the ability to mold the market, though other partnering configurations are also an option.

With this clear view of market potential, we can move to the last step in the program—formulating market strategy in Chapter 6.

Example 5.18 Summary Strategic View

U.S. Printing Press Industry

The first figure is an industry value map, while the second presents a summary of strategic fit.

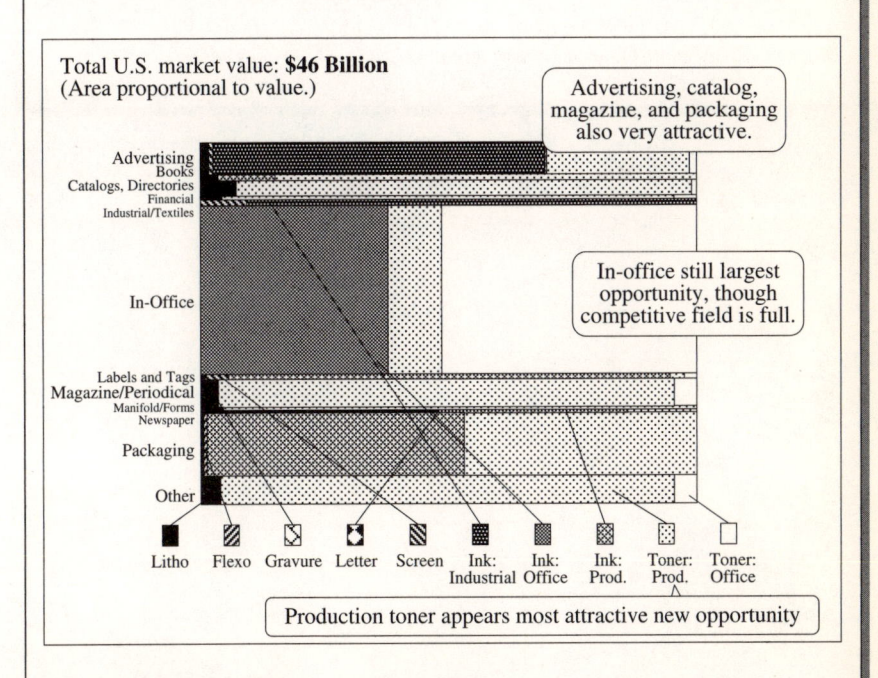

Total U.S. market value: **$46 Billion**
(Area proportional to value.)

Advertising, catalog, magazine, and packaging also very attractive.

Advertising
Books
Catalogs, Directories
Financial
Industrial/Textiles

In-Office

In-office still largest opportunity, though competitive field is full.

Labels and Tags
Magazine/Periodical
Manifold/Forms
Newspaper
Packaging
Other

Litho   Flexo   Gravure   Letter   Screen   Ink: Industrial   Ink: Office   Ink: Prod.   Toner: Prod.   Toner: Office

Production toner appears most attractive new opportunity

Source: Business Intelligence Associates LLC.

> Digital players are advantaged in offer and brand.

	Advantages	Challenges
Offer	**Digital is both viable** and out of reach of traditional players.	**Full solutions need to be configured** to match traditional players.
Brand	**Brands strong and recognized**, business relations already exist with customers.	Trust is not at same level enjoyed by traditional players.
Distribution		**No correctly targeted sales organization** or relationships.
Capabilities	**Technical skills strong**, especially in digital.	**Management not versed in needs of commercial** printers or broad solutions.
Economics	Economic proposition to customers proven and increasingly attractive.	
Supplier Access	Suppliers not powerful, and components are reasonably accessible.	

> Established sales organization needed.

[Key Issues]

Source: Business Intelligence Associates LLC.

CHAPTER 6

Define a Path That Exploits
REAL OPPORTUNITIES

Market profit pools deliver an unparalleled view of where the best value-creating opportunities are likely to be across markets. The only need that remains is to formulate a market strategy that maximally captures value for your business.

This chapter addresses exactly that need. In it, we explore a market strategy formulation process specifically designed around driving business value, and incorporating very powerful techniques and tools. In the past 20 years, particularly since 2000, the science of strategic decision making has made some insightful advances; we have included some of these, including "real options" valuation techniques that allow uncertainty to be easily incorporated into decision making. Sadly, these advances have been cloaked in an aura of complex mathematics to date, and presented primarily in technically oriented literature. This has seriously inhibited widespread adoption—although, to be fair, some of the tools have only recently reached usable levels of robustness and ease of use.

We use and illustrate these new techniques simply and clearly at an executive level, and have taken pains to avoid the underlying mathematics and theory. The idea is that you need to use these techniques for strategic understanding and action, but need to avoid getting mired in the mechanics of the tools. Let's face it, as of the past five years, those skills can be bought; what can't be substituted is your understanding of your market, your business, and the choices available—and, of course, you leading your business along a value-creating path.

At the core of this strategy formulation process lie forecasting and uncertainty estimation, decision mapping, the discounted cash flow (DCF) technique (to figure out the value of business propositions), and real options (to value and navigate decision paths).

We start at the ground floor and characterize the basics of value-maximizing strategy formulation. We then step through the market strategy formulation process, addressing the issues in a sensible order and using a fictional example of a business, Samsung, considering its future in the United States. A new entrant to the branded U.S. in-office digital printer market, Samsung is a part of a larger Korean company and is a rapidly rising electronics business. It is aggressive and has useful strengths to bring to bear on a challenging market.

Business Value and Making Strategic Choices

Thought leaders and academicians will tell you that business management is about making the right decisions and getting them executed well; from a business leader's standpoint, that execution is primarily through persuasion and influence. It follows that the business leader intent on maximizing shareholder returns will search out and choose the path forward that generates the greatest intrinsic value for the business (from Chapter 1, the present value of future cash flows) and will turn to facts and solid rationale to persuade others in the business to charge up that same path.

As we saw in Part One, market strategy has the greatest impact on business value by a long way—implying that business leaders must be willing to invest the effort needed to get it right in particular. The basic approach to strategy formulation is to identify opportunities and then evaluate and choose among them in a way that delivers the greatest value-add. It seems that value-maximizing business leaders are fortunate; they have a single, higher-order business objective—something that streamlines an otherwise complex and political task of choosing among market opportunities. Figure 6.1 illustrates the basic idea.

Every business has a baseline warranted value, labeled "as-is" in Figure 6.1, against which different market strategy opportunities will deliver more or less business value; represented by A, B, and C. Naturally enough, there are a number of ways of getting things done, depicted as strategy variants on the right side of Figure 6.1, in this case relating to variants of the highest value opportunity, C. In the past, to the extent that this value approach was included at all, the effort would also attempt to recognize uncertainty and give a best case, an expected case, and a worst case.

Outside of those somewhat arbitrary guesses, the issue of uncertainty and how to deal with it has always gone largely unaddressed. In fact, it has mostly been seen as a serious negative and much is done to avoid it altogether. The world has moved on in recent years and adopted the view that risk is actually limited to *negative* uncertainty; that is, when it leads to losses. Positive uncertainty is something to be identified, understood, and embraced. The trick is to be able to identify them separately and act on them differently.

Value Impact Market Strategy Opportunities

Intrinsic Business Value
($ Billions)

Strategy C appears to offer most value.

$16 —
$12 —
$8 —
$4 —
$0 —

Adds value — Reduces value — Adds substantial value

Value "as-is" | A | B | C

Market Strategy Opportunities

Market Strategy Variants and Scenarios

Intrinsic Business Value
($ Billions)

Variant C1 has a narrow value spread while C4 actually has downside risk.

$16 — Best Expected / Worst
$12 — Best Expected / Worst
$0 —

Best Expected / Worst | Best Expected / Worst | Scenario range — Best Expected / Worst

C1 | C2 | C3 | C4 | C5

Market Strategy Variants

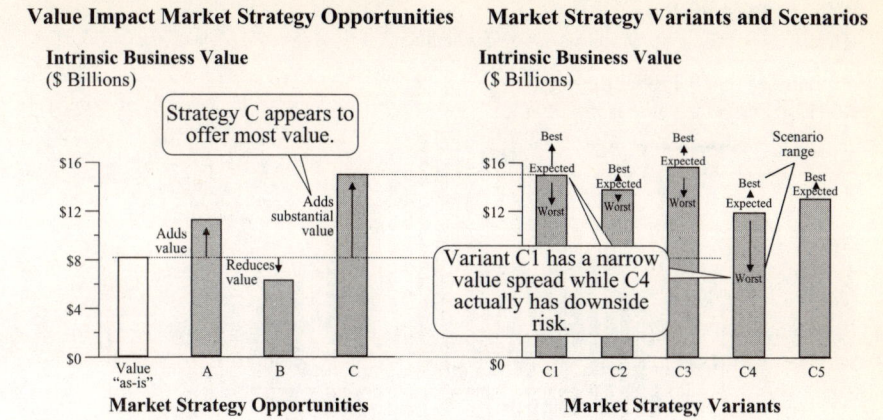

FIGURE 6.1 Choosing the Value-Maximizing Market Strategy
Source: Business Intelligence Associates LLC.

In large measure, it is the 'problem' of uncertainty that has been overcome in recent years. It turns out that uncertainty is not a problem at all, but something to be explicitly recognized and included in the decision cycle. Market and internal uncertainties, which managers intuitively know and recognize, can be included in economic valuations to deliver business value estimates *along with uncertainty profiles*, specifically indicating whether an uncertainty is a risk or an upside. For example, Samsung has the opportunity to enter the U.S. book printing press market, and one of the ways it could do so would deliver a business with an expected value of $13 million. This information, however, is far more insightful when accompanied by its probability profile, as in Figure 6.2.

A quick look at Figure 6.2 reveals that $13 million really is only the *expected* value. In fact, to a 95 percent confidence interval (that is, we're sure it will be somewhere in that range), there is a chance that the strategy will have a value as low as $–3 million and as high as $28 million. Looking at it from a probability point of view, the strategy has an 8 percent chance of being in negative territory—something to think about when management comes to compare it against some of its other opportunities.

This uncertainty perspective is actually just the first in a sequence of insights. From here the uncertainty profile is easily summarized and used as an input to a real options assessment, which brings together several business propositions and basically figures out what value-maximizing business leaders would do in the full range of outcomes. This and other strategy formulation techniques are reviewed later in this chapter, and we do not want to get too far ahead at this point. With that said, it is worth introducing

Probability

Probability that value is *negative*: 8%

Probability that value is *positive*: 92%

Expected value

−$3

$28

95% confidence interval

$0 $10 *$13* $20 $30

Value of Business Proposition
($ Millions)

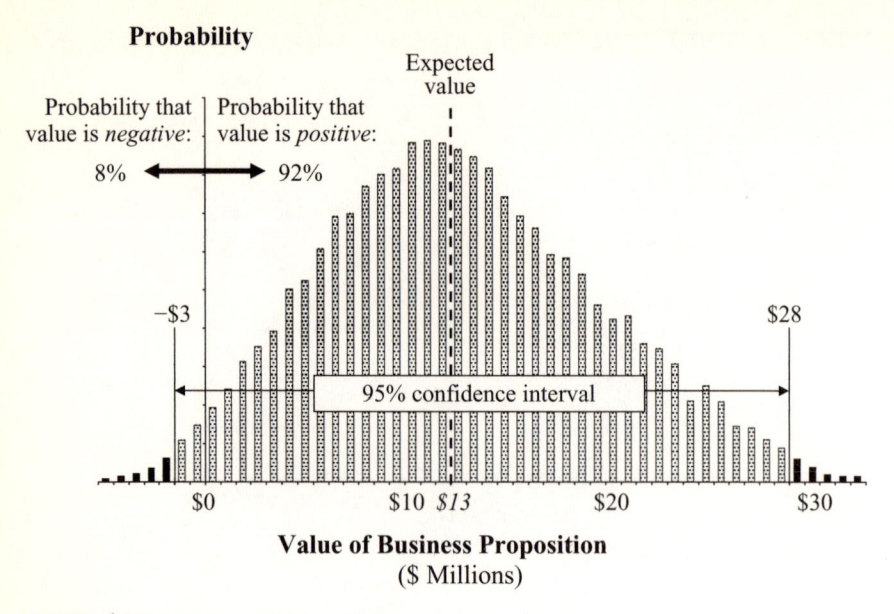

FIGURE 6.2 Profile of a Business Value
Source: Business Intelligence Associates LLC.

the basics of real options now, as we will be referring to them and their needs before we actually use them in the next section.

What Are Real Options?

The term *real options* refers to the application of a now well-known financial market technology (options) to the real world: valuing the right, but not the obligation, to make an investment at some time in the future, at an amount set today. Well, that's the technical definition. In short, real options techniques give us the economics we need to make decisions where there is uncertainty and choice. In ordinary-speak, this approach figures out the circumstances in the future when one course of action is worth more than another; it then assumes management makes the appropriate course change at those times in the future, and calculates what the entire venture is worth with those sensible decisions. It delivers a summary value estimate that is critically important in strategy formulation, as we use it to compare opportunities against one another.

Before real options were recognized and included, value-maximizing businesses only had tools that put a value on a specific course of action, such as the DCF valuation, as though business leaders didn't have the flexibility to change course—like abandoning a loss-making business. Take the case of a pharmaceutical firm with a plan to launch a drug. The economic projection shows several initial investments and a subsequent series of cash flows growing into the future, giving an attractive valuation as a result. Now, there is a real chance that regulators will not approve the drug, raising the question, what would you do as the business's leader in that event? Obviously, you would shut the project down and avoid the planned marketing and production investments (especially if you had been paying attention to granular, cash profit performance).

While that and other scenarios can be individually modeled in the DCF approach, they cannot be brought together or merged with other opportunities and scenarios in a way that allows valid economic comparisons. There has been some use of DCF values in decision trees in the past to consolidate decision path values, but the technique uses discount rates that are rendered inappropriate when decisions change the risks involved. And cutting out downside risk, as in the pharmaceutical case just mentioned, changes the risk profile substantively. Decision trees also suffer from the use of probabilities that are arbitrary and excessively discrete. For example, the technique forces a choice between two or a few outcomes, each having a probability; it cannot address real-world uncertainties, which come as a continuum and are in many variables.

Real options techniques solve these problems. Uncertainties are established much more accurately and directly and are associated with each valuation as a measure of its *volatility*. Since volatility is used, discount rates are neutralized within many real options tools by converting calculations to using risk-free discount rates. And armed with the value and volatility for each business proposition, the real options tool plots out the probability of every asset value in all future periods. It is with this probability-based view of the how the future unfolds that the real options tool delivers a value estimate for the entire opportunity, including all potential decision paths.

Explaining such things as real options without examples may make them seem dry and arcane. Later in this chapter we see the vital role real options have in strategy formulation, and how real options tools are used and how they work. We start by reviewing the market strategy formulation process itself.

Formulating a Value-Maximizing Market Strategy

Although there are many ways to formulate market strategy, this approach is specifically designed around maximizing business value while being flexible enough to capture the wildest and most creative ideas for strategic moves in the market (and, to a certain extent, it encourages their consideration). When it is done right, this approach has a track record of delivering timely and unambiguous action plans. The approach and the six tasks contained in it are described graphically in Figure 6.3; we have used it as a map to structure this chapter, and we will walk through each task sequentially.

1	List and Define Opportunities	• Generate a list of market and business opportunities. • Rationalize the list, eliminating the unviable and non-value-creating.
2	Flesh Out and Map Opportunities	• Add detail to each opportunity. • List variants, scenarios, and alternatives. • Create decision maps, capturing key uncertainties and decision paths.
3	Characterize Outcomes	• Characterize expected outcomes for each business proposition in each decision path. • Explicitly enumerate outcomes and uncertainties.
4	Evaluate Economics	• Use discounted cash flow techniques to value business propositions in decision paths. • Use real options to value decision paths and entire opportunities.
5	Define Path Forward	• Rank-order the value creation potential of decision paths and opportunities. • Characterize qualitative inputs (risk appetite, management capabilities, etc.) • Compile integrated path forward.
6	Plan and Execute	• Develop detailed plan of execution (actions, timing, investments, management tasks).

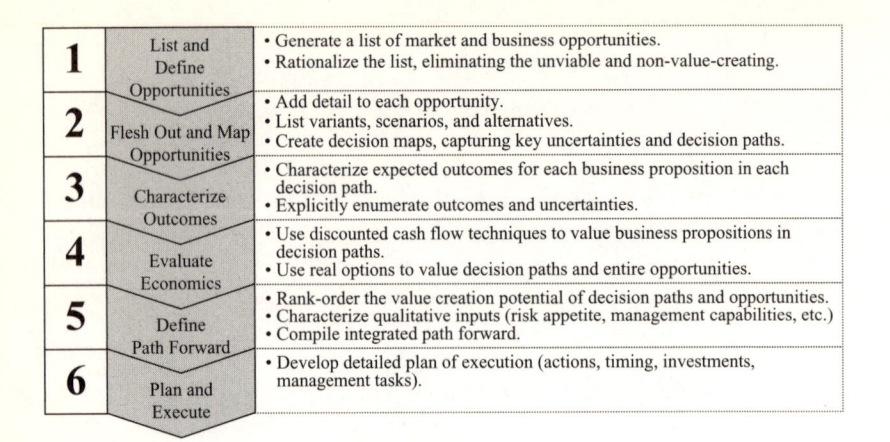

FIGURE 6.3 Value-Maximizing Market Strategy Formulation
Source: Business Intelligence Associates LLC.

First, a list of the opportunities available is compiled, leveraging preceding work on internal and market profit pools to characterize ongoing business performance, and existing and potential markets. In the second task, meat is put on the bones of the opportunities by adding specifics and detail, capturing the various ways they can be put together in a market strategy, and using decision maps. From there, in the third task, the expected outcome of each mapped path is further characterized in terms of market and operational metrics, together with a characterization of the uncertainties involved. These are brought together in the fourth task by running the numbers and determining the value creation each path will deliver as part of a market strategy. This task uses DCF valuation techniques to value business propositions, and real options analysis to bring these valuations together to value entire decision paths, and so sets the stage for integrated decision making. In the fifth task, those economics are weighed by decision makers, including preferences and appetites for risk; the path forward is agreed upon and the market strategy stated. An action plan is defined in the sixth task, setting out tasks, timing, investment and resources requirements, and contingencies and event indicators for business leaders to keep their eyes on.

As we step through this process in the sections that follow, we illustrate key concepts and tools using an ongoing example—actually formulating a market strategy as we go. To do this, we reach back and use the U.S. printing press industry illustration used throughout Chapter 5, and formulate a market strategy for Samsung, a new player in the U.S. in-office digital printer market. Samsung's initial situation is introduced in Example 6.1. We

Example 6.1 Introducing Samsung's Current Situation

Challenges of a New Entrant

Samsung is new to the U.S. in-office digital printer market, currently confined to low-priced toner desktops. Its presence is just discernable in the accompanying figure as a thin sliver in "Units Sold" under "Printers: Toner Mono"; it is so small it can't be seen under "Multifunction." Since its prices are so low (the thick line at the bottom of unit price charts) it is also not visible in revenues charts at all.

However, Samsung is a huge toner printer engine manufacturer, with nearly a third of the global market; large players go to Samsung to fit their own offerings.

Also, there is Samsung's brand. In the 1990s, it was seen as a cheap electronics manufacturer. However, since 2001 that has changed dramatically; in 2006 the Samsung brand was 20th on the Interbrand ranking, with a value of $16 billion, up from 42nd and $5 billion. Samsung is now ahead of Dell, Xerox, Kodak, Panasonic, and many others; it is getting close to printer leader Hewlett-Packard's (HP) $20 billion brand value.

Finally, Samsung's parent, Samsung Group, is a very large industrial manufacturer with relationships with many global businesses (many of whom print or use packaging), and an established U.S. sales/distribution infrastructure.

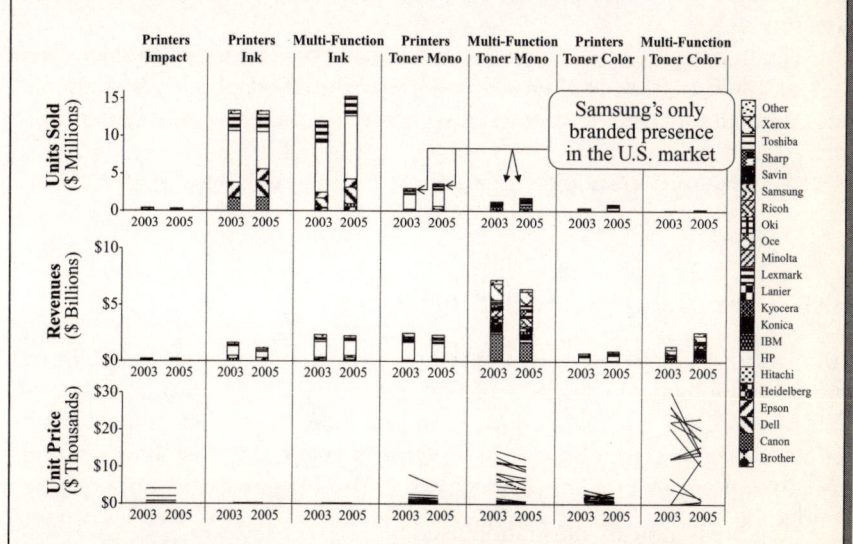

Source: IDC 2007; Interbrand; Business Intelligence Associates LLC.

are obliged to point out that we compiled and use this information without the support, encouragement, help, or even knowledge of Samsung. Those in the market hoping to pick up a few nuggets of strategic information are warned: Much of it is simply wrong—do not rely on it.

It is clear from Example 6.1 that Samsung has only a small U.S. presence—but even small players are blessed with the opportunity to grow business value. Indeed, without the Warren Buffett problem (where his capital base is so large that the universe of investment candidates with substantive value growth potential is extremely small), small players have a relatively larger number of opportunities. So what does Samsung have to build on? Well, since it makes so many toner printer engines, it knows the business well; not a unique capability by any means, but one that levels the competitive field significantly. Also, with this capability they are in the advantaged position of being able to integrate controller circuitry right on the engine itself, leading to a less costly product to produce, and potentially better protected from third-party supplies substitution.

In raising the Samsung brand they pulled off a stunt almost unparalleled in business history. And its trendy cell phone line has placed the brand into the pockets of many consumers or their friends. But that's consumer electronics, while much of toner desktop digital printer market is business-to-business; so how is any of it useful? It turns out brand recognition in office printer purchasing is key, again leveling the playing field and limiting the advantages existing digital printer market leaders would naturally assume.

Finally, its parent Samsung Group's access to customers and sales capabilities could be powerful factors in industrial markets; both are shortcomings all digital players have to deal with, should they choose to enter those markets.

We now turn to strategy formulation, starting with Task 1.

Task 1: List and Define Opportunities

An obvious thing to do, one might think, is to step back and simply list out all those things the business could do in the market. In practice, however, it is a task that is largely overlooked in just about all market strategy efforts in favor of going with one or two people's gut. Unfortunately, those guts usually belong to powerful executives in the business, and opportunities tend to become limited to verifying the legitimacy of one or two known and preferred choices. And with that one piece of organizational acquiescence, huge amounts of value are ignored, very often left to hungry new entrants and competitors. In this task we look at the benefits of a dedicated and creative effort to explicitly list opportunities, and suggest ways to generate opportunity ideas and record them.

Time and again, anecdotal evidence has pointed to this first task as being one of the most valuable parts of the entire process. A freewheeling creative process that crafts a wide list of opportunities always comes up with new and unique ways to put things together, enabling improvements in all sorts of strategy areas, from improved offering definitions to improved competitive positioning and even internal operations.

A useful tool to use to generate opportunity ideas is the market strategy types framework of Chapter 5, which we have applied to Samsung's case in Example 6.2 to create a list of opportunity ideas, albeit the most obvious and simplistic ones. Naturally, any players seriously contemplating these markets should expect to generate a more creative list; they are most likely in or near the market, so they have a useful vantage point and are familiar with their organization's strengths. While frameworks help in idea generation, the most useful approach is to set up an opportunity formulation work environment that encourages out-of-the-box perspectives, perhaps leveraging tools such as "war gaming" (essentially a form of role playing), envisioning, brainstorming, and others. Again, the market strategy classification framework is effective in jogging ideas, but it shouldn't be relied upon as the extent of the creative process, as we have done here.

Example 6.2 Listing Market Strategy Opportunities

Example Market Strategy Opportunities for Samsung

An example of a *game follower* strategy for Samsung might be to acquire and offer ink printers to their existing consumer market. In a *market follower* strategy they might drive into the corporate market with their toner offering. Or they might pursue a *risk-taking follower* strategy, and both enter the corporate market and offer ink printers or new toner-based production printers. In terms of third-level, higher risk/reward market strategy ideas, Samsung could pursue opportunities largely uncharted by others—*disruptor* and *pioneer* strategies discussed in Chapter 5. We focus on Samsung's pioneer opportunities later in this chapter.

Samsung's Market Strategy Opportunities List in Printing Presses

Market Strategy Opportunities				Where Compete?	How Compete?
Level 1: Existing	Exploiter	Milk business	1	Stay within consumer, toner mono market	Stop investments, extract cash over time
		Follow market leader	2		Keep up offering/ business model improvements
		OEM only	3		Withdraw as end-product vendor; OEM
		Invest big	4		Invest for share, lead product improvements
Level 2: Charted	Game Follower	Enter ink	5	Acquire ink offering, stay in consumer only	Deliver mid- or higher-level quality
		OEM ink	6	Acquire ink engine, sell ink engines OEM	
	Market Follower	Enter corporate market	7a	Develop/acquire corporate offering	Deliver low-cost solutions
			7b		Deliver mid- or higher-level quality
	Risk-Taking Follower	Enter ink/ corporate	8a	Acquire ink offering, enter corporate market	Deliver low-cost solutions
			8b		Deliver mid- or higher-level quality
		Production/ corporate	9	Develop corporate production offering	Deliver mid- or higher-level quality
Level 3: Uncharted	Disruptor	Low-cost supplies	10	Stay within consumer, toner mono	Sell based on low-cost supplies
		Low-cost suppies/new	11	Develop/acquire corporate offering	
		e-paper	12	Stay within consumer	Develop/acquire reimageable paper
		e-paper/new	13	Stay in consumer, and enter Corporate	
	Pioneer	Big press profit pools	14	Enter high-value press markets with toner	Deliver digital presses in a partnership with traditional players
		Small press profit pools	15	Enter second-tier press markets with toner	

Source: Business Intelligence Associates LLC.

At first, we develop a list of opportunity building-blocks, the core and basic ideas, such as those for Samsung in Example 6.2. Once they have been identified they are ready to be commingled, disassembled, integrated, and nested—potentially combined in creative ways as components of some larger plan, or part of some multistep plan.

An example would be for Samsung to first acquire a production printer offering for the in-office market (number 9 in Example 6.2), and from there move into a traditional printing press market after a year or two (number 14 or 15). In practice, this sort of sequencing is always how things actually end up, and this mixing up of opportunities must be explicitly listed and recorded. It is difficult to do this in a structured way without losing nonlinear thinking, and often it is best to simply list them out as they surface, perhaps with short descriptions. Naturally, these lists continually change as strategy formulation proceeds and ideas continue to evolve; new ones will warrant inclusion, while others drop off as problems become apparent.

Finally, there is one set of opportunities not explicitly recognized in the market strategy types framework—and that is a market exit. This is clearly always an option and there are always a number of ways to get it done. A market exit must be included in the evaluation, if only to be sure that it has no merit. Shareholders deserve to know if there is a better way to employ their capital, and business leaders should always be the first to know when that is the case!

Before moving on to the next task, it is important to stage-gate the process and qualitatively rank-order opportunities in terms of viability, difficulty, and value potential. Naturally, the idea is to keep these lists to a manageable length, using intuition to limit wasted effort and drop obviously unworthy ideas.

Task 2: Flesh Out and Map Opportunities

Ideas are one thing, but a well-researched and thoughtfully crafted market strategy is quite another. While too few of today's market strategy initiatives start with an explicit effort to list high-potential opportunities, fewer still are taken to the next levels of coloring in and evaluating alternatives. In this task we identify what is actually needed by, and expected from, each opportunity, setting up subsequent tasks of quantifying outcomes and translating them into economic results.

Fleshing Out Opportunities with Specifics

Putting the specifics to each opportunity is important, not just because it helps lay out the economics, but because it also forces all those involved to go through the necessary thinking—injecting a healthy dose of realism, enhancing buy-in, demanding discipline to ensure internal consistency, and stirring further creativity. That creativity leads to more useful and robust opportunities, perhaps developing additional opportunities, too.

We can see this process at work by looking at one of the opportunities for Samsung. In particular, the initial version of the small press profit pools strategy is explicitly written up in Figure 6.4. When this write-up was done, quite an amount of further thinking emerged—driving subsequent, iterative development.

The initial small press profit pools strategy idea was to pursue the smaller market profit pools for digital presses in the hope that by focusing on them, Samsung would be able to dominate them and extract a larger share of their value. That thinking evolved with the recognition that some market profit pools will evolve faster than others, and the first, books, is already well under way—far ahead of other opportunities. This strategy opportunity developed into using books as a stepping-stone, a platform to unlock the larger profit pool opportunities—effectively merging the small press profit pools strategy idea with the one above it on the list, the big press profit pools strategy, in a sequenced plan. Perhaps some conditional indicators need to be tracked to help make the call to move to that second step, or perhaps the economics of the small press profit pools strategy would only be attractive given the opportunity to move on to big press profit pools.

A common element in both the big and the small press profit pools opportunities is the potential to work with an existing market player (one that now offers traditional presses only) to boost results. Variants of this include an acquisition, a partnership, or a joint venture. Each opportunity and its variants warrant evaluation for likelihood of success, expected market results, investment needs, and other factors that define their future economics. In fact, this sort of review even helps to understand contingencies and alternative decisions, such as the price at which an acquisition is worth pursuing.

No matter the business or situation, there is always a wide array of opportunities and variants. Again, for the practical purposes of moving forward, building-block opportunities are best captured in some structure and fleshed out to the extent possible, as in Example 6.2. Higher-level strategy ideas that integrate building-blocks need only be captured and described ad hoc, so that they can be included in the assessments later.

Before turning to decision maps, we first take a quick detour to look at the need to bring in widely recognized rules of thumb and ideas to the strategy formulation process. This is especially important in value-maximizing initiatives, since there are several known strategy formulae that have powerfully demonstrated their value over the years. We'll examine a couple of high-impact ones on the way.

17: Small Press Profit Pools

	Where?	**How?**
Market Strategy	Enter second tier printing press market profit pools (books?); stay within toner offerings.	Deliver toner digital presses; work with player already in traditional press market?

- Drive into traditional press markets with toner.
- Immediately acquire existing player for sales/distribution, offering development, and brand.
- Books set to emerge with digital first; education?
- Use as stepping stone for moves to other profit pools.
- Develop offer and launch within 12 months.

Key Elements of Business Plan

Customer Markets	Offering	• Hi-speed toner in existing press. • Initial focus on books/education. • Launch within 12 months.
	Brand	• Leverage existing high-end brand together with Samsung digital messaging.
	Distribution	• Leverage existing high-end player's sales and relationship capabilities.
Internal Operations	Operations	• Leverage existing high-end player's operations in new joint and integrated operations.
	Economics	• Acquire traditional press player. • Invest in new offer development. • Protect supplies profit model.
Supplier Access		• Leverage existing capabilities: Samsung vertical integration, other supplier relationships.

Expected Book Market Fundamentals

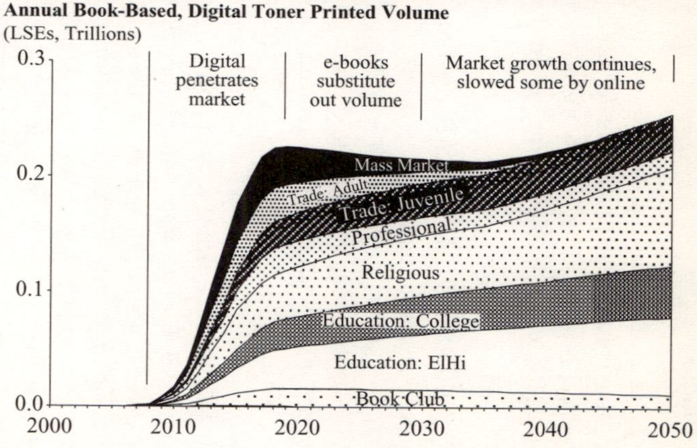

Annual Book-Based, Digital Toner Printed Volume (LSEs, Trillions)

Digital penetrates market | e-books substitute out volume | Market growth continues, slowed some by online

Mass Market, Trade: Adult, Trade: Juvenile, Professional, Religious, Education: College, Education: ElHi, Book Club

- Market profit pool review set out expected demand for equipment and supplies: MIEs, volume, margins, probabilities.
- Competitive and share performance need to be forecast.
- Education has high probabilities, volumes, and homogeneity.

FIGURE 6.4 Example Opportunity Summary—Samsung in Digital Book Printing Presses
Source: Business Intelligence Associates LLC.

High-Value Rules of Thumb

Although we are not yet at the point in the strategy formulation process to evaluate economics, the value-focused mind-set should never be far from thinking about expected returns. The following are a few generalizations that can be very useful to design into strategies from the outset.

FIRST-MOVER RETURNS ARE USUALLY THE GREATEST One thing about digital presses in the U.S. book printing market (the subject of Figure 6.4's opportunity summary), is that they are not much of a leap from ordinary high-speed production digital printers. In fact, it would take only a few relatively minor adjustments to incorporate inbound paper handling and outbound book-binding capabilities. With that in mind, it is no surprise to find that there are already competitors with offerings in the digital toner production printer market (largely high speed office printing and copying); including the usual suspects HP (with its 2001 Indigo acquisition), Xerox, Canon, and latterly Kodak (with its NexPress business). Some of these players have already fielded trial solutions for short-run book manufacturing.

In value-oriented market strategy terms, this is a significant disappointment for our subject, Samsung. In the vast majority of markets and situations, the first-mover position carries with it a disproportionately large share of market value—sometimes as much as half a market profit pool's projected value in many sectors, when observed from the time the market emerges. There are several reasons for this, as conceptually illustrated in Figure 6.5: First movers stake out the largest share slice, which tends to have longevity; they also tend to recognize and move on opportunities ahead of the pack, moving development at a higher cost rate, though cumulatively lower cost overall; finally, they also tend to be able to carve out the high-premium portion of the market for themselves, a substantial boost to long-term cash flow.

For Samsung in the book market, however, it looks like these spoils are not available. Indeed, with this market evolution in mind, the book-based digital press opportunity cannot strictly be considered a pioneer market as defined in the market strategy types framework. However, it is so new that it remains uncharted, and it will be as challenging to navigate as a pioneer market.

PRICE ECONOMICS IS AS IMPORTANT AS PRICE ELASTICITY In any market occupied by a few large players, it always pays to spend that incremental energy on increasing price rather than on squeezing out more share; it's easy to see why in Figure 6.6.

The continual inflexions in the in-office market (discovered in Example 5.8) are a godsend to its market leaders—who, if they have any

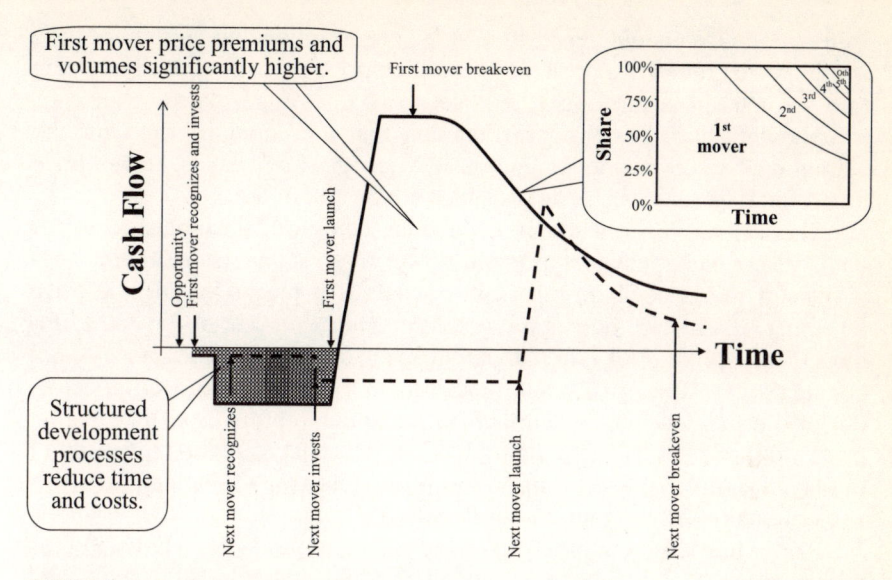

Define a Path That Exploits REAL OPPORTUNITIES 147

FIGURE 6.5 First-Mover Returns
Source: Business Intelligence Associates LLC.

When margins are high …

Greater profit potential in increased *share*.

Generally, set price to increase share when:
- Margins are high.
- Market is growing fast.
- Current share is low.
- Scale economies exist.
- Competitors are slow.

When share is high …

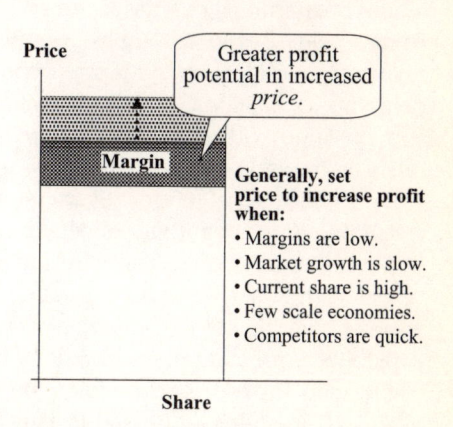

Greater profit potential in increased *price*.

Generally, set price to increase profit when:
- Margins are low.
- Market growth is slow.
- Current share is high.
- Few scale economies.
- Competitors are quick.

FIGURE 6.6 Price-Share Trade-Offs
Source: Business Intelligence Associates LLC.

value-oriented strategic perspective at all, are planning and hoping for their continuance. Take HP's position in in-office printers; with such dominating sale volumes from the outset, it is set to receive huge returns with each incremental price hike. However, entrants that subsequently come into the market have to cover operating costs and quickly show results, and so price low to grab as much share as possible. What can HP do?

The answer lies in a sort of reverse elasticity. Understanding customer demand/price elasticity is important, however, so is understanding the economics of the price/share trade-off. For HP, that means finding the price level that cedes share only at a rate that maximizes its cut of the entire (future) market profit pool. Often, that may mean actually reducing prices—not cutting them to a rate that would "teach them a lesson" to scare competitors out of the market, but just enough to maximize returns from that market profit pool. While market bullying has the potential to reduce the number of players, it invariably ends up in lost profitability for all. Better to keep an eye on maximized long-term cash flow.

And when a new market inflexion comes around, the whole process begins again. As fast movers, dominating players (that is HP, Canon, and others in the printer market) resecure their share positions again at attractive prices, then guide price declines to optimize the price/share trade-off. Of course, the really smart players are creating their own market inflexions.

OTHER TIPS Many value-maximizing generalizations come under the heading "take the money sooner, rather than later." Given the fact that capital has a time-proportional cost associated with it, it always pays to be in possession of cash as early and as long as possible, *all other things being equal*. As this relates to market strategy, it often comes down to adjusting investments to delay tax obligations, developing market approaches that exchange some sort of value with customers but result in earlier payment, or structuring business models that increase possession of cash. This philosophy coincides with the legal axiom, "Possession is nine-tenths of the law."

While a business that delivers on its expected cash flow is a nice thing, investors expect more. They are interested in value growth, and that only comes with *growth in expected cash flow*. Chapter 7 addresses the important issue of building in a cash flow growth engine. Lastly, focus in organizational capabilities, reputation, and/or skills has an uncanny history of being associated with superior performance, both in the market and in organizational results. This is also addressed in Part Three, in Chapter 8.

Decision Maps

Decision maps characterize the decision paths to be considered in an opportunity, plotting out the variants and decisions along each. Later in the process each viable decision path will be assessed for its value creation. Decision maps have a crucial role in explicitly recognizing decision paths and setting out the elements that make them up.

Before exploring how decision maps are used, it is worth touching on a couple of useful process-related tips. First, great care is needed to separate nonlinear thinking that creates new ideas and opportunities from the rigid structure demanded by decision maps. Specifically, when decision mapping starts, attention unfortunately diverts to the mechanics of the mapping process itself and adherence to the structure it demands—usually at the expense of creativity. This is especially true for tasks at the front end of the strategy formulation process. However, by the time outcomes need to be defined in the next task, all opportunities and their variants will have to fit into disciplined, well-structured decision maps.

With that said, much of strategy formulation is a chaotic and iterative process, comprised of finding a stake, putting it in the ground, understanding its implications, and then going back to adjust and improve. Unfortunately, chaotic and iterative processes tend to be lengthy and resource consuming. As a result, after the creative opportunity definition process is complete, it helps to draft and analyze decision maps as stand-alone building blocks, only mixing and matching opportunities and variants in differing configurations afterwards. A healthy amount of trial and retrial must be expected, even planned in.

Finally, it is also worth pointing out that some of the most dynamic and interesting thinking in the process is at the decision-mapping stage and the two tasks following it. Here, opportunities are developed well enough to be tangible, while the issues at hand are complex and high-stake. They are also the principle responsibility of the leaders of the business—and few others. This is apparent as we take a look at the development of a decision map for Samsung's U.S. book printing press opportunity, number 15 from Example 6.2, which happens to be at the building-block level. When the opportunity was captured in Figure 6.4, a number of variants were also captured in an ad hoc list, primarily dealing with execution alternatives (though they can just as well include product configuration or other issues). They included acquiring an existing market player or partnering with one, perhaps starting with a partnership and moving to an acquisition later, or building a sales organization from scratch. With this list and some disciplined thinking, we can map out the decision options and different ways they can unfold into decision paths. The decision map of Figure 6.7 shows a typical initial output.

Each decision path has its own termination point on the right. Note that all the variants discussed earlier for this opportunity are addressed by at least one decision path—additional paths get added as the sequencing of implementation and other issues are thought through. Let's take a look at some of the specifics in this draft decision map.

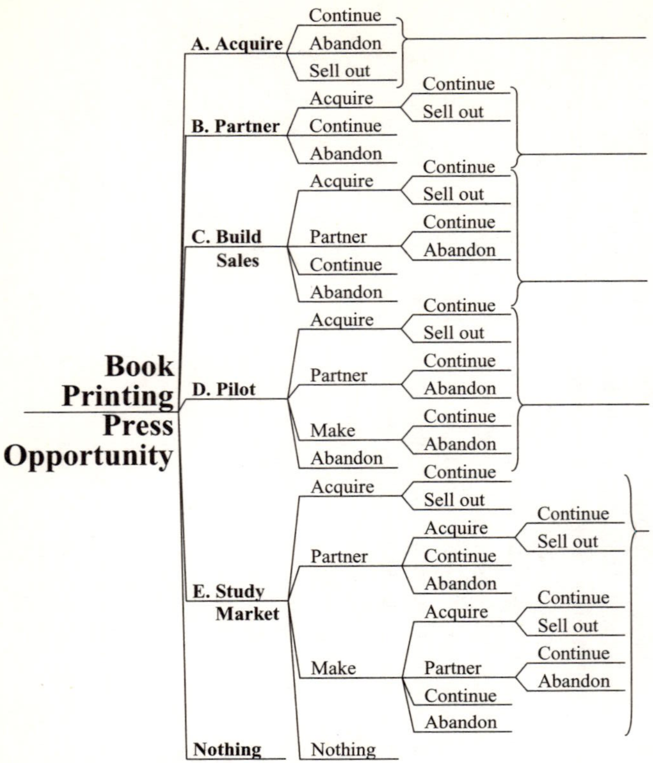

Path/Variant	Basic Option	Secondary/Subsequent Options
1. Acquire	• Samsung immediately acquires existing player to rapidly secure sales/channel capabilities and market presence.	• Samsung can divest if the situation proves unattractive. • A divestment recoups some capital and avoids losses.
2. Partner	• Samsung immediately partners with existing player to rapidly secure sales/channel capabilities and mkt presence. • Profit sharing likely required.	• Samsung can double-down and acquire market player. • Samsung can exit to avoid losses if situation proves unattractive.
3. Build Sales	• Samsung immediately builds sales/channel capabilities, so retaining all profitability.	• Samsung can 'double-down' in acquisition or partnership. • Samsung can exit to avoid losses if situation proves unattractive.
4. Pilot	• Before investing in R&D and sales, Samsung runs a pilot and conducts market research.	• If sales org. is effective, Samsung can build it up. • If sales org. is ineffective, can acquire, partner, or avoid investment and losses.
5. Study Market	• Before investing in R&D and sales, Samsung conducts research on the market.	• If the market is attractive, can acquire, partner, or build, and double-down later. • If market proves unattractive, Samsung can avoid investment.
Nothing	• Samsung decides the opportunity doesn't warrant investment.	

FIGURE 6.7 Draft Decision Map—Samsung's Options in the U.S. Book Printing Press Opportunity

Source: Business Intelligence Associates LLC.

Samsung's option to acquire an existing market player is represented by the first branch, "Acquire"; this is actually an opportunity *variant*. It is likely a valuable variant as it quickly gives Samsung an established sales and channel capability with full control and boosts prospects for share gains. Should things not work out, however, reselling the acquired business would limit losses. Further, one might think that after an acquisition, if things were not working out, Samsung could decide to divest and then try its luck on its own or perhaps partner with another player. On reflection, divestment without exiting the market doesn't seem a viable option as management would face substantial political issues with shareholders, as well as practical problems with the market and channel partners, and a noncompete agreement is likely to be a condition of the sale. Consequently, this branch/variant has only three continuing decision paths: maintain the business, abandon it, or exit by divesting the acquisition.

The second variant, "Partner," captures Samsung's option to create a partnership with an existing player, thereby obtaining the sales/channel capability it needs, albeit with less control than an acquisition. In this case, however, Samsung would have the option to double-down later and acquire the player concerned, perhaps even some other player. Again, dropping the partner and subsequently building a sales organization from scratch is probably not a viable option here for some of the same reasons that applied in the first branch.

And so the variants go on. The next one reflects Samsung's option to build its own sales/channel organization, and includes further options to expand through acquisition or partnership. The fourth variant captures the idea that Samsung doesn't have to fully commit now, postponing the decision and conducting a pilot to learn what is needed operationally and how the market responds. Finally, the last of the variants also delays the decision, but in the meantime Samsung only conducts a market study. As a result, it receives updates on the market, but learns little on operational needs (which means they may choose an inappropriate configuration at launch and find that they need to change later). Again, Samsung always has the option to do nothing—the ultimate loss limiter.

Now we turn to populating decision maps with quantitative estimates of what is likely to happen along each decision path, bringing in market forecasts and estimating operating performance. These realities invariably alter the draft decision map.

Task 3: Characterize Outcomes

As we see later, while each decision path has a unique set of decisions and assets in it, it usually also has elements shared with other decision paths. In most cases, at least one of the assets is a business proposition, likely a new business being considered for inclusion in a market strategy. Other assets can be included, however, such as intellectual property, the salvage value of an ongoing business, real estate, and the like, though these have values that are usually already known or readily discernable.

Figuring out the warranted value of business propositions is a key deliverable of the valuation estimates of the next task. In this task, the information needed to conduct those valuations (outcomes information) is compiled and processed in the decision map.

What Do We Need to Know?

The key role real options have in evaluating the economics of our strategic opportunities was outlined at the start of this chapter. We also saw that to use them we need to know the value of the various assets under consideration—and to the extent those assets are business propositions with uncertainty, we need to know both value and the volatility of that value.

Discounted cash flow valuations give us the intrinsic value of business propositions. When DCF models are built dynamically in spreadsheets, they can also be used by Monte Carlo simulation tools to figure out volatility, as set out in Chapter 5. Again, to do that those models need to be robust enough to give valid results even when inputs, such as price, share, and the like, are changed dramatically and assume extreme values—thanks to the way Monte Carlo simulation tools work (some of their trials are at the extremes of the probability continuum).

WHAT IS NEEDED TO GET EXPECTED VALUE As pointed out in the Introduction, this book is intended for business leaders, and as such the technical aspects of constructing DCF valuation models and gathering the information they need as inputs is not addressed (except for the market forces and factors approach for market profit pool valuations, set out in Chapter 5). With that said, the basic outcomes information needed by DCF valuations to get cash flow projections are volume sold (perhaps determined using market share), price, profit margin (often price and profit margin are combined into unit profits), and capital investment needs.

The approach to estimating these for each business proposition is similar to that used to forecast overall market cash flow in Chapter 5. In that approach, forecasts are developed for the factors that shape demand, competitive intensity, offering efficacy, and supplies, based on their underlying drivers and expected future events. Again, historical precedents are also useful to trace likely future performance when circumstances are similar. An example of this might be to observe the typical share gains of previous new product introductions, and to use those profiles to forecast upcoming launches. As they say, history has a tendency to repeat itself.

Unfortunately, forecasting can quickly get overly detailed. For the lengthy 15- to 20-year forecast horizon we are interested in, it is sufficient to work at a relatively high level. This is in contrast to near-term forecasting for market tactics, which tends to demand much specificity and often requires information at a detailed market subsegment level, rather than using averages. In contrast, for strategy formulation, sensible judgment by tenured executives is all that is needed; they are, after all, among the few experts available on their respective markets. As in all aspects of strategy formulation, the process needs to be iterative; as more is discovered and learned about business models and other factors, forecasts need to be adjusted.

WHAT IS NEEDED TO GET VALUE VOLATILITY Creating business proposition outcomes forecasts for use in DCF valuation models is not enough, however. Real options techniques need to incorporate uncertainty, specifically in terms of value volatility. To determine this, we turn to the same tool used in Chapter 5 to determine the uncertainty in market profit pool values—the Monte Carlo simulation. This tool is used in the same way here. As the inputs to the DCF valuation (share, price, costs, and all the others) are keyed into the spreadsheet, the tool asks for the uncertainty of each input amount, cell by cell (in fact, repeated uncertainty information can be readily copied across similar cells). With all of these captured, it runs a series of trials and provides a profile of the business proposition's expected value, along with a probability curve and its standard deviation, from which we get the 95 percent uncertainty range.

A business proposition's value volatility, as required by real options techniques, requires one more step. Volatility is defined as the standard deviation of the rate of return; so before the Monte Carlo simulation is run, an additional formula has to be added to give the rate of return. As it conducts its trials, the Monte Carlo tool can then also track rate of return and report its standard deviation—the business proposition's value volatility.

Although there are a couple of steps involved and several statistical-sounding words, the process is surprisingly simple; today, the process is greatly automated, making it quick, and well worth a little staff time. Moreover, in most cases there is much similarity between the business propositions under consideration (which are mostly variations on themes), significantly limiting the analyst time needed, as we see next in the process to populate decision maps.

Populating the Decision Map

So far we have outlined the fundamentals of decision maps and reviewed what information is needed to conduct the economic evaluations of the next task. The two now come together, and the process by which that is done is best described by illustration; again, we return to the example of Samsung's opportunity in the U.S. book printing press market.

While the decision map of Figure 6.7 gives us a first cut of likely decision paths, it is short on the specifics needed to run the economics. What performance and results can we expect? What timing is realistic in each decision path? How much capital needs to be invested? For that matter, will any of these realities alter the decision map's structure? These and other factors need to be specified if decision paths are to be sufficiently described for the economic evaluations of the next task.

Of course, this sort of information is situation-specific and needs to be thought through. Example 6.3 gives a simplified example of the type of operating performance information needed for each variant (or decision map branch). In it, only two variables are forecast for each business proposition: market share, specified in terms of the peak share achieved, and unit profitability, specified in terms of a proportion of the market's average. As the decision map is populated, new factors and congruencies are uncovered, likely leading to some level of restructuring of the original draft.

Furthermore, capital investment needs also have to be plotted throughout the decision map. Example 6.4 sets out an example of this, including asset values (such as acquired businesses and divestment values), build-out expenses (such as R&D and organizational builds), timing issues, and deal conditions.

Example 6.3 Example Outcomes by Branch/Variant

Samsung's U.S. Book Press Opportunity (January 2008)

A. *Acquire*. An acquisition will take one year to close. A further six months is needed to prepare, resulting in a launch in mid-2009.

Market share is expected to peak at 15 percent in four years; Samsung is late entering the market, after HP and Xerox. After that, share declines as others enter the market. Uncertainty in the share estimate is lognormally distributed, autocorrelated 90 percent, with the lower 95 percent certainty boundary at 70 percent of expected share.

Margin is expected to be at 90 percent of the market is average; the acquiree's brand gives a good price, but below HP and Xerox. Uncertainty is normally distributed, starting with a 95 percent certainty boundary at 20 percent above and 20 percent below the expected margin, and gets wider 1 percent each year. It is also autocorrelated 90 percent.

Define a Path That Exploits REAL OPPORTUNITIES 155

> B. *Partner*. A partnership also takes one year to establish and six months to launch; target date mid-2009.
>
> Share is expected to peak at only 8 percent in four years, as Samsung doesn't have full control over the partner's sales capability. Margins and uncertainty profiles are similar to "Acquire" above. Profits will need to be shared 50-50 with the partner.
>
> The option to double-down and acquire the partner will take one year to decide and another to close, implying 2012 is the earliest launch date. This would lift peak share to 13 percent only, as the market will have tightened since 2009.
>
> C. *Build*. Again, the earliest launch is mid-2009; 18 months are needed to establish sales.
>
> Share is expected to peak at 2 percent in four years, as Samsung will not have a competitive sales capability. Further, as Samsung is an unknown, price will be low; margin is likely 70 percent of the market's average, with a similar uncertainty profile as in the preceding routes. Double-down options have outcomes similar to the double-down option in "Partner."
>
> D. *Pilot*. Should the pilot green-light any of the three expansions, the result in market performance is very similar to the double-down options previously named, in timing, expected share, and margin. The pilot just avoids near-term commitment, saves $1 million of a later build-out, though the delay reduces attainable peak share. However, it is informative, such that a double-down option is unnecessary.
>
> E. *Study*. The market study postpones major investments and options one year.

Example 6.4 Example Capital Investments Needs

Samsung's U.S. Book Press Opportunity

> *R&D/Offering Development*. To meet planned timelines, an incremental $10 million in R&D spending is needed immediately for acquire, partner, and build strategy variants. Note, this is a present-value amount; it is $10 million no matter when it is spent. (A side note for students of financial theory: This investment has no market-related risk, and so is discounted using the risk-free cost of capital rate.)
>
> *Acquisitions*. Seven decision paths call for an acquisition of an established player, each one having its own timing for the transaction.

> Further, the acquisition price changes over time, resulting in price differences between paths, and the acquired business can be divested later, capping downside exposure. The acquisition price in 2009 is $280 million and has two parts:
> 1. The selling price of $200 million, the present value of cash flow from the traditional press business.
> 2. An $80 million premium.
>
> For Samsung, the first part is a wash; it is a fair value for the business's cash flow, and there would be no net loss in a resale. However, investment bankers believe the premium's value will fall to $50 million over 15 years (declining $2 million per year); and in a resale, only 95 percent of the sell year's value would be obtained.
> <u>Partnerships</u>. No capital investments will be required for partnerships.
> <u>Build sales</u>. Two different sales force building programs are in the decision map:
> 1. A full build-out; requiring an immediate $20 million, to hire, train, and establish.
> 2. A pilot, requiring an immediate $3m for a localized team. If a full national build-out follows, that will require a further $19m.
>
> <u>Study</u>. The market study costs $1 million.

Samsung's first option, to acquire a player with an existing presence in traditional printing presses, has the attractiveness of being likely to capture the most market share—particularly if launched immediately—as well as delivering relatively high margins. And, since Samsung will own the business, it gets to keep the entire cash flow stream, directly contributing to its own value. However, it is also taking on the management of another business, a traditional printing press manufacturer, of which it only actually wants to use part. This is a risk that needs to be considered carefully, given the tendency for acquisitions to take on strategies of their own. Risk is mitigated by Samsung's ability to resell the business at some point in the future; however, as noted in Example 6.4, the *floor* (that is, the sellout sales price of the premium) falls away over time, as the price declines at $2 million annually and has a 95 percent recovery rate.

All of these factors have to be used to recast the earlier decision map of Figure 6.7, this time with timing, sequencing, and the key economic parameters we are interested in. From before, these parameters include capital investment amounts and operational performance metrics, such as peak share forecasts and per unit profit margins.

In the process of thinking through the variants and how the situations would unfold in Examples 6.3 and 6.4, two pieces of information surfaced that significantly restructure the decision map. First, to conduct the study, only a small immediate investment is needed of $1 million; however, all other variants require an immediate $10 million investment to develop an offering. Second, to obtain the use of an external sales and channel operation, such as through an acquisition or partnership, Samsung must immediately start a search and negotiation process. However, to *build* a sales and channel operation, full scale or pilot, an additional capital investment is needed, of $20 million and $3 million respectively.

These two pieces of information have the effect of regrouping the decision map's branches. The "Study" variant is alone in requiring only $1 million up front. The "Pilot" is also alone, though it requires both $10 million in R&D and $3 million up front to build a small sales group. The full "Build" also requires $10 million for R&D and a further $20 million for the build itself. Finally, the "Acquire" and "Partner" variants also call for the $10 million R&D spending immediately, only splitting into separate paths in 2009, when they each need different commitments. After these, a range of other options become available at various times, including the ability throughout to simply abandon the investment, business, or asset at any time. Also, after an acquisition is made, it can be divested to recoup much of that capital investment; in such circumstances an explicit profile of the value of the salvage is needed for each year going forward. Figure 6.8 illustrates how the top branches of the original decision map would be recast.

Capital investments and performance numbers relating to each decision path are captured in the table on the right of the chart in Figure 6.8, ready for consideration in the economic evaluation of the next task. The acquisition and partnership variants have much in common, certainly in initial periods. The acquisition offers higher control and consequently a higher peak share; it also comes with a substantive capital commitment. The partnership option has the distinct disadvantage of sharing the venture's cash flow stream. Clearly, this has a direct impact on the value of the business proposition, and a key variable will be in negotiating what the cash flow stream split actually is. A key benefit of evaluating strategic options in this process is that we can easily back into answers, such as finding a profit share split ratio that would make the partner proposition worthwhile. Beyond that, the attractiveness of the partnership option is obviously the ability to avoid investing a great deal of capital, while still being able to leverage the capabilities of an established market player.

Turning to the other opportunity variants (decision map branches), the "Build" option needs $10 million for R&D and $20 million for the build itself. Since the market's structure will already have been established, and new entrants are expected, this variant simply doesn't have time to build

[Figure 6.8 diagram content:]

In this branch the initiative starts immediately, with $10m R&D commitment.

Immediate action needed; search for acquisition[1] or partner.[2]

Business proposition expected operating performance:
• Expected peak shares: 15% with acquisition from 2009.
  13% with acquisition from mid-2011.
  8% with partnership from 2009.
• Expected relative margins: 90% in all cases shown.

2008　2009　2010　2011　2012　2013

Acquire　Launch Business
　Acquisition　Sell Out
　　　　　Acquire Acquisition Launch Business
　　　　　　　　　　　　　Sell Out
Partner　Launch Business
1. External　Partnership
   Sales　R&D　Abandon

Book Printing Press Opportunity

	Capital Expense / Initial Investments (To be discounted at risk-free)			Business Performance Variables	
	R&D	Org. Build	Acquisition[1]	Peak Share	Relative Margins
1	-	-	$80m	15%	90%
2	-	-	-	-	-
3	-	-	$75m	13%	90%
4	-	-	-	-	-
5	$10m	-	-	8%	90%
6	-	-	-	-	-

Option to sell acquired business at any time after acquired (realistically, after new business is launched); substantially limits investment capital in jeopardy.

Option to abandon initiative at any time after start; limits losses to just those incurred before abandonment.

Each decision path has its own investment needs:
• $80 million to close acquisition[1] in 2009.
• $75 million to close acquisition[1] in 2011.
• No capital needed for partnership.[2]

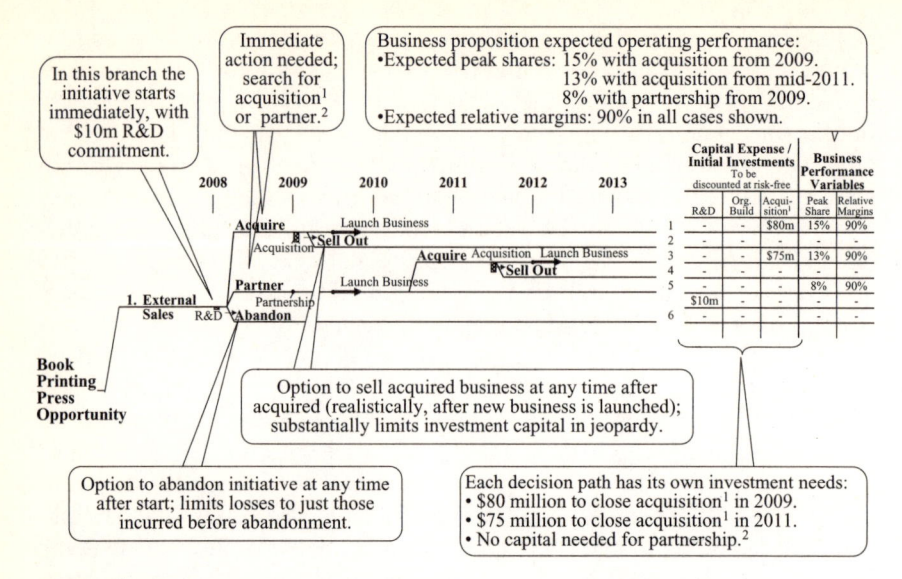

FIGURE 6.8 Populating the Decision Map—"Acquire" Decision Paths

Source: Business Intelligence Associates LLC.

[1] Acquisition price in 2009 is $280 million, based on an $80 million premium and $200 million for expected future cash flows from the traditional printing press business (an independent value source that can be excluded from consideration). Note that the premium's value declines $2 million annually, and its salvage value is 95 percent of that year's forecasted acquisition price.

[2] In partnerships, Samsung is assumed to share profits 50-50 with the partner.

up much market share. Traditional printing press vendors will divert their established share elsewhere as they find digital solutions; a new sales force is unlikely to have much impact given historical precedent in similar markets. The option to double-down may be useful; an acquisition or a partnership with an established vendor is possible.

Also, on the face of it, it isn't unreasonable to think the pilot would offer Samsung the ability to get better insights into the opportunity's direction. Unfortunately, the pilot will not launch earlier than the other options, as R&D is on the critical path, and the smaller-scale sales force will also need time to get built; only after both of these happen can the pilot get under way, implying that results will not be concluded until mid-2010. The pilot doesn't just delay launch a little; it will not be possible to make a full launch for four years. By then, market potential will have diminished, even for the double-down options. Finally, the "Study" option just punts, putting the entire decision path back a year, and no operational experience is gained at all.

The restructured full decision map, together with all of the outcomes information, is set out in Figure 6.9. Although uncertainty information is not

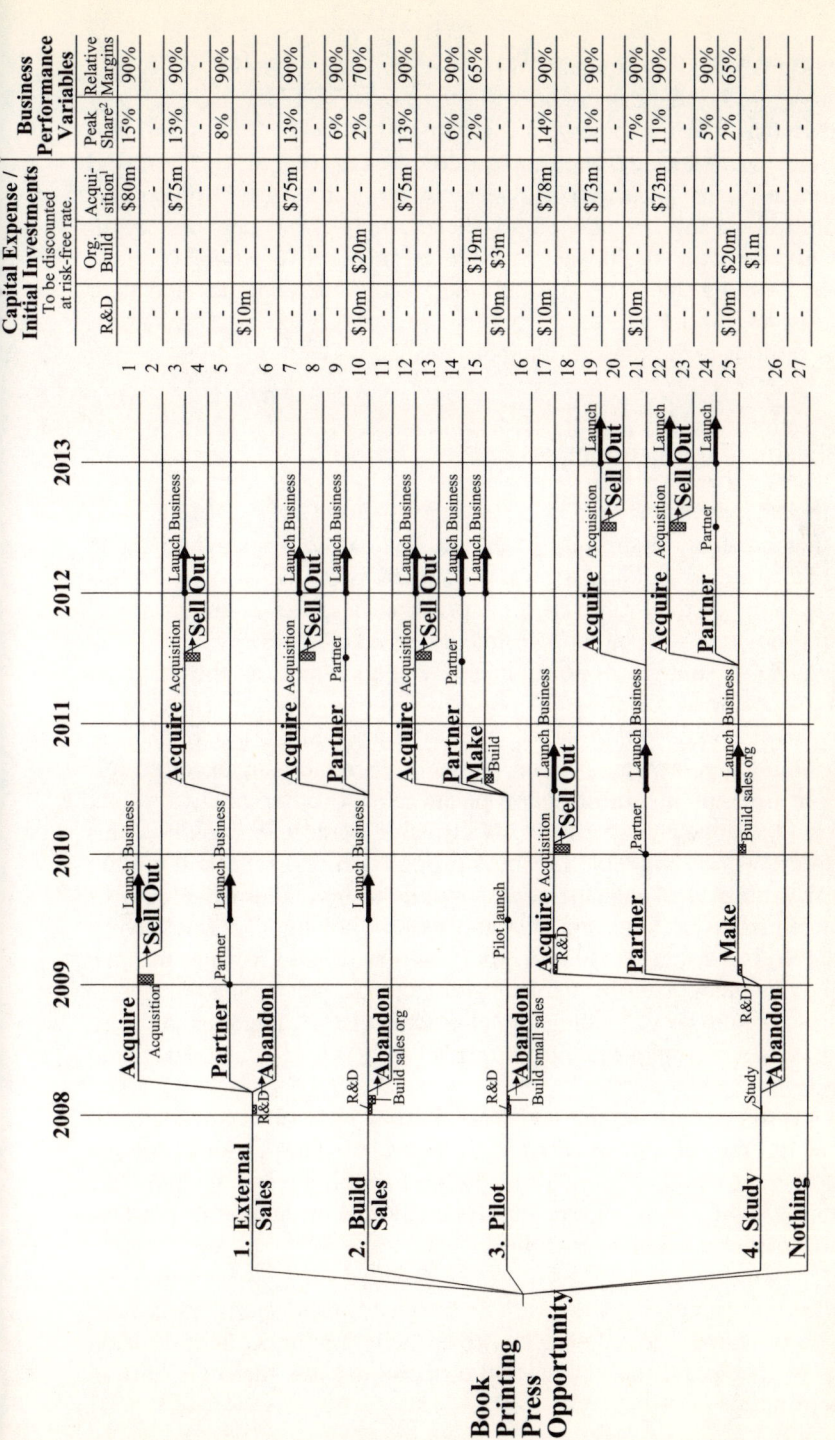

		Capital Expense / Initial Investments (To be discounted at risk-free rate)			Business Performance Variables	
		R&D	Org. Build	Acquisition[1]	Peak Share[2]	Relative Margins
1		-	-	-	-	-
2		-	-	$80m	15%	90%
3		-	-	$75m	13%	90%
4		-	-	-	-	-
5		$10m	-	-	8%	90%
6		-	-	-	-	-
7		-	-	$75m	13%	90%
8		-	-	-	-	-
9		-	-	-	6%	90%
10		$10m	$20m	-	2%	70%
11		-	-	-	-	-
12		-	-	$75m	13%	90%
13		-	-	-	-	-
14		-	-	-	6%	90%
15		$10m	$19m	-	2%	65%
16		$10m	$3m	-	-	-
17		$10m	-	$78m	14%	90%
18		-	-	-	-	-
19		-	-	$73m	11%	90%
20		-	-	-	-	-
21		$10m	-	-	7%	90%
22		-	-	$73m	11%	90%
23		-	-	-	-	-
24		-	-	-	5%	90%
25		$10m	$20m	-	2%	65%
26		-	$1m	-	-	-
27		-	-	-	-	-

FIGURE 6.9 Summary Decision Map—Samsung's US Book Printing Press Opportunity

Source: Business Intelligence Associates LLC.

[1] Acquisition price in 2009 is $280 million, based on an $80 million premium and $200 million for expected future cash flows from the traditional printing press business (an independent value source that can be excluded from consideration). Note that the premium's value declines $2 million annually, and its salvage value is 95 percent of that year's forecasted acquisition price.

[2] In partnerships, Samsung is assumed to share profits 50-50 with the partner.

included, it gives a good summary of the decisions on the table and is very useful for organizational discussion and buy-in.

At this point, the outcomes information and associated decision maps that we have compiled are enough to draw conclusions on the best and most valuable course of action. However, without a structured economic evaluation, few people are able to run these numbers mentally and get to the right answers; those who are capable of such a feat would certainly stumble in working their way through the various uncertainties and their implications. We undertake that structured process in the next two tasks, using real options techniques to integrate results.

Task 4: Evaluate the Economics

So far in this chapter we have stepped through a market strategy formulation process that created opportunity ideas and increasingly quantified them, with a view to understanding the value-creation potential of each. In this task, we determine that value-creation potential for use as an economic input in the next task—compiling an integrated market strategy.

The value of strategy opportunities is not the same as the value of business propositions. Business proposition value is based exclusively on cash flow streams expected from a specific venture, while opportunities are potential high-level strategic actions, of the type set out in Example 6.2, and include investments, business propositions, and other assets, brought together in decision paths with the added value of decision *options*. This is very different from a simple business proposition and reflects the often substantial value-add of management's options to take alternative courses of action, which is at the core of real-options thinking. Options have a substantial and measurable value in their own right, and a value that the capital markets recognize (this explains, for example, why some businesses have market values far exceeding straightforward DCF valuations and represent the expectation of a significant upside, such as for Google, eBay, and others).

So opportunities are not the static choices they were once considered to be. It turns out they comprise decision paths, each having various business propositions and/or other assets (which could simply be loss limiters, like discontinuing a business). As a result, the economic evaluation in this task has two distinct and sequenced components:

1. Finalize the valuations of the various business propositions and assets.
2. Put these values, together with investment amounts, into decision maps to determine the values of the decision paths that make up an opportunity.

We review each of these in turn in this section, illustrating both with the continuing example of Samsung's U.S. book printing press opportunity.

Underlying Business Propositions and Their Value Profiles

In the previous task, specific market and operational outcomes were forecast for each business proposition. From there, with one analyst and a relatively robust spreadsheet-based DCF model (there are now many software packages that do valuations), these outcomes can be quickly transformed into expected values. When further armed with Monte Carlo simulation software, your analyst can also accompany valuation estimates with their volatility counterparts.

The decision paths of Samsung's U.S. book printing presses opportunity are recast again in Figure 6.10, this time with summary information for each decision path: capital investments, valuations, and volatilities.

The phrase "Launch Business" reflects the start of business propositions as going concerns, possessing intrinsic value on account of the future cash flow they represent. Note that capital investments in R&D, acquisitions, and other investing that precede the going concern are not part of the business proposition's valuation; each is a point around which management might change course (abandon, scale up, scale down, etc.) and so must be kept apart and used separately in the real options valuation of decision paths. As a result, they also do not have market-based risk, and need to be discounted at the risk-free rate.

Valuing Decision Paths

Unfortunately, the value of an opportunity cannot be determined by simply adding up asset values along its decision paths. Why? Because, among other things, decision paths are mutually exclusive. You can't, for example, acquire a business while simultaneously partnering and competing with it. Real options techniques have been developed to deal with this very conundrum—combining the values of mutually exclusive courses of action. In this discussion we show how these techniques put a value on each decision path; these are the last economic inputs to the strategy formulation process, and they lay the basis for strategy choices to be made in the next task.

HOW REAL OPTIONS TECHNIQUES DETERMINE DECISION PATH VALUES So why do real options techniques succeed where other approaches fail? In short, real options techniques value decision maps and their branches without deciding *now* which decision paths to take, but instead by using probabilities (uncertainty) to combine values. Take the case where Samsung makes an

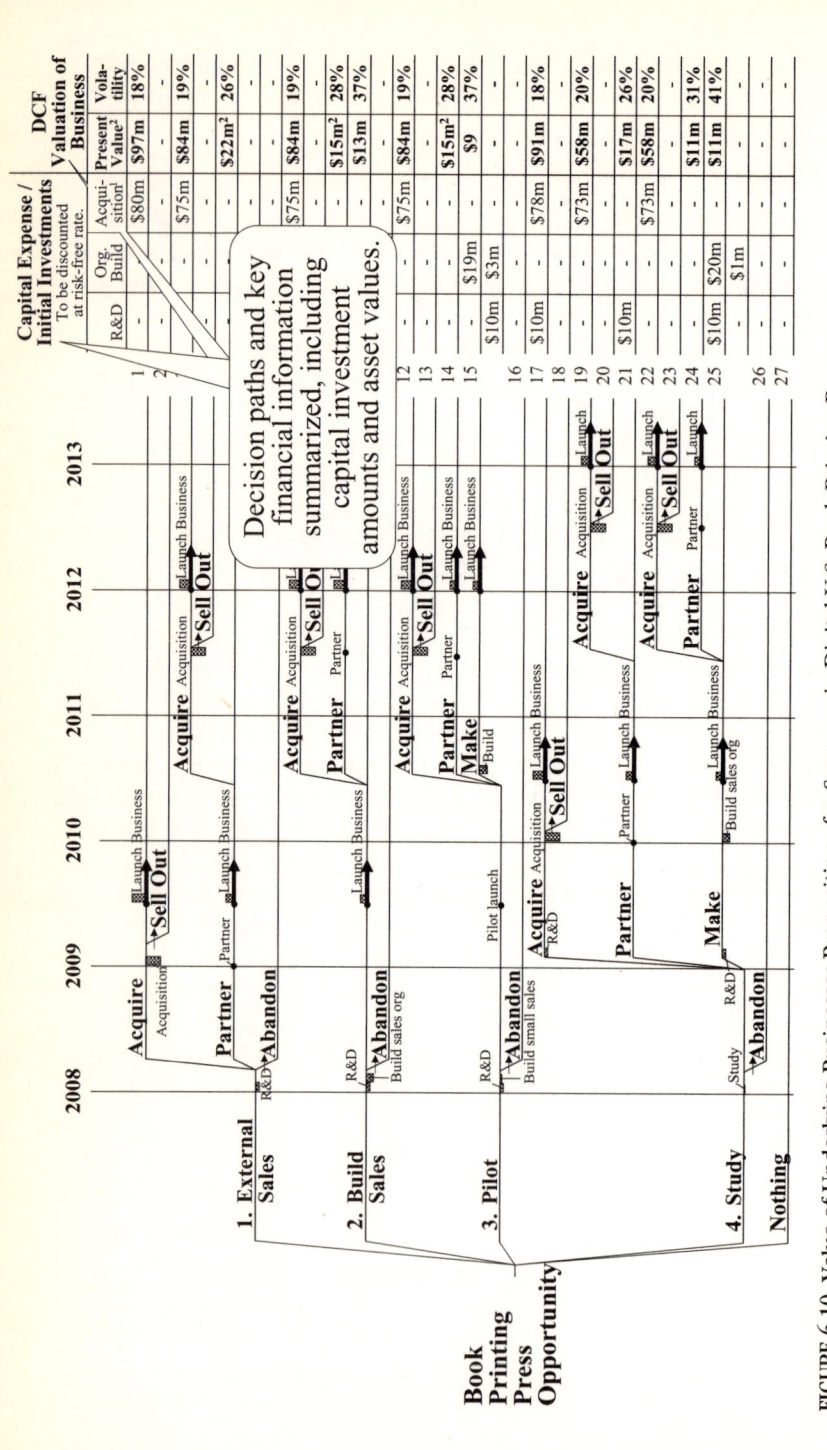

FIGURE 6.10 Value of Underlying Businesses Propositions for Samsung in Digital U.S. Book Printing Presses

Source: Business Intelligence Associates LLC.

[1] Acquisition price in 2009 is $280 million, based on an $80 million premium and $200 million for expected future cash flows from the traditional printing press business (an independent value source that can be excluded from consideration). Note that the premium's value declines $2 million annually, and its salvage value is 95 percent of that year's forecasted acquisition price.

[2] In partnerships, Samsung is assumed to share profits 50-50 with the partner.

acquisition for its U.S. book printing press opportunity. There is a chance that the market will turn out poorly and future cash flow never goes positive; after all, market assessments left open the door, albeit with a small probability, that margins could be much smaller than expected—such as where the supplies profit model is destroyed. Other influential factors also had low-side estimates, such as digital adoption, market share, and others; should they all coincide, the situation would indeed be poor and any business proposition's value would be negative. In the real options approach, *all of these uncertainties have been processed in the valuation of the business proposition and are captured in the value's volatility measure.*

Now, should the situation go sour before the acquisition is closed (paid for), management would rightly abandon the plan then and save themselves a lot of value. Another evolutionary path is where the market is considered sour after the acquisition. In this situation, management would exit the venture and divest the acquired business for its salvage value, thereby limiting losses. Although mutually exclusive, these and all other possible scenarios are plotted out and evaluated for the most valuable course of action in each eventuality.

So, how do real options tools accomplish such a complex challenge? There are several possible approaches, though the most mature and readily usable one is the *binomial lattice*. This tool plots out the values of all assets, according to their probabilities, into the future on a set of lattices. In the special case of assets with uncertainties, such as business propositions, the lattice starts with its present value and then lays out the expanding uncertainty of values using the volatility metric. Next, the tool looks through all the assets and their probable values over time, identifies the highest-value, one at each point, and puts that value in a new "solution" lattice. For example, when the salvage value exceeds the going concern value (which may happen to some level of probability, at some point) the tool assumes management would then abandon the business and recoup the value remaining in the salvage. The tool then reworks the solution lattice back to the present, choosing only these higher-value decision results to determine the new value for the opportunity. Appendix C provides an excellent executive review of the binomial lattice tool, and uses a simplified version of the Samsung book market opportunity as the example in the explanation.

UNDERSTANDING AND USING REAL OPTIONS VALUATIONS The most important insight real options techniques give us in market strategy formulation is that management's ability to make choices increases the value of the underlying business proposition. This is especially useful in two ways. First, business leaders get a more accurate view of value, such as a business with an abandonment option. Second, in situations where there are several strategic alternatives with assets of similar magnitude values, incorporating the value of the option helps separate the choices. (This works both ways, however; where there *is* an order-of-magnitude difference between two business propositions, and similar uncertainties, the relative impact of the option's value is greatly reduced.)

Also, it is interesting to note that uncertainty actually works to increase values! Since management can be relied on to cut short loss-making businesses (particularly if they use highly granular, cash-based techniques), then the value of a highly uncertain business increases, since the downside is cut off and only an upside remains. Of course, these uncertainty profiles need to be well plotted out. Further, real options techniques also help confirm other sometimes intuitive rules of thumb, such as the real value of having choice, the usefulness of leaving capital commitments to the last moment, and others.

Let's see how these valuation issues play out in the case of Samsung's acquisition in the U.S. book printing press opportunity. Here, Samsung would start the initiative by committing $10 million to develop an offering in R&D, and would take one year to find a target company and bring it to the deal closing table. In that time it would have the option to abandon, which it might use if the market suddenly appeared unattractive. This is captured in the partial decision map of Figure 6.11 in the "Abandon" path 6, and is a choice that continues forever. Once the deal closes and the funds are transferred (just focus on the $80 million premium; the balance of the $280 million price is a wash, reflecting the value of expected cash flow from the traditional press business), an additional option becomes available: to divest the acquisition. This is captured in Figure 6.11 as "Acquire," path 1, and the divestment is "Sell Out," path 2; both can continue forever (although once sold, the acquisition's value obviously can't be reinvoked).

Now, in a straight DCF valuation, the value of the acquisition would simply be the present value of the business proposition, net of the R&D investment and the acquisition price, or $10.9 million. However, when the options to abandon and divest are included, many downside scenarios are excluded from possibility, while upside scenarios remain (there is a chance the new business will strike it rich!). Recalculating the value, using the same present values for the business proposition and acquisition payment, the real options approach gives a value of $12.6 million—nearly $1.7 million more. This is a substantive change in valuation, some 15 percent of the DCF value.

Let's look again at the "External Sales" branch, this time isolating Samsung's option to proceed in a partnership with an existing player. In this case, Samsung would again start the initiative by committing $10 million for R&D, and would also take one year to find a target company and close the deal. In that time it would still have the option to abandon; this is

Define a Path That Exploits REAL OPPORTUNITIES 165

A DCF valuation would simply subtract R&D ($10.0m) and acquisition ($76.1m in today's value) costs from the business proposition's value ($97.0m) to give **$10.9m**.

Real options valuation includes value to abandon the initiative in any circumstance where value is less than zero, or to sell the acquired business for its salvage value:

Acquisition and Salvage Values [1] of Targeted Acquisition
Nominal values (not present values) in millions:

	2009	2010	2011	2012	2013
Acquisition	$80.0	$78.0	$76.0	$74.0	$72.0
Salvage/resale	$76.0	$74.1	$72.2	$70.3	$68.4

Value with options: **$12.6m**

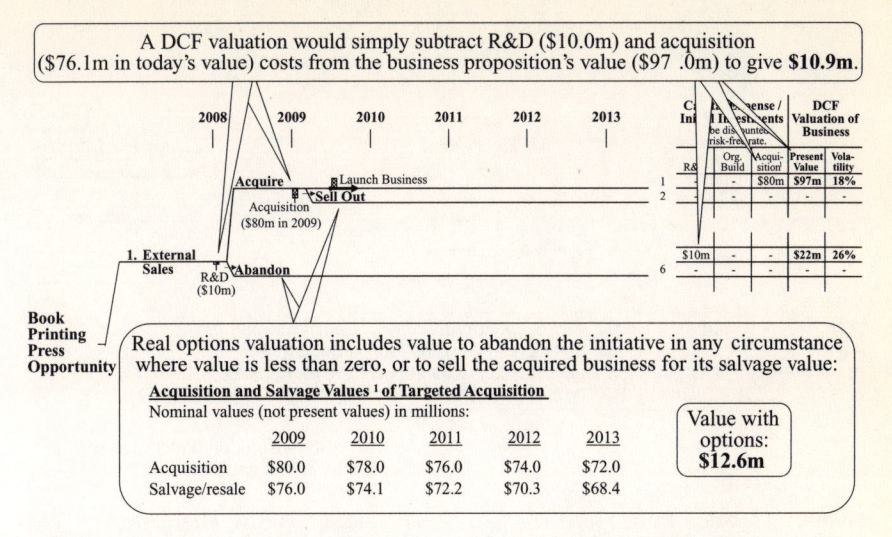

FIGURE 6.11 Value with Options Included—Abandonment and Salvage

Source: Business Intelligence Associates LLC.

[1] Acquisition price in 2009 is $280 million, based on an $80 million premium and $200 million for expected future cash flows from the traditional printing press business (an independent value source that can be excluded from consideration). Note that the premium's value declines $2 million annually, and its salvage value is 95 percent of that year's forecasted acquisition price.

captured in Figure 6.12. The "Abandon" path 6 remains, though in this case the partnership does not have an investment requirement—just a profit-sharing business proposition, represented by path 5. However, Samsung may choose to double-down and acquire its new partner (which comes with its own divestment and abandonment options), and that is captured in Figure 6.12 by another "Acquire" and "Sell Out" fork, this time in paths 3, 4, and 6.

In the same way a DCF valuation cannot incorporate the value of abandonment, it also cannot account for mutually exclusive management actions (such as continuing in a partnership, and possibly acquiring that same partner). With that said, we can dissect the paths to see where value originates from. The present value of the underlying partner business proposition is $22 million. A DCF valuation would simply subtract the R&D investment ($10 million) to get a value of $12 million. Curiously, the real-options value of only paths 5 and 6 give $12 million also (in fact it is just a little greater). In this case, the value of abandonment is almost zero; the upside volatility (uncertainty) of the partnership business proposition value is not enough to make much difference. However, including the option to double-down

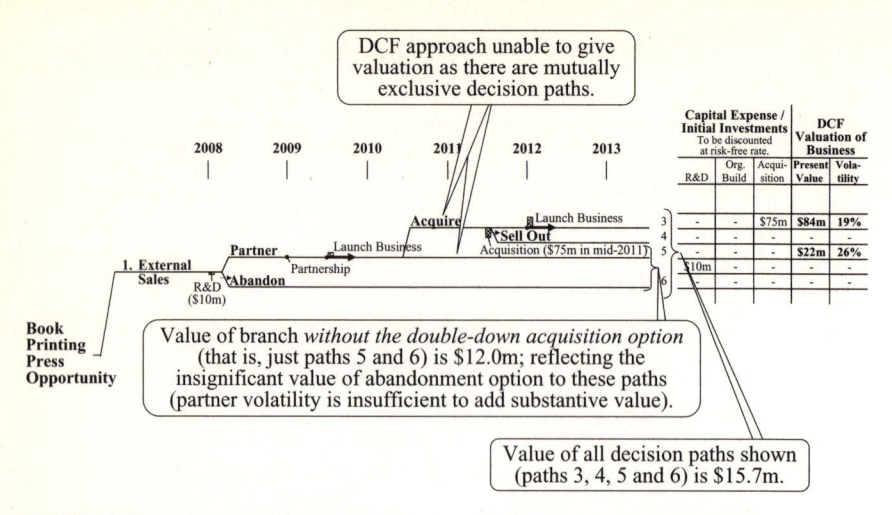

FIGURE 6.12 Value with Options Included—Multiple Substantive Alternatives
Source: Business Intelligence Associates LLC.

increases the upside dramatically (that is, including paths 3 and 4), resulting in an overall value of all these decision paths of $15.7 million. This is a substantial increase and simply could not be evaluated using DCF techniques.

With these insights into the sources of value within the "External Sales" branch, when the entire branch is valued—including all the options to acquire, partner, partner then acquire, and all the others—the result shows a value a little over $15.7 million. The paths included are depicted in Figure 6.13. It is not surprising to find the value is a little over the "Partner then Acquire" option reviewed in Figure 6.12. That turns out to be the dominating value contributor; the other options add minimal value for outlying, lower potential scenarios.

All other branches in decision maps have been evaluated in the same way—initially in their subcomponents (as we did for Figures 6.11 and 6.12), then consolidating them (as in Figure 6.13), and finally pulling them all together. In terms of the Samsung U.S. book printing press opportunity, the other branches did not have as high values as the "External Sales" branch offers. The highest alternative was for a path that started in the "Make" scenario, and also called for a double-down acquisition in 2010; it had a value of $14.9 million. As a whole, the opportunity offers a value of $15.8 million, when all options are incorporated.

In this task we have seen that flexibility has a value, and that value can be quantified to a specific dollar amount. With that, we went on to value actions that include flexibility, and use those results to come to a valuation for entire market strategy opportunities.

Define a Path That Exploits REAL OPPORTUNITIES 167

							Capital Expense / Initial Investments To be discounted at risk-free rate.			DCF Valuation of Business	
	2008	2009	2010	2011	2012	2013					
							R&D	Org. Build	Acquisition	Present Value	Volatility
		Acquire	Launch Business						$80m	$97m	18%
			Sell Out								
			Acquisition ($80m in 2009)	Acquire	Launch Business				$75m		
		Partner	Launch Business	Sell Out						$84m	19%
1. External Sales			Partnership		Acquisition ($75m in mid-2011)						
		R&D Abandon ($10m today)					$10m			$22m	26%

Book Printing Press Opportunity

Value of entire "1. External Sales" branch (decision paths 1 through 6) is a little above[1] $15.7m, reflecting dominance of partner plan with double-down option (decision paths 3 and 4).

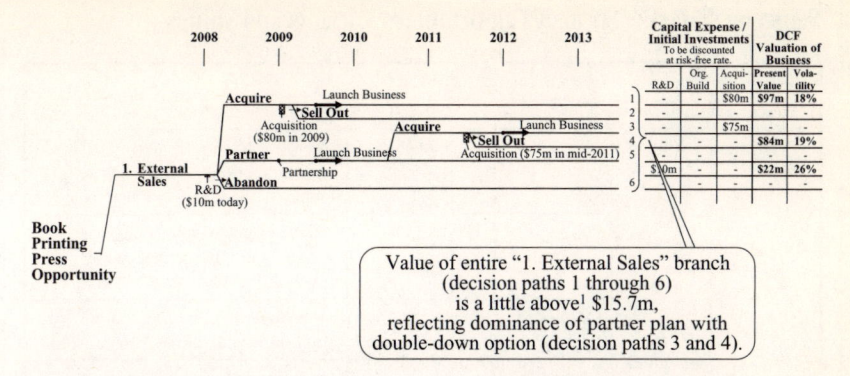

FIGURE 6.13 Value with Options Included—Consolidating Values within Entire Branches

Source: Business Intelligence Associates LLC.
[1] Actual value is $15.73 million.

Task 5: Define the Path Forward

Armed with the value contribution offered by each opportunity, we are now in a position to define a path forward in a market strategy. Three factors have a role to play in this task: the economics and value contributions of the various opportunities, the appetite for risk and the potential for unspecified future options, and qualitative organizational considerations.

What Do the Economics Say?

The "Evaluate Economics" task gives business leaders a view on the value of each strategic opportunity, and the sources of value within each. From here a mix-and-match process is needed to compile a path forward (of course, always keeping our options open!).

The key to defining the path forward is in the decision maps. At the outset, a list of building-block opportunities was compiled in Example 6.2, together with ad hoc outlines of how they might work together at the strategy level. As the process has evolved, two things have happened to the decision maps: (1) The highest value variants (branches) have been identified, and (2) new variants have been assembled using combinations of those high-value branches. More often than not, these combined variants are contained within building-block opportunities, though this is not always the case, and whole new strategy opportunities sometimes need to be added to the list.

For example, one building-block opportunity (number 15) called for entry into small press profit pools, while another (number 14) called for

Example 6.5 Summary of Samsung's Opportunities

Samsung's Market Strategy Opportunities Variants and Values

Market Strategy Opportunities				Value[1] ($ Billion)	Variant/Discussion
Level 1: Existing	Exploiter	Milk business	1	$0.06	Use price to exit. Options: Focus on specific markets; sell as salvage at end.
		Follow market leader	2	$0.12	Balance price to take share from leaders. Options: Target quick follower position.
		OEM only	3		Destroys value; existing market position is valuable asset to be kept.
		Invest big	4		Capital investments will not accelerate value growth (volume or profit growth).
Level 2: Charted	Game Follower	Enter ink	5	$0.32	License ink offering and leverage existing share position; in parallel with #8.
		OEM ink	6		Technology investments cannot be recovered; destroys value.
	Market Follower	Enter Corporate Market	7a	$0.04	Not much incremental value over customer. Option upgrade to #7b difficult.
			7b	$0.15	Leverage existing offerings; little channel investment needed.
	Risk-Taking Follower	Enter Ink/ Corporate	8a	$0.06	In parallel with #5. Option upgrade to #8b difficult.
			8b	$0.14	In parallel with #5.
		Production/ Corporate	9	$0.02	After #7b. In parallel with #15.
Level 3: Uncharted	Disruptor	Low-cost supplies	10		Destroys significant value in existing print business, globally.
		Low-cost supplies/ new	11		Destroys significant value in existing business. New capital investments are lost.
		e-paper	12	$0.02	Develop e-paper solution; estimated 20-year time frame. Options: Target display technologies.
		e-paper/ new	13	$0.05	Develop e-paper solution; estimated 20-year time frame. Options: Target many press markets.
	Pioneer	Big press profit pools	14	$1.68	After #15: Target packaging, magazines, and catalogs; perhaps advertising?
		Small press profit pools	15	$0.02	Enter books in 2008 in partnership. Options: Acquire partner; expand to labels?

Define a Path That Exploits REAL OPPORTUNITIES 169

Interrelationships between Market Strategy Opportunities

```
                        Exit
                         (0)              ───── Related
  Small press profit pools   Milk business  ───▶ Sequenced
                  (15)   (1)              ····· Contradictory
  Big press profit pools (14)
                             (2) Follow market leader
        e-paper (13)
                             (3) OEM only
     e-paper/new (12)
                             (4) Invest big
 Low-cost supplies/new (11)
                             (5) Enter ink
    Low-cost supplies (10)
                             (6) OEM ink
                       (9)  (8)  (7)
   Enter corporate with production    Enter corporate market
                         Enter
                       ink/corporate
```

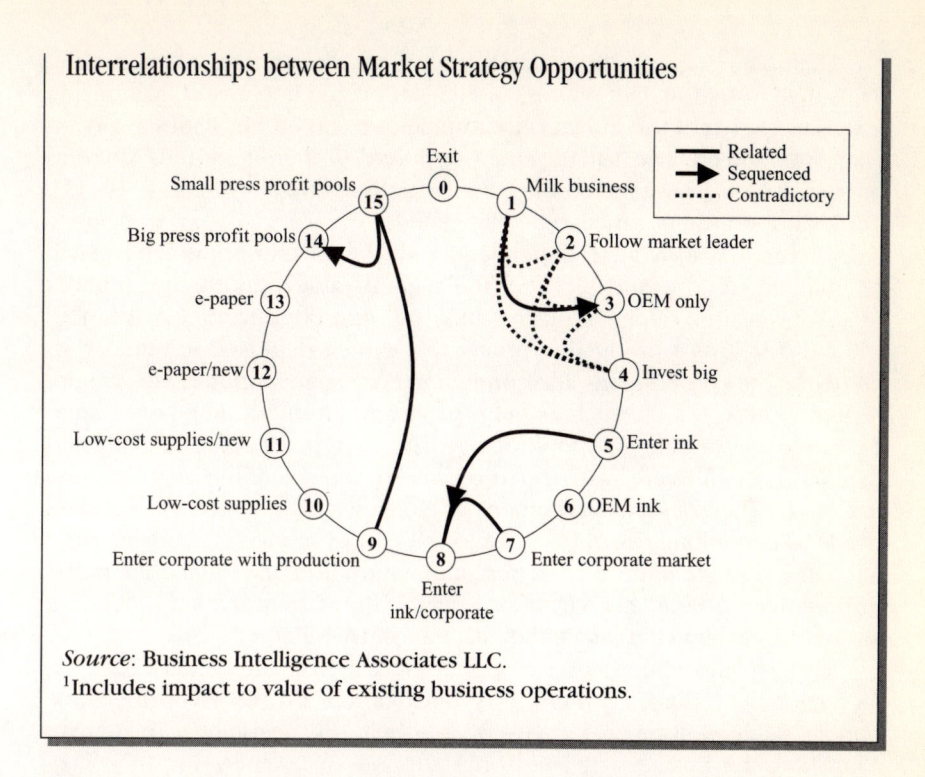

Source: Business Intelligence Associates LLC.
[1]Includes impact to value of existing business operations.

entry into larger ones. As each was mapped and assessed, the highest-value variants were identified. In the case of the small press profit pool opportunity, it was pursuit of the U.S. book digital press market in a partnership; in the case of the big press profit pool opportunity, it was pursuit of the U.S. packaging digital press market (with options to expand into magazines and catalogs)—using the book opportunity as a stepping-stone. As is typical, the opportunities morphed as the specifics were thought through; in this case, one opportunity was nested within a variant of another.

Example 6.5 summarizes the results across all the strategy opportunities in our Samsung illustration. It reports the value of the highest-value variants in each opportunity and how they morphed—including how they merged and adjusted in their definitions, what the key subsequent options are, and the sequencing and dependencies between them. The good news is that a detailed and outrageously sized decision map is not needed. The work conducted in the preceding task to identify the variants in each opportunity that contributed the most value can be leveraged to simply eliminate variants that add no value, even as options. And since we know for the remaining paths where the sources of value emanated from, they can be merged and morphed to redefine opportunities.

Example 6.5 goes a long way to unlocking the market strategy for the Samsung illustration, in a process of elimination, judgment, and maximizing economics. Five of the fifteen opportunities we started out with have been eliminated already; no variant could be found in them that adds value to the existing business, and so they are not options (numbers 3, 4, 6, 10, 11). The exit opportunity can also be eliminated.

There are also related, dependent, and sequenced opportunities, such as numbers 15, 14, and 9. Here, the highest-value opportunity, number 14's $1.68 billion, depends on the entry into the book market by number 15, and develops a production printer that can be deployed in number 9's entry into the corporate in-office printer market. Some opportunities are not related to others at all, such as the e-paper opportunities, numbers 12 and 13. These are long-range opportunities that may replace paper one day and their current values are small (but this is mostly a result of the long timelines involved). They deserve investment in their own right, since the business needs to be looking down the road to stay ahead of market inflexions and in control. Note that these are different in nature from the low-cost supplies opportunities 10 and 11, which also disrupt the current market model but are not viable strategies since they have negative values.

These relationships between opportunities help create bundles of strategic action. Of course, contradictory ones cannot be placed in the same bundle, such as number 4, investing big, being inconsistent with number 1, milking the business. Related ones support each other, and their economics need to be updated to understand what that value-add is. The following summarizes key bundles based on the situation for Samsung in Example 6.5:

1. With one exception, the existing business opportunities, numbers 1 through 4, are contradictory and cannot be bundled. Since they are also unrelated to other opportunities, the highest value path forward should simply be selected and adopted: number 2, follow the market leader.
2. Two opportunities, numbers 5 and 8, call for entry into the ink market (beyond Samsung's existing toner presence). Samsung will need to acquire an ink solution, and the most viable variant is to buy ink printer parts and sell them under its own name, subsequently acquiring its own ink technology.
3. Two opportunities, numbers 7 and 9, call for entry into the corporate in-office toner market (beyond Samsung's existing consumer presence). This is relatively easy to accomplish, since many channel and other similarities exist. Both are value creating, though on its own, number 9 is marginal.
4. Again, numbers 14 and 15 call for a staged entry into the U.S. printing press markets. The option to include number 9, entering the corporate

market with toner production printers, increases the added value of all three opportunities, spreading R&D investments and positioning the brand more extensively in the business-to-business market.

So what do the economics tell us? First, the existing business will add the most value by following the leader into and out of market changeovers, and using price to incrementally take share from the leader. This should probably be adopted as a market strategy element.

Second, the huge $1.68 billion value-add in the big press profit pool opportunity, number 14, would override other choices, if there was conflict. This override is subject to organizational considerations, discussed in a moment. The book market opportunity, number 15, is included as an integral part of big press opportunity's value. This also looks like a highly viable market strategy element.

Third, several incremental opportunities, mostly level 2 "charted" types, also add value. The highest priority is in expanding the offering to consumers to include ink (opportunity number 5), which has a value of $320 million. Further, entering the corporate market with midmarket/upmarket offerings in the existing toner business (opportunity number 7b) and ink (opportunity number 8b) together add $290 million. These opportunities offer a solid value-add, though they are more subject to other business priorities than the preceding two opportunity bundles.

Finally, the e-paper opportunities, numbers 12 and 13, are really variants on the same theme, and share the same decision path throughout the R&D phase in the next 10 years. These should be initiated; initial investment amounts are not substantive, though the market opportunity in 20 years will be. These will be developed and refined as time progresses.

In short, the economics assessments have told us where the value is created, and their associated market reviews have told us how the opportunities relate to each other. Most important, the real options review has told us that as time goes forward, *an open mind is the greatest asset*, and flexibility in decision path choice and timing is paramount. Next, we finalize the path forward and construct a strategy statement by considering risk and organizational issues.

What's Your Appetite for Risk?

Risk assessment has always been a principal concern for business leaders and others tasked with making investments. However, the level of understanding of risk, until the past decade or so, has not been at a level to quench the need to manage it, while the tool bag to deal with it practically has been distinctly empty.

Now business leaders have several practical tools with which they can gain insight into the nature, magnitude, and source of risk in potential investments. Although what has become available is by no means enough, it has advanced the cause substantially. The tools are the same as those used to formulate our market strategy:

- *DCF valuations.* As DCF techniques were being adopted widely in the 1980s, the greater accuracy in absolute valuation of business propositions significantly added to the investor's view of what the business was worth, versus what was being paid for it. Furthermore, the technique itself recognizes risk (in the discount rate), and to properly use it demands an appreciation of the underlying relationship between risk and the expected rate of return—delivering an education on risk in its own right.
- *Monte Carlo simulation.* Now business leaders can add substantial insight into their view of riskiness, with probability-based uncertainty profiles provided by Monte Carlo simulations. In contrast to the past, where business leaders could only contemplate the risk of a few factors in a limited way (such as, will product market prices get to the level expected?), they can now get a very specific and value-focused picture of end results, such as that in Figure 6.2. Now business leaders can ask, "What is the probability the outcome will be a negative value?" or, "Will the option to partner with player X reduce the likelihood of a negative value?" In fact, a range of new insights can be gleaned, such as probabilities that one business proposition's minimum value will be greater than another's. Comparisons of upside potentials can now also be added to the discussion. By having market managers add probabilities to their forecasts, which can be robustly rooted in historical precedent, tremendous insights become available with which to manage investment risk.
- *Real options valuations.* Ultimately, backing the wrong horse is a risk in itself, and the insights provided by real-options thinking give explicit recognition to the value of having options. For example, when a business, a technology, or anything else is referred to as a "platform," it has option value that is very tangible. Quantifying that option value can change the thinking dramatically.

In short, taking the time to add these tools, even just the thought pattern they demand, to the effort to define the business's market strategy sheds needed light on the sources of upside potential and downside risk. Of course, while each business must characterize risk, from there it's down to management's own tolerance for it in their decision making.

Organizational Considerations

The role organization-driven issues play in defining market strategy cannot be underestimated, given the impact the organization has on the shape and nature of the business. While it is impossible to second-guess the situation in your business, three frameworks can contribute greatly to the consideration of the business's market strategy.

1. *Play to the organization's strengths.* The business model assessment framework of Chapter 5 is needed again, this time to deliver a more detailed and quantitative report on the suitability of specific strategy opportunities and bundles presented by the economic review.
2. *Incorporate the human factor.* This chapter outlines a mostly fact-based approach and tool set to help define a market strategy. To act without regard to the human factors, however, would be foolhardy—a fact well recognized by all good managers. With that in mind, those factors can be characterized and mapped against the needs of key strategy options. Three maps of the business are useful: the organizational structure (including individuals' skills, hierarchies, and head counts); the economics in the business (where value creation is concentrated, and associated with which executive); and the organization's political structure (outlining where relationships and power lie). While there is no direct linkage between these maps and the market strategy decided on, the process itself delivers useful insights on what the organization will be able to deliver, and how best to configure it to improve the chances of success.
3. *Prioritize—value versus implementation.* In theory, all opportunities that create value should be pursued; capital is freely available—it's just expensive. Naturally, in the real world, organizational and management constraints force a focus. No organization can take on all the value-creating opportunities it faces; indeed, many will have a problem taking on even just the one greatest value-creating opportunity. In the end, prioritization is needed to make the call on what opportunities to pursue, and that prioritization must depend on a recognition of the *implementation effort* and *value-creation potential* of each opportunity bundle. Simply arraying them out in these two dimensions helps separate out the most attractive ones, as illustrated for the Samsung example in Figure 6.14.

In this way, several levels of priority emerge, generally driven by higher-value, lower-effort opportunities. If attainable, extremely valuable opportunities like number 14 deserve extra effort, even if it means stretching the organization. Beyond that, the existing business is usually also a top priority. Then trade-offs are needed, to choose between strategy bundles based on combinations of value-add and effort needed

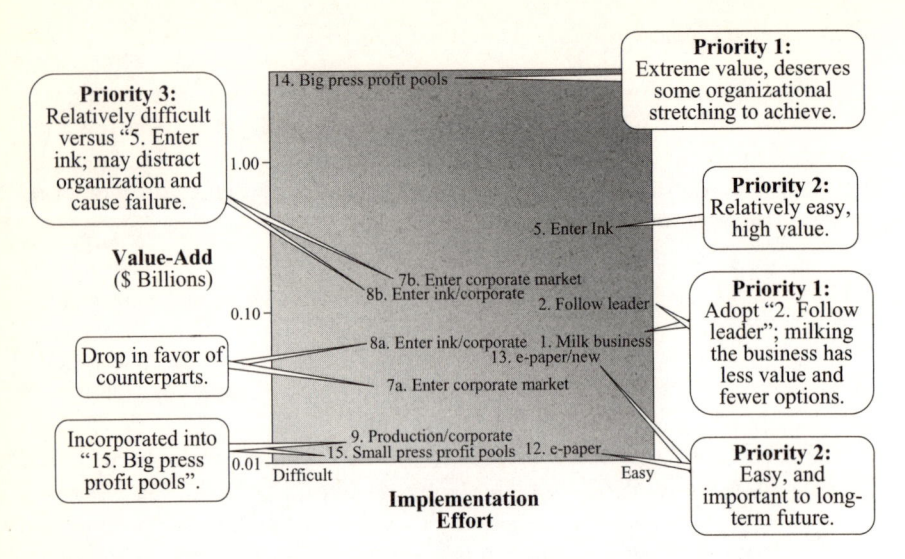

FIGURE 6.14 Prioritizing Market Strategy: Value versus Implementation Effort
Source: Business Intelligence Associates LLC.

to get done. For example, there is such a trade-off between opportunity number 5 and the bundle of numbers 7 and 8. If the organization can cope with them both, then there is not an issue. However, that may not be the case, and the value-effort profile of number 5 is more attractive (greater value, less effort).

Organizational considerations are the outstanding consideration in the market strategy formulation process. From here it is up to managers to decide what they can bite off, in line with what they think they will get in financial returns and how much risk they and their shareholders are willing to take on.

Summarize the Market Strategy for the Organization to Sail By

Although maintaining flexibility and making value-maximizing choices at each point in time is a basic tenet of value management, the intended direction of the business in the market has to be explicitly stated, so that line managers all haul in the same direction and investors know what they are investing in. That market strategy statement is best understood and used by the organization when it sets out, with specificity and detail, where the business will compete, and how it will compete in those areas. In the Samsung example, the U.S. market strategy statement might be summarized as follows:

"Samsung is a digital printing solution provider, serving both consumers and commercial printers of books, packaging material, magazines, and catalogs. Our offerings have the highest reliability, at reasonable prices."

This captures the intention to remain in the consumer market, perhaps extending into ink, though to also serve specific parts of the commercial printer market. No mention is made of corporate in-office printing, as this is assumed to be too much for the organization to take on at this point. The reference to reliability focuses on a single, critical market positioning, which has been used to drive market share forecasts.

Naturally, the knowledge base underlying the market strategy must also be frequently updated, reflecting changes in MIEs and forecasts. While this enables and empowers proactive decision making, the strategy statement itself cannot be changed regularly, since organizations need stability. If confusion is to be avoided and results are to be achieved, turning the ship must happen infrequently, and with a thoughtful communications plan.

Task 6: Plan and Execute

Even the most valuable strategy is worthless without effective implementation. Superior implementation and how to achieve it is a topic outside the intended scope of this book, but is addressed very well in many other texts. There are two groups of issues that must be included in implementation planning:

1. *Actions and responsibilities*. Although it may seem obvious, an explicit statement of the actions needed to execute the market strategy and their timing is a baseline requirement. This must resemble the original economic evaluation closely, in terms of timing, expected action, and other factors. Visionary strategies that set out intended actions but are not followed up with specific and detailed action plans stamped by business leaders have a documented tendency to not get done. This is particularly true for acquisitions, where the underlying drivers for the acquisition have been recorded as getting discarded within even just a year of the transaction. With an explicit time-based action plan, however, success rates increase exponentially—even more so when the names of specific executives are associated with deliverables.
2. *Resource needs*. Here also, open recognition of the financial and human resource needs has the effect of making sure that the plan is grounded in reality. It also increases the chance that the resources will actually be made available. Politically, it signals that the strategy will receive the organizational support it needs in order to be successful.

Return on Effort

With these six tasks, from listing opportunities to determining their economics and formulating specific actions, business leaders have some of the most proven approaches to getting their businesses to maximize long-term cash flow and intrinsic business value. While there are many other actions businesses can take to drive cash flow, it is market strategy that gives the greatest value-creation leverage for the management resource and effort expended.

PART III

Sustaining Value Growth

Parts One and Two of this book showed how to use market strategy to add value to a business, first by finding and focusing on internal profit pools in today's business, and then by finding and focusing on market profit pools to create value in tomorrow's business.

Finding profit pools is one thing, but actually *capturing* them is quite another. That typically requires organizational and other change, usually a lot of it, and that change is always needed quickly if opportunities are to be robustly exploited. Unfortunately, the larger a business grows, the more specialist are employee skills and the more complex the organization becomes; managing change becomes exponentially difficult. In fact, many well-established businesses become very good at *suppressing* change, so that the tried-and-true methods that are making money today are not disrupted by defect-creating variance. But if a business is going to succeed in leveraging the power of market strategy to boost value, then the entire organization has to become proficient in both seeking value and managing continuous change.

This is what Part Three is about. In these two chapters we address two critical topics: what is needed to sustain value growth, and how to configure the business for value-maximization.

- Chapter 7 shows why established businesses often struggle to capture new sources of value, and presents a proven framework for driving value growth through systematic corporate renewal.
- Chapter 8 outlines how to identify the principal areas of value creation within an organization, and how to use structure to focus on and systematize value creation.

CHAPTER 7

Corporate Renewal and New Business Management

With Jim McCreary

"Nobody ever got fired for buying IBM." Anyone who was around in the mid-1980s will remember that phrase, emblematic of the high reverence in which IBM was held. In truth, IBM's most salient reputation was for its investment attractiveness. It was a solid bet, predictably turning out value growth throughout the 1970s and 1980s; it was the darling of every solid portfolio. After all, it was "Big Blue," the bluest chip around.

Then came the stumble. The first hint came after the 1987 crash; the value growth machine started a sideways shuffle. Then, between February 1991 and August 1993, it crumbled; the share price dove from $140 to $41. In two years, nonreinvesting shareholders saw their invested capital shrink 71 percent! What happened? The answer is simple, and most observers were aware of it *as it was happening*: IBM failed to keep up with changes going on around it. Over 30 years the organization built a finely honed machine around delivering a specific proposition; everyone focused on making the machine deliver that proposition in a better way—and it worked for a long time. Its business leaders also succumbed, and when change on the outside finally started to just go by IBM, those leaders couldn't accept it. In the end, it took a determined new boss like Lou Gerstner and the organizational equivalent of shock treatment to drive through the needed change.

IBM is one of many to have struck gold with an exceptionally performing business model or offering, only to grow entrenched to the extent they don't see or can't respond to change. Consider the following cases:

- Digital Equipment Corporation, 1974–1987 versus 1988–1991.
- Westinghouse, 1980–1985 versus 1986–1990.
- Xerox, 1959–1979 versus 1980-present.

These are three of many examples, historically considered blue-chip. They are not unusual in that they delivered a considerable run of spectacular shareholder return performance which then abruptly turned into an ignominious market-value implosion, the post-implosion business being a shadow of its formerly high-flying self. While it's easy to look back and point to the entrenchment that drove respective downturns, the key question is, How can entrenchment, as predictable as it is, be avoided? How can businesses of all sizes achieve the continual renewal that sustains above-average value growth?

In this chapter we first look at the fundamental drivers for sustained value growth, and then turn to see how it is achieved by understanding the challenges involved and learning from past successes and failures. That is followed by a discussion of *how* to achieve sustained value growth and corporate renewal, including a review of best practices in the corporate development process.

How Is Sustained Value Growth Achieved?

While intrinsic business value requires businesses to successfully execute and to deliver cash flow into the future as expected, value growth requires an even greater challenge—that businesses find ways to grow that future cash flow stream. The existing stream, as difficult as it may seem to keep it going, is already expected. Moreover, since investors also expect their capital to appreciate, business leaders are *obliged* to deliver value growth. Table 7.1 outlines three financial tenets of business management, together with their implications for what the business model must deliver to achieve the desired result.

Viewed this way, the secret to sustained value creation is pretty simple. The basic requirement is for a base business with a return engine that generates the expected future cash flow. Then value growth is achieved by using that base business to grow cash flow, leveraging a thoughtful market strategy to grow high-return sales. Finally, recognizing that *all* business models are subject to diminishing returns (high returns attract competition, which then reduces returns), new businesses must be developed to supplant retiring ones.

In short, *sustained high value growth is only achievable through new business development*. As we saw earlier, few companies have successfully demonstrated the ability to sustain value growth in the long haul. In the next two sections we learn from some of the challenges involved, and from some of the few corporate success stories.

TABLE 7.1 Basic Value Management Insights and Business Model Implications

Financial Insight	Business Model Implication
Investments create value when their rates of return exceed capital costs.	Create a *return engine*—distinctive capabilities (competitive advantages) that allow a business to serve target customers more profitably than competitors can.
Growth creates value *only* when rates of return exceed capital costs (growing losses is not good).	Use market strategy to build a *growth charger* and add customers and revenues that keep rates of return above capital costs.
The longer rates of return exceed capital costs, the more value is created (difficult, as it attracts new capital and competition).	Use market strategy to build a *continuous renewal engine* to generate a continuous flow of new opportunities (as the two above).

Why Sustaining High Value Growth Is Such a Challenge

The key difference between managing incumbent businesses and creating (and managing) new business can be summarized in one word: *failure*. While failure is simply not acceptable in an incumbent business, it is a hard fact of life in new business creation. It just needs to be properly managed. As one might expect, problems arise when incumbents try their hand at new business creation—as they must do for renewal and sustained value growth.

New Business Creation and Failure

The degree to which failure is a fact of life in new business creation is borne out by the fact that only 5 percent of formal new business ideas make it to market launch, and only 4 percent turn out to be value creators. This rate of failure is often quite startling to those managing incumbent businesses, where the prevailing mind-set is that anything less than a 100 percent success rate is unacceptable. Figure 7.1 shows stage-gate survival rates for a portfolio of 6,000 new business ideas generated in a large-company innovation process over seven years, whose performance was tracked for over ten years.

At the front end of the process (at the left-hand side of the chart), only 10 percent of formal new business opportunity ideas are chosen to continue down the process pipeline for further development; *90 percent of initial ideas are killed off*. At each later stage, 15 percent or more of the prior stage's initiatives fail to make the cut and are killed off.

Survival Rates
(Proportion of ideas)

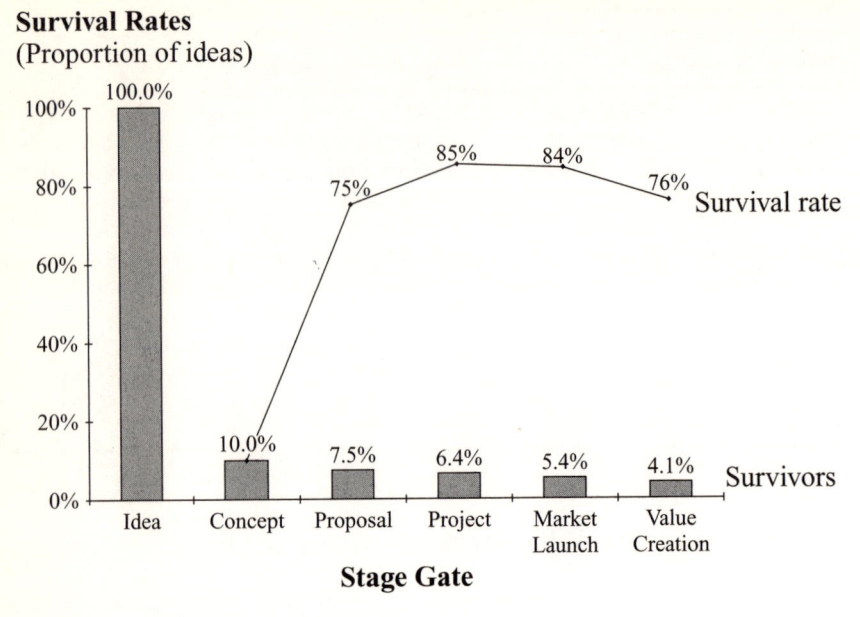

```
100%  100.0%
                                85%    84%
 80%                    75%                    76%
                                                  Survival rate
 60%

 40%

 20%
         10.0%  7.5%   6.4%   5.4%   4.1%
  0%                                               Survivors
       Idea  Concept Proposal Project Market Value
                                      Launch Creation
                     Stage Gate
```

FIGURE 7.1 New Business Survival Rates
Source: Jim McCreary.

    This high failure rate is not just a corporate phenomenon; Figure 7.2 compares the cumulative start-to-exit returns on a venture capital (VC) portfolio (463 ventures backed by a variety of VC firms during the 1980s) against a corporate ventures portfolio (30 ventures started inside several large companies during the 1980s).

    Each point on the lines in Figure 7.2 shows what the overall portfolio rate of return would have been if the portfolio manager had made all the investments to the left of that point, and none of the investments to the right of that point. In essence, each line shows us how much failure each portfolio has to pay for (on the left-hand side of the chart) before the high returns from more successful investments (on the right-hand side of the chart) bring the overall portfolio return above zero. For instance, the bottom 50 percent of the capital invested in the VC portfolio generated an overall portfolio economic profit return on investment (EROI) of –20 percent. For the corporate portfolio, the bottom 50 percent of capital invested earned a return on investment (ROI) of –75 percent. Curiously, the bottom 88 percent of *both* portfolios earned a combined EROI of 0 percent. Clearly, any organization that makes a serious commitment to systematic new business creation needs to learn how to tolerate and constructively manage high failure rates!

Portfolio Annualized Lifetime ROI

[Chart: Y-axis from -100% to 100%; X-axis "Portfolio Capital Invested" from 0 to 100%. Two curves labeled "Corporate portfolio" and "VC portfolio."]

Portfolio Capital Invested
(Worst performers to the left, best performers to the right.)

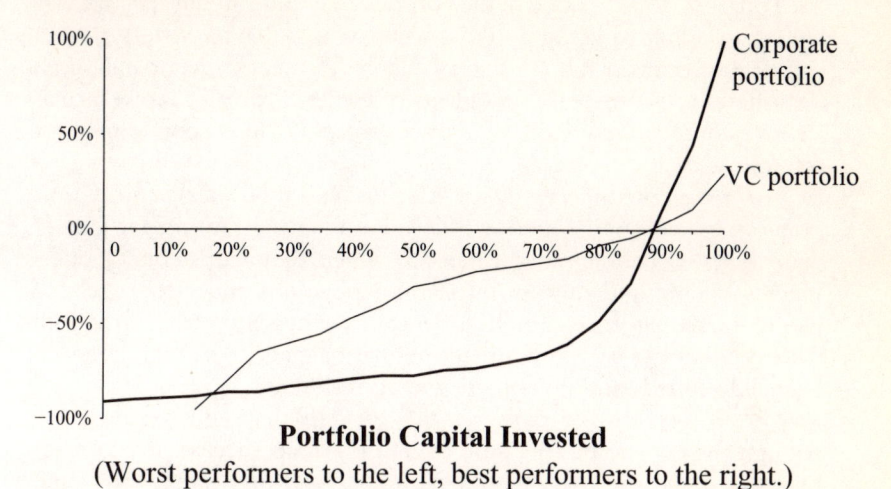

FIGURE 7.2 Comparison of Venture Capital and Corporate Innovation Returns
Source: Jim McCreary.

Five Basic Rules for Sustaining High Value Growth

The VC portfolio in Figure 7.2 provides a useful benchmark to understand key success factors in value growth and corporate renewal programs. Five basic rules for sustaining high value growth can be drawn from the similarities and differences between VC and corporate venture investment portfolios:

1. *Keep your costs low until you have proven small-scale profitability, because most of your projects will fail.* Failure costs were very high for both VC and corporate portfolios. The bottom 88 percent of both portfolios delivered a net zero EROI. Very large successes in the top 12 percent of each portfolio were needed in order to create value by generating returns above the opportunity cost of capital. Reducing the cost per failure in the bottom 88 percent of each portfolio obviously has great potential to increase overall portfolio returns dramatically. This analysis should harden our determination to use low-cost creative demonstration projects to prove each innovation project's profit potential before pouring in large amounts of scale-up cash.
2. *Cut your losses, but allow some mis-strokes.* The long, low belly of the corporate portfolio line clearly signals that corporate investors are much

worse at cutting off underperformers than are VCs. They tend to pour in investment capital in attempts to salvage underperforming (but very visible) projects. In fact, none of the corporate ventures in our data set was willing to admit to being a 100 percent write-off! While every project should be forgiven the occasional failure to meet a major milestone on schedule, alarm bells should go off when a project blows a major milestone delivery more than once, *especially* in corporate renewal portfolios.

3. *Let your winners run, even if they leave the parent business behind.* Corporate winners often generate truly huge financial returns, far greater than their VC counterparts, especially when they can exploit opportunities deeply and quickly by using a powerful and closely related parent infrastructure. Naturally, whenever winners are constrained with the everyday big company organizational baggage, corporate renewal is quickly stifled (and investment averages suffer).

4. *Keep your opportunity pipelines full enough* that you always have enough projects going to assure overall portfolio success. If you don't play this game on a relatively large scale, you may suffer long (and politically difficult) periods of failure before the occasional winner comes in.

5. *Establish and maintain a truth-speaking, truth-seeking company culture,* because straight talk is the only thing that will navigate you accurately through the delicate process of deciding which projects to kill and which to let run. If this process is perceived to be clear and fair, it will keep your would-be innovators motivated to try again in spite of the low odds.

Organizational differences between VC and corporate investment vehicles give insight to ways corporate programs can be improved, as well as areas that can be exploited. Some of the problems in corporate programs include dull or negative incentives, weak deal flow and quality, constrained project charters (due to turf and political conflicts), poor investment management, and concerns over liability and brand exposure. These constraints make it all the more important for corporate programs to actively develop bench strength in innovation management, to apply rigorous economic criteria to new opportunity funding requests, and to exploit corporate resource sharing and scale up advantages aggressively.

Constructively Managing New Business and Failure

As we saw in the IBM case, perhaps the most powerful constraints to systematic value growth and corporate renewal are organizational and cultural. Clearly, high failure rates have to be tolerated, and failures need to become learning experiences; observations about what doesn't work lead to finding something that does. Experienced business leaders in established businesses, beware—*this is almost the polar opposite of the variance-reduction mind-set needed to smoothly operate an incumbent business.*

Punishing failure has an immediate and disastrous effect on the organization's ability to innovate, create value, and grow, and it is not difficult to see it. For a start, everyone sees the negative outcome for the guy who tried something new and failed, and so the general propensity to try something new ever again plummets. The new opportunity deal flow just dried up. This is an insidious problem; it has no visible indicators, and the near-term impact on today's business is actually reinforcing (as it promotes a culture of honing skills). But, as competitors innovate, margins erode and it becomes more and more difficult to justify reinvestment in the business. Sooner or later, the problem becomes extreme, at which point management becomes *very* interested in finding and capturing new profit opportunities. But by that time, the organization has suppressed innovation for so long that it has no deal flow, and no recent experience in managing innovation projects. (These situations are easy to spot; management feels compelled to "do something big" to solve the problem at a stroke, and the results are frequently gigantic fiascoes, like Motorola's Iridium satellite phone venture or Daimler-Benz's merger with Chrysler.)

So how should high-risk new business growth opportunities and ventures be handled? Consider what would happen if, instead of punishing well-intentioned failures, organizations treated them as learning experiences, squeezed each one to extract every possible insight about what to do differently the next time to increase the probability of success, and spotted each employee to "three strikes before you're out" (three unsuccessful, but virtuous, attempts before going into punishment mode). Of course, the organization would try more new things, learn more, and quickly improve its ability to find virtuous change opportunities and manage them well.

In addition to addressing culture, organizational structure adjustments provide a second option, including separating major innovation projects from the organization, or just altering reporting structures. Naturally, there are trade-offs involved, such as the reduced access that new venture projects will get to corporate resources if they are separated out, or the interruption to the incumbent's business operations where these projects are retained internally.

While each organization and situation is unique, two factors that deserve consideration in using structure to promote the prospects of major innovation projects are: the nature of today's culture and the role of the new project(s):

1. *The culture in today's business.* As we have seen, the prevailing culture in today's business can have a stifling effect on major innovation projects. In fact, problems can also go the other way, where innovation

projects disrupt the finely honed processes needed to serve existing market needs. The two questions are: To what extent will the existing culture allow and promote the new project? And to what extent do we actually want the existing culture to change? There are often surprising answers to the second question, especially in markets where competition is tight and finely honed continuously improving processes are required.

2. *The role of the innovation project*. Innovation projects come in all shapes and sizes. Some are opportunistic bets, and there are those that have strategic import to the existing business, such that they are expected to be as large as, perhaps even replace, today's business. The opportunistic plays tend to be attempts to exploit corporate strengths, though they are not central to the incumbent's future. The strategic plays, however, can be quite distracting, since they address the same markets or operations and could easily be seen as a threat to the existing organization in some way. A useful example of this might be the threat perceived by managers in bricks-and-mortar book retailers such as Borders and Waldenbooks, and the hostility that an Internet retailing venture would have been given in the late 1990s.

The following framework (illustrated in Figure 7.3) has been adapted from the work of Dexter Hendrix et al. in *MetaCapitalism*, by Means and Schneider (Wiley, 2000). There are three possible configurations to

Business Substitution Potential

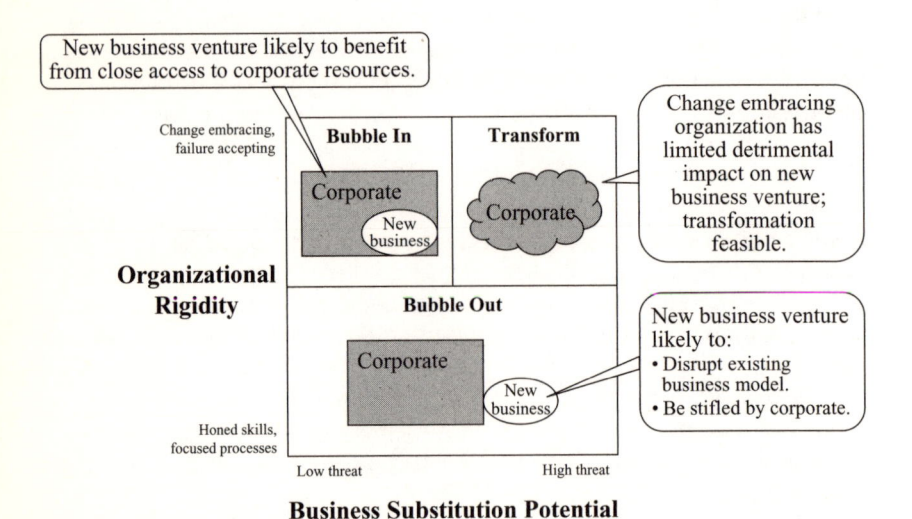

FIGURE 7.3 Where to Grow the New Business?

Source: Adapted from *MetaCapitalism* (Wiley, 2000). Reprinted with permission of John Wiley & Sons, Inc.

structuring corporate-based new businesses. "Bubble in" refers to growing the new business within the incumbent's organization—physically co-located, administratively supported (sharing systems and infrastructure), and commercially and managerially integrated (perhaps subordinated to some parent business unit). "Bubble out" refers to having the new business outside the incumbent, though there are obviously degrees of separation in each of the key areas—physical, administrative, commercial, and managerial. Finally, the new business can actually be a "Transformation" of the incumbent itself.

Figure 7.3 outlines how the incumbent's culture and the new business's role should be considered in organizational structure decisions. In cases where the culture is change embracing and failure accepting, there should be a greater propensity to retain the venture within the incumbent—though very few established businesses can boast these traits. Here, "bubble in" or "transformation" probably represents the best structural solution, though transformation is really limited to cases where the endgame is widely recognized and proven. In cases where the culture is, or needs to be, more finely honed and tuned to a specific process or business model, the propensity should be to separate the venture out.

Culture and organization issues are among some of the most difficult to deal with, not least because they are intangible and much of their effort cannot be measured. This is especially true for the leaders in a business, who probably have some considerable tenure in the organization and are unable to see these unmeasured issues. The goal of growing value through corporate renewal is an important and honest one which deserves a great portion of executive time and effort. Much is at stake.

Having seen the challenges inhibiting long-term value growth and corporate renewal, we now turn to cases of demonstrable and sustained success.

It *Is* Possible to Sustain High Value Growth Performance

Companies that have delivered high rates of shareholder return over very long time horizons have tended to choose one new-business-building configuration and stick to it. Some of these are exemplified in Table 7.2.

All of these companies grew into and sustained greatness by developing management methods that systematically searched for, found, and captured high-value new business opportunities. They did this by innovating in multiple dimensions, ranging from fundamental process cost reduction, to dazzling product breakthroughs, and to bold entry into difficult new markets and regions.

Note how many of these companies preferred the bubble-in approach. Coca-Cola, General Electric (GE), and Microsoft used transformation

TABLE 7.2 Example Business-Building Configurations

Company	Time Period	Business-Building Configuration
Coca-Cola	1981–1987	Transformation
	1987–1996	Bubble in
General Electric	1981–1986	Transformation
	1986–2000	Bubble in
Intel	1982–2000	Bubble in
Johnson & Johnson	1984–2001	Bubble in (pre-commitment)
		Bubble out (launch/growth)
Microsoft	1985–1995	Bubble in
	1995–2000	Transformation
Wal-Mart	1972–1992	Bubble in

approaches only when driven to it by visionary leaders who clearly foresaw major threats to business-as-usual, and who forced their organizations through a Transformation phase as an expedient way to restore flexibility. Once they restored flexibility, they reverted to the less traumatic bubble-in approach, for reasons that GE Chairman Jack Welch summarized by observing that "change has no constituency. People like the status quo."

During the second half of Jack Welch's tenure, GE provided a very high-profile example of corporate success in bubble-in value growth and corporate renewal. During Mr. Welch's tenure, GE demonstrated that systematic, value-seeking management methods can create huge amounts of value. In the 20 years he was at the helm, GE's shareholder returns (stock appreciation and dividend reinvestment) were 5,000 percent—that's fiftyfold!—bringing its market capitalization up to $400 billion. Some of that certainly came from cost cutting early in his tenure (when he was referred to internally as "Neutron Jack" for the neutron-bomblike effects his initiatives had on employment at high-cost GE facilities). However, costs can't be cut below zero, and so most of this value growth had to have been created by finding and capturing major new opportunities in both existing and new businesses.

General Electric faced a classic post-restructuring challenge in the late 1980s: With easy-to-get profitability gains from cost cutting mostly captured, how could the company generate value-creating profitable growth on a massive scale? After considerable experimentation, GE derived a systematic approach that very effectively adheres to the five basic rules for sustaining high value growth outlined in Figure 7.2:

- Several large, sustained, CEO-led initiatives like "boundarylessness" and Six Sigma, backed up by consistent executive leadership behaviors, created a culture in which seeking and speaking the sometimes unwelcome

and complete truth was formally expected, and rewarded much more reliably than in most companies.
- By pushing profit and loss (P&L) responsibility far down into its organizations, and then giving each P&L manager stretch goals that could not be met by incrementally improving business-as-usual, GE created a large cadre of managers who were highly motivated to try a lot of new and different things to grow (and advance their careers). This gave many people chances to learn how to bake innovation resources into conventional budget structures and to manage those efforts well enough so that something produced significant financial good news during the budget year. This structure produced prodigious quantities of the essential fuel for profitable innovation: opportunity deal flow. It also tended to keep the cost of any single failure relatively low from a corporate portfolio perspective.
- The performance measures used generally rewarded value-creating behaviors, so consistent winners advanced reliably (as in "let your winners run"), and consistent nonwinners did not (as in "cut your losses").

Many additional details and nuances of GE's value-seeking management systems have been chronicled in the business literature and a wide variety of books over the past decade, so we will not pile on. With that said, GE has become a relentless opportunity seeker and a prolific initiator of ambitious, well-chartered, well-managed innovation projects, many of which find a way to succeed. By systematically creating quality deal flow, a truth-seeking culture to manage it well, and processes that reward success (and quickly learn from failure), GE has built a value-seeking engine of continuous business renewal. This will doubtless deliver above-average rates of return and above-average growth rates for as long as its leadership team continues with its current culture.

Johnson & Johnson (J&J) also has a long history of success in creating exceptional value systematically, by creating tightly focused business units, giving leaders generous discretionary resources, and requiring extraordinary growth *and* profit performance from each. Life is excellent for J&J business unit leaders who make their numbers consistently. Johnson & Johnson also does an excellent job of limiting the costs of failure, by the simple expedient of firing business unit leaders who consistently fail to meet extraordinary performance expectations. This combination of resource flexibility, powerful upside incentives, high accountability, and immutable downside consequences has proven effective for J&J in business after business, year after year.

By studying these and other examples of sustained value-creation excellence, we can derive a general framework for how to convert an episode of good value-creation performance into a long-running series of value-creation successes.

Reconfiguring New Business Development to Deliver Value Growth and Corporate Renewal

Most of the literature about shareholder value focuses on how to use value-based management principles to optimize return-growth trade-offs over three- to five-year time horizons in large businesses that already exist. Once the optimization is done and value is maximized, this literature tends to end with the business equivalent of "and they all lived happily ever after."

The rest of this chapter presents a specific framework and set of processes for how to continue to deliver above-average value-creation performance over time frames in the "ever after" period. These processes can't be put in place overnight, and they require lots of managerial care and feeding, so they are not easy to implement. But when implemented carefully and managed well over long time horizons, the compounding effect of time creates truly exceptional value for the company's shareholders, and for its managers and employees as well.

Today's New Business Development Process

While many businesses have new business development programs, few of them are explicitly tasked with delivering value growth and corporate renewal. In most cases, new business development programs primarily aim to deliver additional revenue (perhaps profitability) by exploiting existing strengths or market opportunities. Indeed, in large measure, the design of the program itself reflects this intended mission. The typical process starts with opportunities being presented and, if the proposal meets broadly stated business development hurdles, it is converted into a formal project. It then makes its way through an unspecified and unique development process and is subsequently launched into the market. Figure 7.4 sketches out this typical process.

The process often has many beneficial management practices, several of them originating from the VC community (from which many corporate development staff started their careers). These include active deal-flow development, stage-gate deal-flow management, value-focused business models (outsource some activities, and the like), creative and sophisticated small-scale market testing, creative low-cost promotion and distribution methods, and others.

```
    Ideas ▷
                    ┌─────────────────────────┐
                    │ Opportunities           │
                    │      Projects  Ventures ▷   Incremental
                    │                             corporate
                    │                             value
    Ideas ▷         └─────────────────────────┘
```

                            New businesses
                    ───────────────────────────────▶

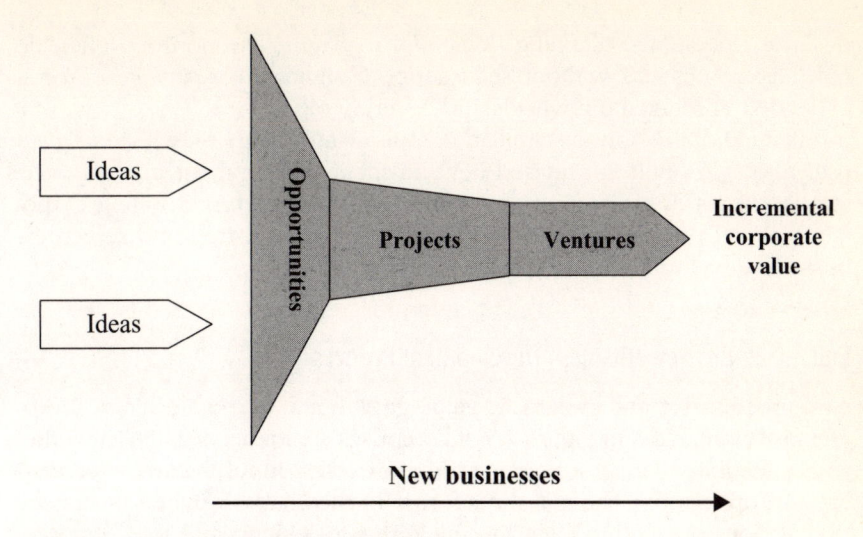

FIGURE 7.4 Typical New Business Development Process
Source: J. McCreary, Business Intelligence Associates LLC.

The typical process, however, also has significant problems. Goals for overall new business development performance are rarely and poorly defined, usually resulting in unfocused and somewhat irrelevant deal flow and investing. For example, in a recent interview, one executive leading corporate development for a well-known company described his goals as limited to "Figuring out how to meet the corporate 15 percent annual sales growth target, and the 15 percent EBIT margin targets they've given us. Right now, we're looking at significantly less than that. So, we're trying to develop new markets ... for our existing product line." While not unusual, this declaration signals unfocused efforts and rudderless strategic direction. While it does have profitability and growth goals, capital requirements are not addressed at all (which seriously jeopardizes value creation), and the growth goal appears to totally ignore market growth. Further, while there is a nod at market focus (new markets for existing products), there is no indication that specific profit pools have been targeted.

The typical new business development process also has issues with how it is operated and organized. For the most part, project solicitation and approval processes are not closely linked with market strategy, to the extent that market strategy has been tightly defined itself. Facilities to design ideas that proactively accomplish market strategy plans (not to be confused with near-term market tactics) fall far short of what is needed for corporate renewal. Further into the process, formal mechanisms for incubating new business operations, retaining skills, and managing the portfolio often do not exist at all; and without such support, significant scarce resource is expended in reinventing wheels and covering old ground.

If some of this sounds familiar, the following discussion will be of great use. In it, we outline a revised new business development process—one that leverages the best practices found in several high-performing corporate renewal programs. The lessons apply across industries and serve new business development programs of all sizes and types.

Enhancing the New Business Development Process

A comprehensive and systematic value growth and corporate renewal program is summarized in Figure 7.5. It comprises six formal activities, together with a feedback loop for learning and an explicit input from market strategy. An opportunity starts at the left side of the chart, designed in strategy formulation, originating from the market as a demand-pull idea, or originating internally as a capability-push idea. It then flows through the funnel from left to right; when it gets to the right it is a proven, profitable new

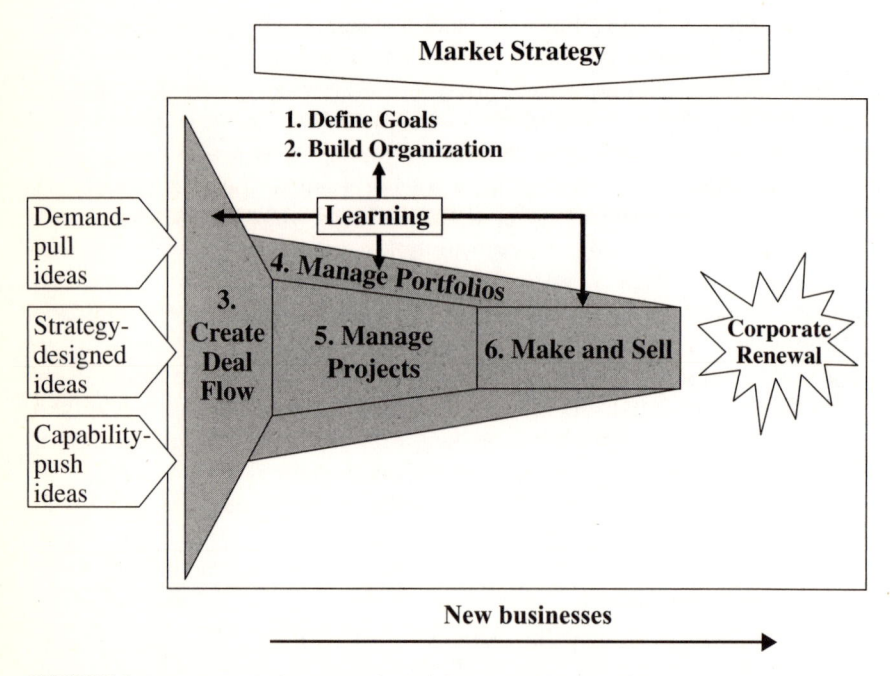

FIGURE 7.5 Systematic Value Growth and Corporate Renewal Program
Source: J. McCreary, Business Intelligence Associates LLC.

business, new offering, or new process. Whatever its form, it, in turn, generates lots of new ideas which are routed back to the front end of the funnel. Of course, the funnel shape reflects the significant attrition in each activity along the way; as we saw earlier, only 1 in 20 ideas makes it all the way to the end.

In today's world economy, for any person or business with distinctive skills, opportunities to make money by applying those skills to consumer or industrial market needs and wants are literally everywhere. The great challenge is not to find a good opportunity to pursue; it is to identify and sift through the thousands of available opportunities, to find a handful of ideas that you have the resources to pursue effectively and which will give you high value if you pursue them successfully.

Each of the program's seven activities has a significant role to play in value growth and corporate renewal:

1. *Define goals.* The program's business goals are specifically defined by market strategy (which sets out where and how the business will compete) and include growth and profitability targets that are too ambitious to be met by incremental improvement on business-as-usual.
2. *Build organization.* As illustrated by the GE example, it is important to create a formal organization and informal culture that can manage today's business efficiently but is not afraid of change and will systematically find and capture high-value opportunities.
3. *Create deal flow.* Given goals and strategy, a proactive search for high-value opportunities is an essential activity deserving significant effort and resources.
4. *Manage portfolios.* The organization must choose, monitor, support, and in many cases kill projects, using transparent and logical methods that are broadly perceived by the organization's rank and file as intelligent—keeping failure costs low, success rates high, and deal flow strong.
5. *Manage projects.* Each chosen portfolio opportunity needs to be organized and managed as a specific project, using well-understood innovation-management good practices.
6. *Make and sell.* The point of each project is to prove the opportunity's profit potential and scale it up so that it transitions into a stable, profitable, and continuously improving process or business.
7. *Renew and refresh.* As processes, product lines, and businesses mature, they have the potential to generate many new ideas and new opportunities which a value-seeking organization can use to renew and refresh itself, by resetting goals, refreshing the organization, generating fresh deal flow, and finding and sponsoring the next generation of high-potential new opportunity projects.

In the following material we walk through each program activity, outlining its role and highlighting best practices. Note that this framework can be applied to managing any type of innovation project—a new process, a promotion or distribution channel, product, service, market, region, or entire new business, whether developed internally or acquired externally and rejuvenated.

ACTIVITY 1: DEFINE GOALS The most important component of any value growth and renewal program is an explicit statement of what needs to be achieved. This statement must be driven by market strategy directly and needs to specify goals for both strategic and opportunistic projects. Overall program goals are needed in four areas (individual project goals are dealt with in Activity 5):

- Participation (market focus).
- Profitability.
- Growth.
- Core operating process performance.

Unfortunately, goals at this level of detail and specificity are sorely lacking in many of today's new business development programs.

Participation Goals Participation goals have to come first, because they determine where in the vast sea of consumer and industrial markets you will aim the wide mouth of your idea-generation funnel. A good participation strategy defines, in concrete terms, where the business is competing today and where it intends to compete in the future. It will state what the business will include or will consider as desirable targets to add over time, both for today and for a long-term desired future.

- *Offering types.* Identification of specific product and service interest areas, describing such issues as functionality, differentiation, future developments and potential, existing and future compatibilities and partnerships, and so on.
- *Customer types.* Identification of specific customer groups (including channels), using quantified customer attributes (such as demographics for consumers), behavior patterns (brand responsiveness), and so on.
- *Geographies.* Identification of specific target areas, region, country, territory, and local areas descriptions (inclusions and exclusions).
- *Internal configuration.* Identification of targeted value chain activities and targeted technologies.

For practical purposes, participation strategy targets need to be translated into simple decision rules for considering new business and innovation

Participation Area	Identified Targets
Offering Types (products and services)	• Digital radio chips • Driver software • Design-stage technical support • After-sale technical support
Customer Types (including channels)	• All the large mobile phone handset manufacturers • Large electronics hardware contract manufacturers • Wi-Fi hardware manufacturers where we have entrée or can get it • Large system integrators who are developing large-scale RFID systems
Geographies	• United States (Chicago, San Jose) • European Union (Finland) • Japan • China • Korea, Singapore
Internal Configuration (value chain, core technologies)	• Value chain areas: Sales and marketing; hardware design and rapid prototyping; software development and testing; pilot manufacturing (with fast transfer to low-cost contractors); B2B downstream technical support • Core technologies: Digital systems design for production in standard silicon circuitry (special emphasis on small size, low power consumption, and low cost)

FIGURE 7.6 Example of Specific Participation Goals—Wireless Components Business

Source: J. McCreary, Business Intelligence Associates LLC.

ideas. These rules will be helpful to both bearers of potential proposals and internal project evaluators, and need to result in answers as simple as "Yes, we'll consider this idea," or "No, this is too far beyond our scope." Figure 7.6 provides an example targeting profile for a wireless components business.

Profitability Goals   With target markets identified, new business organization and investment profitability minimums need to be set forthrightly—after all, growth that isn't profitable simply destroys value.

Now, profitability goals can be simple, but they must be economically robust. As we have seen throughout this book, though perhaps most pointedly in Chapter 4, there are two dimensions to value: the cash flow from operations, to be sure, but also the amount of capital invested (which carries with it its own cost). One of the most practical and readily estimated profitability measures for major innovation projects is economic profit return on investment (EROI). As we saw before, any number greater than zero means the business is *economically* profitable and may be a candidate for growth investment; however, any number less than zero means that the business is economically unprofitable, and must improve or show where improvement is expected before it can be a candidate for growth investment.

Because most new business ventures are relatively uncomplicated, EROI can be easily determined from contribution-level income statements and balance sheets. Technically, it is after-tax operating profit, divided by the net capital tied up by the business (both working capital and fixed assets); the discount rate (the time-based cost of capital) is then subtracted from the result. Care is also needed to ensure the distortions outlined in Chapter 4 are resolved, but since we are getting a business-level EROI (that is, not calculating segment-level profitability, and so not making allocations), it is usually a simple case of removing depreciation from operating profit.

Note that standard GAAP-based margin goals undercharge for key expenses, such as marketing and sales, while ignoring or mistreating the cost of capital; this allows many businesses to march proudly forward, meeting goals but destroying value (and eroding stock prices). Again, the goal itself is very simple when EROI is used, limited to a single percentage measure, such as in the following statements:

- "Overall, the new business program must deliver 10 percent EROI, measured each January."
- "Late stage investments must achieve over 15 percent EROI to qualify for growth capital."
- "Investments not achieving a positive EROI may be subject to termination within two quarters."

It is worth pointing out that profitability goals that do not include all key expense areas or a charge for capital in a single measure tend to get blurred. If the goals in the preceding sentences are rewritten with separate references to standard profits, marketing charges, capital usage, and the others, it is not difficult to see the possible problems. An effort to keep the measures simple will reap tangible and intangible rewards, avoiding reports like "Well, we met the goal for capital but . . . next period OP is on target . . ."

Growth Goals Aggressive growth goals for the new business organization have two essential roles to play:

1. Keep short-term new business managers from gutting future prospects by cutting growth investments to run up today's EROI.
2. Force long-term new business managers to actively search for, and invest prudently in, high-potential renewal projects.

After locking the back door shut by setting ambitious profitability goals, as previously discussed, a growth goal can be as simple as a revenue growth rate. Ideally, expected growth rates of targeted investment areas are known, and growth goals for the new business organization can be set as the targeted industry/market growth rate plus some increment. Growth rates of 3 to 5 percent above the industry average are typical and achievable, depending on the specifics involved. Higher growth goals can be risky; businesses that try to sustain far-above-industry growth rates in perpetuity often wind up provoking destructive price wars or the like, even triggering fraudulent behaviors (as we have seen with Bausch & Lomb, Enron, and others).

Once again, there is much to be said for simplicity, and revenue growth goals are needed only for the new business organization overall, as well as its key target investment areas. With that said, if a target investment area is opaque or too chaotic to measure, then overall revenue growth rates will have to suffice. However, the loss of insight in relative performance risks underperformance and/or unintended behaviors, and should only be accepted, on an exceptions basis, if it's impossible to reach consensus on a reasonable approach.

Core Operating Process Goals In addition to the profitability and growth goals just discussed, it is generally desirable to get ambitious improvements for each existing business's core operating processes as well. For instance:

> *Our idea development process historically has taken us 18 to 24 months, and then another 18 to 24 months to go through our new-product development process. This is clearly not competitive enough to bring new ideas to the market fast. We're now working on an Idea to Production (ITP) process which we hope will cut the new-product development cycle time from 24 months to 24 hours! Obviously we have to change the whole structure in order to do that.*

This is an excellent example of an operating process goal that clearly can't be met by incremental improvements to business as usual. An executive-level call for an order-of-magnitude cycle time reduction like this is also an executive-level call for, and endorsement of, radically creative thinking to enable a major out-of-the-box change. Setting a goal like this will force an organization to innovate ambitiously.

ACTIVITY 2: BUILD ORGANIZATION Goals don't mean much until you build an organization that is capable of pursuing and achieving them. So it's necessary to build and maintain business units that have the formal and informal organizations, skills, performance measures, and reward structures needed to:

- Operate profitably in today's business.
- Find and manage new opportunities effectively.

There is abundant business literature on how to design and build high-performance organizations, which we will not attempt to duplicate or even summarize here, other than to point out that most of this literature presumes either the relatively stable conditions found in already well-established businesses, or the extremely turbulent conditions found in new ventures.

Unfortunately, good organizational practice in large, stable businesses is in many ways the complete opposite of good organizational practice in new ventures. Ventures become large businesses by managing rapid change well enough to find and grow into one or more profitable niches. In venture settings, unconventional thinking, unconventional behaviors, intuitive leaps, and shortcuts often lead to success, recognition, and large rewards. As these ventures succeed and become large, the practical realities of operating on a large scale require them to become more rigid, and they begin to *suppress* changes that get in the way of large-scale operational efficiency. As they gain proficiency at suppressing change, they tend to lose proficiency at finding and capturing new opportunities effectively. As large organizations ossify, the career advancement rules tend to simplify down to "Don't screw up the system."

Breaking through this efficiency-versus-creativity conundrum is the most essential management challenge in achieving sustained value growth and corporate renewal. To sustain superior growth *and* profitability *and* value creation over long periods of time, you have to build an overall organization that can *suppress operational variance* (manage large-scale operations with precision inside narrow total quality management process control limits) *without suppressing the organization's desire and ability to find, develop, and capture new opportunities effectively.*

Naturally, every situation will differ in the details of how to do this well. However, complex organizations that consistently manage change well tend to emphasize the following good practices:

- *Truth and clarity.* Without forthright and complete truth, an organization can't recognize and learn quickly from mistakes, so failure costs accumulate and ultimately kill it. Clear and simple organizational structures minimize the time and energy the organization spends fighting within itself.
- *Accountability.* Organizational clarity also enables task accountability. Every major task or project should have a specific individual owner, with a specific target completion date. He who delivers consistently advances; he who does not, does not. Beware the doctrine of "shared resource efficiencies;" resource sharing dilutes accountability. Organize for clear accountability unless the economic case for resource sharing is overwhelming, *and* the shared resource is chartered to stay competitive in cost, quality, and response time with outside providers of the same services.

- *Flexibility and teamwork.* New opportunities tend not to respect fixed organizational boundaries, so the ability to put together opportunity-specific cross-functional project teams quickly, give them strategic freedom from the operational total quality management (TQM) variance suppression rules, and support them flexibly, is essential.
- *Market orientation.* Technologies and functional skills are tools used to serve customers properly. When in doubt, design the formal organization to serve customers well, and communicate your way through the resulting functional coordination issues.
- *Cash flow orientation.* Ultimately, any organization creates value by building and growing sustainable cash flow streams, so every organizational unit, whether defined as a profit center or as a cost center, should measure how much cash flow value it contributes to, or consumes from, the consolidated business total. Measuring value contribution in fine granularity generates many insights for market strategy, and gives each value-center manager the opportunity to use his virtual business to create new opportunity deal flow and compete for growth resources.
- *Recognition and advancement* as rewards. Large organizations generally do not have the flexibility to give innovative employees and work groups cash payouts that are competitive with independent-venture equity payouts. But they can offer very powerful incentives in the form of executive-level recognition, career advancement, and increased managerial autonomy for work done well. Organizations like Mary Kay and Wal-Mart clearly show how effective and inexpensive a motivator air time with the CEO can be.

The sections that follow will present more detailed discussions of how to organize and execute the activities needed to effectively find and manage new opportunities.

ACTIVITY 3: CREATE DEAL FLOW In this activity the organization actively seeks high-potential new business opportunities that combine both a large-scale return engine (major competitive advantage in an area that customers will value) and a large-scale growth engine (attractive value proposition with powerful distribution into potentially large target markets), and then develops these opportunities into specific investment proposals. These opportunities can include any or all of the following, either singly or in combination (new ideas almost never make it without being combined with others and with existing capabilities):

- Internally developed new products, services, or processes.
- Acquired or in-licensed products, services, or processes.
- New ways in which to serve existing customers.

- New market segments or geographic regions to enter.
- New distribution channels.
- New advertising and promotion channels and methods.
- Any other creative combination of ideas that might add profitability or growth to your company.

It's important to remember that *deal flow* is a VC term, and business should think of it more broadly as *opportunity flow*. What constitutes an opportunity depends on your participation strategy, capabilities, and aggressiveness. A good deal-flow engine has three major components:

1. Active Idea-Generation Processes   The original, classic idea-generation process is a suggestion box. The lowly suggestion box has become a business cliché because it doesn't actively reach out to develop new ideas, and because its contents generally aren't acted on in any sort of visibly fair and wholehearted way.

Therein lies the key to success in generating deal-flow: *Make it the full-time job of enough people, for enough time, so that they get to be good at finding and accurately screening large numbers of high-quality opportunity ideas*. This requires unwavering high-level executive sponsorship, because many cost-cutting types will view a deal-flow organization as a dead-weight cost with a huge travel bill and no visible output. But in a well-managed innovation pipeline process, the deal-flow organization will literally discover a company's next big thing, again and again.

The idea-generation processes should actively pull in many kinds of ideas from across the entire functional spectrum, for both incremental and radical change, in both the base business and in many potential new businesses. Marketing, sales, supply chain, technology, engineering, administration—frontline people in all these areas are teeming with latent ideas for both incremental and radical change in customers and regions served, products and services, pricing, marketing, promotion channels and tactics, operating and management process, technologies, and many others. A set of active processes that brings people together, loosens them up, and kick-starts their creative thought processes can tap into this vast reservoir of creativity and produce the building blocks for excellent new deal flow.

2. Fast, Transparent, and Inexpensive Processes for Scoping and Routing Ideas   An efficient deal-flow engine will need to filter out a very large percentage of the ideas generated early, but intelligently, for low relatedness or low potential value or both. This requires fast, transparent, and inexpensive processes for scoping the ideas for potential, so that they can be routed into appropriate idea-development channels or rethought or shelved.

Fast and *transparent* are essential for motivating frontline idea generators to continue to participate in these processes over time. Since most ideas don't make it very far down the pipe, the process must show the idea contributors fair and logical reasons why their ideas are being shelved. If it does this well, it will remotivate people to rethink, come back, and try again with better-quality ideas. In a fully mature system, many people in the company will become very skilled at prequalifying ideas, generating consistently high quality in the new-opportunity proposals. *Inexpensive* is essential because the process will be dealing with large numbers of ideas. If it takes $500 of analysis time to scope every idea, the deal-flow engine will rapidly become unsustainably expensive. Given a clear participation strategy (see Activity 1), assessing relatedness is a snap. Each assessment should take no more than five minutes, and preferably should take only one or two.

- Ideas that suggest incremental improvements in some part of the existing business can be routed directly into the appropriate functional change management processes.
- Ideas that propose radical changes along one or more dimensions of today's business (customers, channels, product and service capabilities, revenue models, technologies, production facilities, supply chain, or processes) should be held aside for review.
- Ideas that propose to adapt some or all of the business's capabilities to create an entirely new business (new customers and distribution channels, new products and services, or new technologies) need to be compared against the participation strategy. Ideas that fit some part of the participation strategy should be held aside for review. Ideas that don't fit the participation strategy in any significant way should be returned to the idea contributor with a brief explanation, along with a clear statement of what the participation strategy actually is.

Reviewing each idea held aside can be a bit more challenging, but still must be done quickly and simply. Accept the proposer's concept unchallenged, use success-case assumptions, and apply five minutes or less of simple economic analysis to assign a potential value to the idea. Document the estimated value and the key assumptions in a simple ideas database. Above a prespecified dollar threshold, route the idea into the qualified-ideas database. Below that threshold, return the idea and the quick analysis to its originator with a challenge to find a way to make it worth more.

3. Fast, Inexpensive, and Uniform Opportunity Analysis and Investment Advocacy Processes Proposals reaching this point undergo a more extensive and labor-intensive review. For each idea from the qualified-ideas database, assemble a small advocacy team of one to four people to work part-time to develop and prove out the idea. Success for this advocacy team is to deliver, within two to four weeks, a decision to shelve the idea, or to create a specific, investment proposal for the new-opportunity portfolio managers. In most cases, the advocacy team should include the idea generator, a demand-side advocate from marketing or sales, and a capability-side advocate from supply chain, engineering, or technology.

The same basic process works for both in-the-box and out-of-the-box proposals. It should be driven by a standard new-opportunity analysis template, and should resemble a capital project justification project, but with much more emphasis put on proving the existence of both a strong return engine and a large-scale growth engine.

The part-time, volunteer advocacy nature of this process is important. If the idea generator, or other advocates he can recruit, does not believe in the idea enough to devote real off-line time to developing and advocating it, the idea should not advance. And, since these ideas have a long way to go before they reach profitability (if they even make it that far), the whole funnel process has to be very parsimonious about spending real money this far upstream, with so much attrition still to come.

Reducing Risk with Parent Business Relatedness and Flexibility The screening process needs to decide very quickly whether the proposed project or venture fits the current business participation strategy well enough for the business to be an effective sponsor. This issue is so important to risk reduction that it should be carefully and thoroughly rereviewed by the portfolio management team as a key part of the yes/no investment decision process. Here are some guidelines for doing so.

Borrowing and reusing proven business components from a parent business, or from other known benchmarks, can reduce innovation project risks dramatically. The key to whether reuse reduces or increases risk lies in two factors: relatedness and flexibility.

Relatedness can be measured by looking to see if the innovation project and the sponsoring business have essentially the same customers, channels, product and service capabilities, revenue models, technologies, production facilities, supply chain, or processes. Each element that is *essentially the same* enables the innovation project to reduce risk by borrowing and reusing parent capabilities. If it is not, reuse risks escalate—you may be trying to pound a square peg into a round hole.

For each element that is essentially the same and therefore usefully related, ask if that element of the sponsoring parent's business is *flexible* enough to accommodate the likely needs of the innovation project, without seriously reducing or conflicting with the sponsoring business's efficiency and effectiveness. Wherever the answer is "Yes, without a doubt," the project may be able to rent parent resources with great mutual benefit. Wherever the answer is *anything but* "Yes, without a doubt," the project probably will need to pull in one or two key people from the parent in that area to build a parallel capability for the project that does not conflict with the parent's own needs.

ACTIVITY 4: MANAGE PORTFOLIOS In this extremely important program activity, the organization chooses high-potential proposals in which to invest, sets basic goals and milestone performance targets for each project, monitors project performance against goals, and intervenes as needed to renew—or kill off—project funding. It actually comprises several activities, stretching out over a long time period:

- Choosing projects.
- Setting project goals and milestones.
- Monitoring project performance.
- Intervening to re-fund or kill projects.

These activities are the practical equivalent of the role VCs play in launching and sponsoring venture-backed companies. In the corporate world, good practice in managing these activities generally takes the form of well-defined and crisply managed stage-gate processes for managing new product development, new process development, and new market entry projects. There are abundant writings on good practice in these processes, including *Winning at New Products: Accelerating the Process from Idea to Launch* by Robert G. Cooper (Perseus Books, 2001), and at the practitioner level through the Product Development and Management Association.

These knowledge bases are powerfully deep and detailed. However, they also make it very easy to lose track of the strategic big picture and to pursue product development process management for its own sake. Thus they deserve the following seven overriding guides:

1. Successful innovation projects create value, not products. Commercial launch is not success; it is an intermediate step in the process of creating profitable growth and value.
2. Stage-gate processes can be applied to almost all project types, including new products, services, processes, market entries, promotional methods, and so on. Tactical modifications to product-based processes are often needed, but the essential risk management benefits of stage-gate processes are useful across the entire spectrum.
3. The most essential preconditions for committing large resources to an innovation project are:
    - A very strong economic value proposition for both the target customers and the sponsoring business.

- An executive-level commitment from a flagship prospect to support the project and purchase the resulting output.
- Active sponsorship and advocacy from a senior executive in today's business.

4. Keep the project low-profile until it is sure to work. It can have visibility after it signs up a big customer commitment at the senior executive level (note that this can be an internal customer, especially for process innovation projects). This enables customer requirements to override internal politics. It also helps fund the project. These two then attract sponsorship. No internal rival can come in and say, "What were you thinking?" because you can say "I have a flagship customer."
5. Projects that blow the same milestone delivery date more than twice are unlikely to make it. Beware the sidewinder effect, in which an optimistic revenue forecast keeps moving sideways in time.
6. When in doubt about what to do, kill it, to keep the cost of failure low and to avoid the tendency to hang on too long to weak projects. The economic importance of this was shown earlier in this chapter in Figure 7.2.
7. But keep the evaluation and decision processes open, fact-based, and fair at all times, so as not to discourage idea contributors and dry up the deal flow.

ACTIVITY 5: MANAGE PROJECTS In this activity, small cross-functional teams organize specific innovation projects, meet the early project goals, build capacity as needed to meet customer commitments, and drive to market in order to prove viability as commercial new processes, products, services, or businesses. In short, this is where the entrepreneurial rubber meets the road, in four sequential activities:

1. Organize the project.
2. Meet early goals.
3. Build a project team (the project-level equivalent of Activity 2, "Build Organization").
4. Go to market.

The detailed decisions about exactly how to do each of these obviously depend on situation-specific circumstances, but there are many recurring patterns and good-practice guidelines that are derived from good-practice benchmarks. There is an abundance of information available on the Web about how to manage a start-up venture, but much of it should be viewed skeptically, for two reasons. First, almost all of it focuses on how to manage start-ups outside the constraints of a large-company environment. And second, while all new-business ventures start as innovation projects, not all innovation projects are new-business ventures. Corporate innovation projects to test new promotional concepts, administrative processes, and vertical market segments have very different risk profiles and project management success factors than independent new business start-ups.

For would-be project managers working in corporate environments, the Project Management Institute offers both broad and deep tactical knowledge resources in how to manage projects of many different types. As with the Product Development and Management Association, however, this knowledge base is so deep that it's easy to lose sight of the strategic big picture, and the following overrides are warranted:

- Every innovation project should start with a specific charter that clearly defines project goals, decision rights, and resource commitments; an accountable project manager; and an initial team.
- The project manager should be explicitly recognized as having the final decision authority with regard to his business, and to be held P&L accountable.
- You never get enough resources up front—don't waste time talking about what you can't do; do as much as you can with what you've got. Proof of demand from a flagship customer is what will pull additional resources in; you are not running an employment program.
- An intimate relationship with a flagship launch customer will generate lots of immediate customer feedback, so that the project never has to launch something without being sure that at least one major customer will buy it in quantity.
- Recruit self-motivated people with successful project or venture experience into the initial project team so that the project develops a fast-cycle can-do culture.
- Create a high-accountability project culture in which everybody is tested every day. Be realistic, and be brutally clear with people about where they stand.
- Colocate the project team in a location that gives the team significant control over its surroundings. This will give them the psychological freedom to innovate both the small and the large.
- Work through and learn quickly from the inevitable setbacks. Fast adaptation and a willingness to keep plugging away are essential.

ACTIVITY 6: MAKE AND SELL   Here the project proves it can deliver value under real-world conditions, and scale up to transition into a stable, profitable, and continuously improving process or business.

A great deal of business literature is devoted to this activity, so we will not dwell here, other than to highlight the priority of organizational flexibility and a continuous-improvement culture (to adapt to inevitable change).

ACTIVITY 7: RENEW AND REFRESH   In this activity, the large and mature business works actively to renew and refresh itself by resetting goals, recasting the organization, generating fresh deal flow, and finding and sponsoring the next generation of high-potential projects and ventures.

Renewal is the acid test for the management team of a successful new-business venture. Can the team do it all again, as a sponsor this time instead of as a rebellious goal-oriented do-whatever-it takes focused venture? In effect, can the team reseed the front end of the funnel growth and innovation management process with new ideas, and help the best of them grow into their own successful new businesses?

Strong fundamental performance in the early-stage activities (goals, organization, and deal flow) should make this renewal activity occur spontaneously, especially if it is energized by executive leadership that stays paranoid about competitors; uses active processes to rethink, innovate, refresh, and renew the base business; and, above all, shows clear executive support for renewal projects, even if they challenge business-as-usual.

In Conclusion . . .

The first six chapters of this book have shown clearly how a well-developed market strategy can enable a business to create huge amounts of shareholder value by focusing on disproportionate shares of the available market profit pools. This chapter has offered up a framework and process for keeping that value-creation process alive, vital, and fresh over very long time horizons, using market strategy, failure tolerance, and continuous improvement to create a new generation of extraordinary shareholder value creation success stories.

No, it's not easy. And no, it can't be done quickly. But, once in place and working well, it's a very durable form of sustainable competitive advantage—an organization that systematically, reliably, and efficiently finds and captures high-potential value-creation opportunities, learns from its mistakes, and continuously improves its ability to do it better the next time around.

Good market strategy plus continuous value growth and corporate renewal equals extraordinary value-creation performance.

CHAPTER 8

Value-Maximizing the Existing Business

Let's say you own a business that manufactures doors. Over the past few decades you have watched your market grow steadily at approximately the same rate as the economy, and you have succeeded in growing your cash flow at a little faster rate, thanks to some superb competitive plays. The trouble is, you see there is little room left for cash flow growth, since few competitors are left and your business now accounts for a sizable chunk of the market. How do you increase business value?

A large proportion of today's economy is represented by businesses delivering well-established, relatively simple (often mundane) products and services. In many cases, their cash flow growth prospects are limited by some very practical constraints, such as the capacity of the economy itself. The secret to growing value in these businesses, indeed in other businesses too, is to identify the source of value within the organization and exploit it.

And that exploitation has two parts to it; focusing on the source of value—to the extent other areas may actually be jettisoned—and extending that source of value into new revenue areas. For our door manufacturer, known for snug-fitting doors that never have problems, that might mean something like pulling out of the hinge business, and outsourcing door trim-making and other functions. It also raises the question whether a new line of products is warranted, to exploit the business's strengths, perhaps including kitchen cabinets, closets, and even windows.

This chapter reviews how this can be done in a way that maximizes value creation. First, we look at the history of specialization, and how it will evolve going forward. We then outline the key aspects of an exercise to track down the source of value within the business, and discuss ways to release the capital and management distraction tied up in nonvalue-add areas. Finally, we turn to how the value source can be successfully propagated into other areas, understanding what is at the core of where value emanates, and exploiting it to deliver cash flow from adjacent and distant revenue streams.

Business Specialization

Specialization is not a new concept, tracing its roots back to times when mankind first started to live in communities and took advantage of the efficiencies that came with having different individuals focus on specific aspects of daily life. Although things have come a long way since then, the basic drivers for specialization remain, and our economic system continues to reward specialization—when it adds value.

Industry and Specialization

Every business associates itself with an industry, which is itself a form of specialization. As time progresses, all industries deaggregate, such that there is further specialization. Take the case of one of the latest industries to emerge, the computer industry. In just the past 30 years, it has gone from nonexistence to spawning a range of new subindustries and markets. Figure 8.1 illustrates the process as it evolved in the computer industry over each decade.

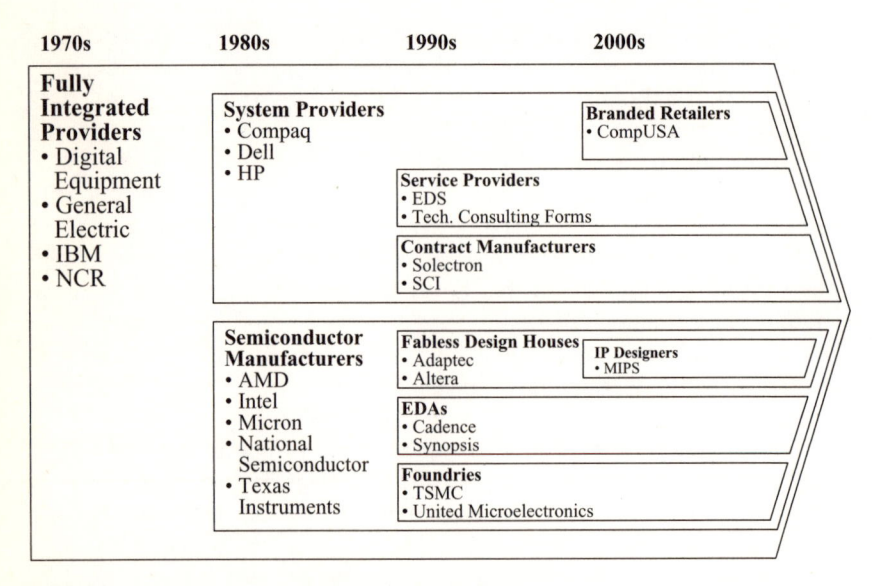

1970s	1980s	1990s	2000s
Fully Integrated Providers • Digital Equipment • General Electric • IBM • NCR	**System Providers** • Compaq • Dell • HP		**Branded Retailers** • CompUSA
		Service Providers • EDS • Tech. Consulting Forms	
		Contract Manufacturers • Solectron • SCI	
	Semiconductor Manufacturers • AMD • Intel • Micron • National Semiconductor • Texas Instruments	**Fabless Design Houses** • Adaptec • Altera	**IP Designers** • MIPS
		EDAs • Cadence • Synopsis	
		Foundries • TSMC • United Microelectronics	

FIGURE 8.1 Deaggregation of the Computer Industry

Source: Adapted from *Collaboration: Using eHubs to Create Value in High-Tech* (IBM Business Consulting Services, 2002); Business Intelligence Associates LLC.

What started as few vertically integrated solution providers, making everything needed to create those bulky machines called computers in the 1970s, has gradually broken up into parts. Increasingly, the large, vertically integrated providers simply ceded parts of their solution to entrepreneurs that could do better—not a difficult eventuality, and likely an inevitable one.

What drives the process? Of course, in many cases a new industry has to overcome the hurdle of creating entirely new inputs, such as disk drives and semiconductors, since there aren't established markets or players providing them already. This is a tough test for new markets, since the only way forward is for the original pathfinding industry players to take on the creation of these new inputs for themselves. However, over time, those players discover that many of these inputs are not areas where they add value, and they increasingly turn to others that will specialize, as in the case of the semiconductor and other industries in Figure 8.1.

This process of deaggregation is simply part of industry evolution. One of the most vivid examples has been in the enormous automotive industry, where Ford was the first to adopt production-line techniques and found itself making a huge variety of vehicle parts; at one point it operated a factory that was the largest covered area on the planet. It needed its parts to work together reliably, and found that the trade-offs favored having control of making the parts internally, over the potential benefits of having suppliers compete over the business. As time passed, however, automotive parts became less of a novelty in design and manufacturing, and communications between business entities improved. As a result, increasingly larger parts of the automotive manufacturing process have been peeled off to parts supplier companies, to a point now where the big manufacturers are primarily brand and design houses that do final assembly. Even these functions are farmed out on occasion.

The point is, specialization is a natural part of evolution, and businesses that are ahead of the process are likely to reap the rewards faster than the competition. Indeed, looking forward, powerful forces are accelerating the specialization process, as we see next.

The Future of Specialization

So what does specialization give a business? The answer is really very brief: Increased focus allows a greater depth in capabilities, which in turn helps in delivering a better result *in the focus area*. And the customer has a tendency to reward increased value (perceived or real) by passing on increased monetary value, whether that is in the form of a premium price or increased demand.

In the past, specialization has been significantly oriented around tangible products and discretely defined services—such as electronic components or systems implementation, respectively, in the case of computer manufacturing. That limitation has been greatly pushed back since the mid-1990s with the emergence of the Internet. Suddenly, every business in the economy was provided an easy way to share large amounts of detailed information in real time. The implications of this watershed development did not go unnoticed, and within a few years, vast amounts of software development resources were applied to business-to-business (B2B) applications, providing a multitude of ways businesses can communicate with each other.

One type of these B2B applications is the value-added community (VAC), a technology-based network that enables automated coordination and trading between businesses. The impact on specialization and business structure is profound; for the first time it is possible to maintain a much higher degree of information intimacy with business partners—opening the door to a far deeper degree of specialization. At last, it is now possible for businesses that are good at making doors to have access to the best in human resources management, the most advanced information systems, and superefficient procurement processes—to name a few.

Over the course of the next 20 years, businesses focusing on these and other operational functions will emerge and grow rapidly, using the Internet as a conduit into the heart of your business. The likely impact of these phenomena was first published in *MetaCapitalism* by David Schneider and Grady Means (Wiley, 2000):

> *Businesses are increasingly recognizing that others have superior infrastructure and/or expertise for functions such as internal accounting, HR management, or the like, and are reaching out to them. An entirely new level of service provision has opened up, and as the communications technology advances, the extent of the functional outsourcing will deepen—driving the business to focus on its core value-add more tightly.*

Figure 8.2 contains a graphical representation on the changes businesses will undergo—an adaptation from the original chart in *MetaCapitalism*.

The traditional, capital intensive business of today, represented on the left of the chart, comprises brand and management functions at the top of the pyramid, lots of capital investment at the wide bottom of the pyramid, and support services off to its side. In the future configuration, on the right of the chart, the capital-intensive business is replaced by a business focused intently on brand and solution management; other aspects of the business are farmed out, thanks to a raft of new service businesses, enabled by VACs that leverage Internet-based technology. Each of these new businesses has its own brand and solution-development focus, honing its skills and tuning its prices in a competitive environment.

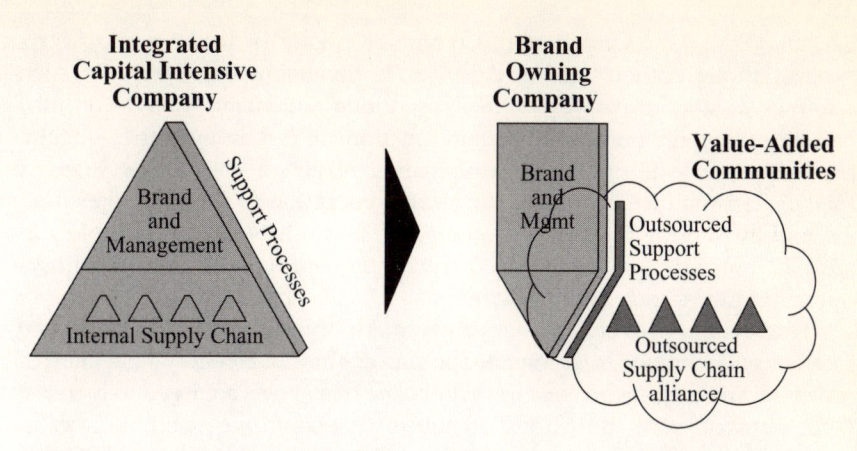

FIGURE 8.2 Deaggregation and Specialization in Business in the Internet Age
Source: Adapted from *MetaCapitalism* by David Schneider and Grady Means (Wiley, 2000). Reprinted with permission of John Wiley & Sons, Inc.

In fact, this sequence has already begun. Value-added communities have started to be stitched together in three forms: *e-markets*, which are independent service providers that connect and conduct B2B transactions in industries; *e-hubs*, standardized interfaces into the information systems of major players in an industry; and plain old *middleware*, software that connects one company's system to another's.

The first model, e-markets, emerged with great fanfare during the bubble just before the turn of the century, and fell into disrepute as a result of an economically irrational rush to grab Internet land and the implosion that followed in 2000. Since then, a more mature evolution has proceeded at a more thoughtful pace. The second model, e-hub, has taken off rapidly since the turn of the century, thanks to there being so many industries with large dominating players. These players have the market power and technological resources to create ecosystems around their businesses. As they farm out whole functions, large service providers, such as EDS, IBM, and others, are extending out to provide those functions as new service areas (call centers, outsourced IT, and accounting are relatively recent examples) and have created standards to plug into customer information systems. Finally, the third model, middleware, has also been developing rapidly, and enterprise software providers have defined their own connections standards, such as SAP's NetWeaver and Oracle's Fusion. As software increasingly becomes a subscribable service, fully standardized connections between companies will only become more prevalent.

Despite the bursting of the bubble and the thinning of their ranks, e-markets have survived and appear to be prospering, such as cc-hubwoo,

E2open, E-Markets, and Perfect Commerce. Many of these are industry-specific, though others exist that provide horizontal marketplaces (for such offerings as administrative supplies, recruiting, and many others). E-hubs have supplanted e-markets in certain functions in certain industries—again, predominantly where there are dominating players in the market, such as Intel in semiconductors and Chevron in the energy sector. Further, outsourcing and off-shoring (that is, outsourcing offshore) have taken off rapidly in the past ten years, with the rise of such companies as Wipro and Infosys operating out of India and elsewhere.

However the evolution actually unfolds, one thing is for sure: The Internet will continue to accelerate the process and degree to which internal functions are outsourced. And as that occurs, businesses are freed to increase their focus on core value-adds. In the next section, we outline a way to proactively manage this evolution—to delineate areas within the business and assess the extent to which they either add value or could be better executed by others.

Focusing on Your Sources of Value

As more business deaggregation options emerge, and as competitive and capital markets' pressure intensifies, businesses will increasingly be driven to focus resources and capital. The fundamental question is, what is your business's real value-add, and what is better done by others?

What's Your Value-Add?

First, value-add comes in many types and shapes, often the results of several organizational functions. Second, value-add changes over time, within industries, markets, and players; as value is created, its sources are found, and natural market forces bring in competition—which tends to normalize the returns from the original source of value. Third, value sources arise out of hard differences, such as physical assets and intellectual property, *and* soft differences, such as organizational culture and management style. With all of this possible variability, it is no surprise that the value-add in business is highly unique—though perhaps with common underlying themes that remain somewhat consistent over time. Each of these three come into play in the following well-known instances, in different ways and to varying degrees:

- *Management style and business portfolio management.* These are not common sources of value-add by any means, though they are two traits that are always associated with General Electric's shareholder value performance over the past couple of decades, certainly since the start of Jack Welch's tenure. General Electric is focused on creating value, and many shareholder value maximization techniques and tools are well deployed throughout the organization, together with that other essential ingredient—philosophical alignment with the idea of maximizing shareholder value. Notably, one critical aspect of the GE management regime is in proactively managing innovation and corporate renewal for value (briefly discussed in Chapter 7).

- *Unique and effective business processes.* Dell Computer has an interesting value-add model; in its case, a flexible manufacturing system delivers tailor-made PCs on demand. In its market, most customers are not willing to pay much more than the market price, so what limited differentiation is possible (such as directly purchased, tailor-made PCs) will only get share, not much of a premium price. For Dell, however, that's fine, since its flexible manufacturing system is also very low cost and results in very attractive profit margins, in an industry that has almost none whatsoever!
- *Trendy lifestyle.* Despite being a computer manufacturer, Apple is actually a very successful example of a purveyor of image and desired lifestyle. Apple achieves this through careful management of its brand and customer experience—from the white iPod and earphone silhouette image on advertising billboards, to its post-sales community management on the Web and in other forums. The result is that customers are willing to pay substantive price premiums, far in excess of the relatively heightened marketing expenses it takes, in order to garner the Apple image and experience.
- *Premium product.* The classic representation of the premium brand, Rolls Royce, delivers the best quality and expression of exclusivity in the automotive business. As with Apple, customers are willing to pay substantive price premiums—though in the case of Rolls Royce, it is not clear that the heightened manufacturing expense is covered by that substantive price premium.
- *Cost efficiency–based culture and careful market targeting.* Southwest's airplane operations efficiency is renowned well outside the boundaries of its own industry for its low cost relative to the major airlines. When it applies this together with a targeting of price-sensitive customers in relatively high-priced routes, Southwest delivers superior financial returns. Notably, a large amount of its operating efficiency is gained by its high-energy and highly flexible corporate culture—which dramatically reduces labor costs and improves process efficiencies.
- *Product reliability and brand.* A significant amount of the value in Kellogg's cereal is in its brand and how it is perceived by the market; consumers are drawn to it as a safe and reliable purveyor of food, and are willing to pay more for it. That's not to say that there is not additional value in the cereal itself, its flavor and the rest, because there obviously is—however, the brand and its management in the market clearly has a sizable role to play

These are just a few, albeit highly successful, value-add models. Obviously, there are as many models as there are businesses; some may be similar between competitors in the same market, and others may be very different. Every business has its own, whether it is explicitly or accurately recognized or not. And while an explicit and accurate recognition is essential for the value-add to be proactively managed, it is not easy to accurately recognize it from the inside. How would you characterize your business's value-add?

Where's the Value Coming From?

What can be said about organizational value-add is that, by definition, it always has a dollar value associated with it. The trick is to figure out where the sources are, and what their dollar value-adds are too.

INTRODUCING VALUE CENTERS This is where a mapping of *value centers* and *cost centers* can contribute. Most business leaders and information systems take a vertical view of business performance, at best—reporting performance in terms of offerings or lines of business. An example of this might be performance reporting on the whiskeys, tequilas, and perhaps a couple of other product lines in a broad-based beverages business. In the value centers model, a combined vertical and horizontal view of the business is taken, specifically to localize and measure value creation within the organization. While it does not paint a complete picture of *how* the business creates value, or *what* that value is, it can certainly help pinpoint *where* it is coming from. To a large extent, that is as much about where value does not come from as it is about where it does. Figure 8.3 illustrates how value centers were delineated in one well-known beverages business.

The departure from traditional vertical performance measures is obvious. The key functional elements that made up the business's processes were called out as separate, horizontal organizations, in line with where value and cost centers were delineated. Any part of an organization can be defined as a value center if it has a replicable counterpart available as a service outside the business. The test of whether an organization part can be a value center is in the availability of a price; if an organization part, such as a service called "Production" in Figure 8.3, can be replicated by an external entity for a contractible price, it can be considered a value center. Conversely, if no external entity is willing to quote a price to replicate a specific part of the organization, it has to be classified as a cost center, and its costs are attributed to value centers as appropriate. This does not mean cost centers don't add value, only that their value has to be incorporated into other areas for purposes of measurement.

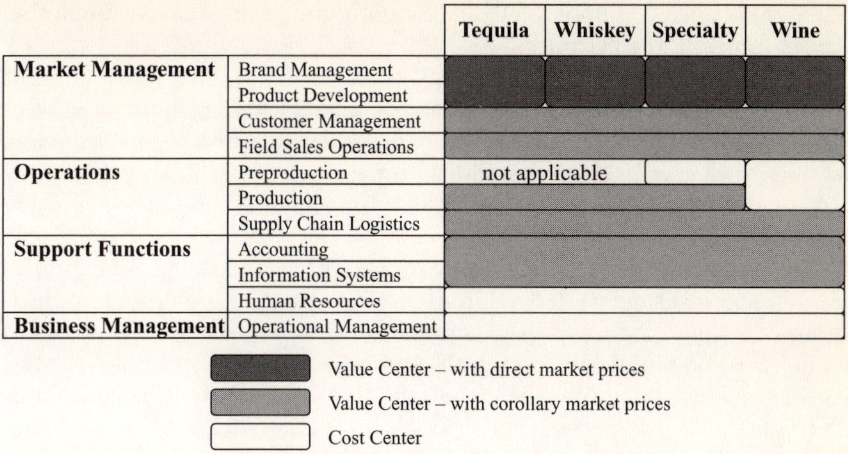

		Tequila	Whiskey	Specialty	Wine
Market Management	Brand Management	■	■	■	■
	Product Development	■	■	■	■
	Customer Management	▒	▒	▒	▒
	Field Sales Operations	▒	▒	▒	▒
Operations	Preproduction	not applicable	▒	□	▒
	Production	▒	▒	▒	□
	Supply Chain Logistics	▒	▒	▒	▒
Support Functions	Accounting	▒	▒	▒	▒
	Information Systems	▒	▒	▒	▒
	Human Resources	□	□	□	□
Business Management	Operational Management	□	□	□	□

■ Value Center – with direct market prices
▒ Value Center – with corollary market prices
□ Cost Center

FIGURE 8.3 Value Centers Map of a Specialty Beverages Producer
Source: Business Intelligence Associates LLC.

In the case of the beverages example in Figure 8.3, large portions of the business's processes were available in external markets. The well-established external service markets were in customer management functions (including inbound order taking and record keeping) and production (for the spirits products only). The less-developed external service markets included those for field sales (but existed in other consumer products segments), supply chain logistics (major freight firms were just starting logistics offerings), and accounting and IT systems (also just starting). Of course, the combined brand management and related product development functions set the price for their respective finished products and were value centers in their own rights.

Two of the four cost centers in this example were directly attributable to their respective brand management value centers: preproduction for the specialty spirits business (the key ingredient was especially grown in the U.S. South) and production for the wine business (which couldn't be separated from the brand). The remaining cost centers, HR and management operations, were charged to value centers according to their consumption of resources.

VALUE CREATION PLOTS The process to determine the value creation of each value center is very similar to that used to evaluate internal profit pools, described in Chapter 4. Moreover, if internal profit pools have already been delineated and measured, the effort to get a value center view is an easy case of parsing the numbers a little differently and getting directly applicable price quotes or market prices.

In most mature outsourcing markets, there is a relatively standardized pricing scheme. For example, for spirits manufacturing, there is a baseline unit volume price for production, and then several add-ons for aging, storage, and various bottling options. In most cases, a satisfactory price accuracy can be achieved to give an order-of-magnitude sense of where value creation is driven in the business.

With pricing and revenue known for each value center, and expenses and capital investments derived from recasting internal profit pool information, economic profit can be determined. Figure 8.4 sets out the areas of value creation and destruction in the beverages business example. No surprise, the key source of value creation in this case was the specialty spirits component of the business; this value creation was focused on its brand management activities, and possibly the raw material preproduction input for which a substitute could not be found.

Also of little surprise was the fact that the wine business was a net drain. However, the additional focus provided by drawing a boundary around the wine value center cleared up questions about the extent that logistics was

Economic Profit
($ Millions)

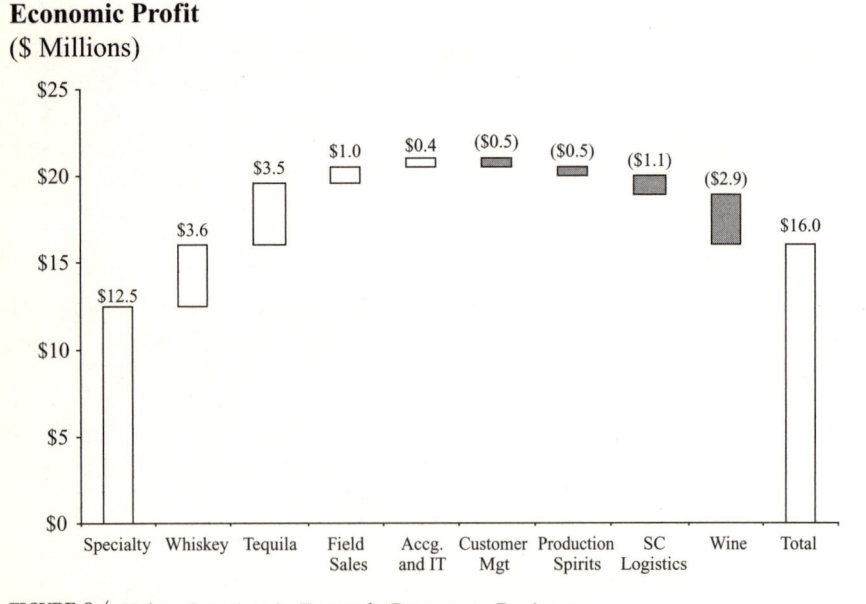

Specialty	$12.5
Whiskey	$3.6
Tequila	$3.5
Field Sales	$1.0
Accg. and IT	$0.4
Customer Mgt	($0.5)
Production Spirits	($0.5)
SC Logistics	($1.1)
Wine	($2.9)
Total	$16.0

FIGURE 8.4 Value Creation in Example Beverages Business
Source: Company reports, Business Intelligence Associates LLC.

dragging its performance down. Unfortunately, the vineyard (preproduction) could not be separated from brand management, since the wine itself came from a name-brand location, and so a more specific view of the value drain's location could not be acquired.

The new information on the supply chain logistics function was very interesting to the business. Not only were the price bids of logistics outsourcers lower than the cost of the internal organization, but the level of service could be dramatically improved and the price would still be lower than internal costs. The logistics provider boasted a degree of scale that was clearly unachievable internally, resulting in bulk scale economies and information systems that were very sophisticated—and highly attractive to the business's customers and suppliers. There was a very real chance that additional market areas would become available as a direct result of switching to the logistics outsourcer, whose costs would be charged as a cost center to each brand management value center.

Improvements in accounting and IT costs and service were also readily available in the market from several vendors. The relationships and effectiveness of the internal field sales operation, however, was a substantive contributor—though there were indications that as that service market evolved, a more capable sales operation could be bought that would deliver increased sales in the years ahead.

Is It Worth Focusing?

The scale of the organizational changes contemplated in the preceding discussion is monumental. Of course, existing businesses would be wise not to move headlong into such changes, though it has to be noted that many new businesses, whether they be start-ups or spin-offs, are increasingly adopting highly outsourced business models from the get-go.

With that said, there is unlikely to be much time before competitive forces will drive these new organizational structures into most industries. While there are always risks to being the first to move, there are invariably good reasons to be the first. While sizable changes of this type are rare, they open up a new dimension in the competitive field and represent an opportunity to boost market position. To a great extent, there is risk that inaction will actually jeopardize the existing business. Any player dragging around a disadvantaged value or cost center will be vulnerable to competitors without that disadvantage. The value maximizing approach suggests you either become competitive in that area or outsource it. Of course, getting competitive in another area is a substantive commitment, carrying its own costs with it, and should be considered very seriously.

ADDRESS MARKET AND OPERATIONAL FACTORS Generally, there are three areas of concern for existing businesses as they consider their outsourcing/organizational configuration options:

1. *Performance uncertainty.* Questions over the level of performance, likely from an external service provider, are always the greatest and loudest concern. Curiously, these questions are also the easiest to resolve, in terms of quick and accurate answers, by simply obtaining historical performance measures and referencing with existing users. In almost every type of outsourced service, one of the basic issues that has to be specified is the *level of service*—your agreed, guaranteed minimum performance needs in a set of explicit performance measures. A tangible example of this is in customer management functions, where call center wait times and resolution rates are specified contractually. The focus, scale, and brand management of outsourcing service providers almost always results in them being able to deliver a far superior level of service for a given spend.
2. *Loss of control.* In terms of managerial control, the major concern is that, in a crunch, the service provider will deprioritize your business's needs in favor of those of others. Another worry is that production line changes or new product introductions cannot be executed with as much management focus and flexibility when crossing a boundary to an external entity. These concerns are valid and among the most difficult to resolve. They are not impossible, however, and the solution is often down to the experience of the service provider and the creativity of the management team. For example, small-scale pilot lines have been used to limit issues in product introductions, and tightened adherence to plans have reduced the need for flexibility in production line changes, and have actually enhanced overall performance. A tapered integration may also work, where significant amounts of in-house capability are maintained, while more standardized elements are outsourced.
3. *Transition problems.* Transitioning a business process to an external service provider is never easy, and anxieties are heightened when mission-critical processes are involved. This concern is often the principal barrier to overcome, and it is a legitimate fear; internal transitions are difficult enough. While many of the same issues in the previous two areas are applicable, the remedies are not as well developed; again, the experience and track record of the service provider are the primary tools to gauge the risks and rewards.

These three issue areas are substantive and warrant careful planning and thought. However, in most cases there is as much to be gained in switching to external specialists, in terms of improved performance, as there is in cost avoidance.

- *Deeper intellectual property* relating to the service, such as knowing the most effective and efficient approach to managing internal accounting or handling inbound call center inquiries.
- *More advanced approaches* and techniques, gained by having the scale to invest into developing new approaches, and the incentive to do so through market competitive forces.
- *More sophisticated capabilities*, gained by having the scale to invest in assets, such as IT systems that make communications easier and processes more effective.
- *Broader relationships* with other service providers and perhaps your (target) customers.

Naturally, a move to adopt a more focused business model is best achieved in measured phases, programmed to minimize risks to ongoing operations and to maximize potential gains. Typically, the first components taken on have limited potential to negatively impact the business in the event of failure, particularly if they are phased in and show solid value-creation potential. With this approach, management gets experience in transitioning to an outsourcing model, while also getting solid results in the immediate term. In the case of the beverages business example, the business first switched to an external customer management services provider, subsequently moving the logistics out; the highly mission-critical spirits production function was reserved until last, while the wine business was disposed of altogether.

DETERMINE THE ECONOMICS OF THE NEW CONFIGURATION Of course, before making the decision to change the business's configuration in any way, the economics of the new configuration need to be estimated to make sure it is worthwhile. This extends beyond cost savings, where the external provider's service is obtained at a price lower than the cost of the internal function, to include measurable changes to the performance in other functional areas as a result of the improvements in performance. An example of this could be improved sales as a result of using a contracted sales force, or reduced production costs as a result of more effective information from the systems of an external IT systems provider.

Extending Your Sources of Value

Perhaps just as important as the capital invested in noncore, low or no value-add areas of the business, is the ongoing investment of management time in those areas. Indeed, it is not unusual for business leaders to devote as much as half their time addressing issues in such areas; although they have little value-add, they tend to demand attention precisely because they draw on resources that are noncore, yet they have to get done.

The question is, what would be the return on those management and other resource investments if they were devoted to identifying and expanding into new areas with the same level of returns as your high value-add areas? In the two preceding sections an important aspect of that thinking was brought to the table: isolating and measuring areas of value-add. From here we step through the three-part sequence to extending your sources of value-add:

1. Characterize your business' value-add, specifically.
2. Identify other markets where that value-add would be suitable.
3. Project the outcomes likely from deploying that value-add into those new areas—economic returns and competitor reactions (and the time to when economic returns are brought down).

Characterizing Your Value-Add

It is not unusual for businesses to have a firm idea of their unique capabilities, and for them to be investing in those areas, only to have a value center review show that those areas actually drive little economic value-add. A useful example of this existed in the apparel industry, where the prevailing wisdom was that raw materials acquisition and garment manufacturing was a highly specialized function, requiring great skill and a tight integration with design. Over time, however, one by one, vendors began to separate out garment manufacturing and, despite its need for precise material alignment, cutting and stitching, and farmed it out to manufacturers thousands of miles away—in the Far East. Those that moved first, including Nordstrom, The Gap, and others in the United States, found ways to neutralize the obvious production complications and benefited from dramatically enhanced business economics. They were also better positioned to invest in design and brand management which, in turn, delivered additional economic benefits.

By contrast, Dell is an example of a business that understood the source of its economic value-add from the outset, the cost advantage of its production system, and has maintained a continuous focus on it. With costs vastly lower than those of competitors as a result, but with end prices only a little lower or approximately the same, the production system drives immense value creation—rather than brand or anything else.

In short, the first step to exploiting your value-add is to properly characterize it—looking beyond the typical focus on rare capabilities and mission-critical activities, to include actual economic rewards. That characterization of areas of value-add needs to be explicit, and it must cite specific elements, including assets in the business (from intellectual property to land and its location), skills and capabilities, and perhaps cultures and outlooks.

In the case of the beverages business described earlier, the key value-add areas were in the specialty beverage, including its raw material source and the management of the three spirits brands. Since brand management and production in the wine line of business were inseparable, it wasn't clear whether the brand management skill was lacking in that market, or whether the market's price simply couldn't support production costs for that particular product.

In terms of this business replicating its brand management skills into new revenue streams, there is evidence that much can be systematized (such as analyzing and modeling consumer behaviors); Procter & Gamble has a globally recognized reputation for doing just that. Indeed, the beverages business examined earlier appears to have already succeeded in transitioning beyond its specialty beverage into whiskeys and tequilas; a strategy that focuses on spirits brand management warrants serious consideration. There are many precedents of source strengths being extended beyond their original form; Chanel extended its image proposition from perfume to fashion, Calvin Kline did the reverse, and Saab extended its design and engineering prowess from fighter jets to automobiles. Furthermore, the specialty beverage's unique raw material source may itself be applied to create new revenue streams. However, it is reasonably clear that, for our example beverages business, expanding its spirits production capability—such as creating a new outsourcing business out of it—will deliver much lower returns, and is likely to be highly distracting for the organization and its leaders.

With knowledge of what the value-add is and where it comes from, the outstanding issue that remains is, in which market areas must that value-add be applied?

What Markets Can Use That Value-Add?

The tools needed to answer this question are outlined in Chapter 5—including evaluating market profit pools, understanding where value is created in each, and assessing strategic fit between a business and a prospect market, using the business model assessment framework. With the insights provided by a value center review, the source of value creation in the existing business is known relatively precisely, and the potential for further value creation can be targeted very specifically.

The most curious effect of having insight into the source of value in your business is that the scope of markets eligible for targeting assessment both expands and narrows. It expands as the realization sets in that the business is actually very different from its historical view of itself. In terms of the previous example, it is not a beverages business, but instead it is a purveyor of branded lifestyle and personal image. The scope of target markets also narrows as the business recognizes that a fully integrated business system is actually undesirable, with its associated distraction from the core value-add, inefficient use of assets and resources, and relatively lower performance in comparison to services provided externally. Again, in terms of the beverages example, the business can now take on brands, perhaps even unconnected with spirits, but not necessarily all the capital-intensive pre- and postproduction capabilities.

Expanding into New Areas

This broadened and narrowed view of markets becomes a starting point for the market profit pool evaluation process outlined in Chapter 5. It also leads to a renewed market strategy formulation process, incorporating the new business model (with focus on high value-add functions and markets) and evaluating opportunities and business propositions with these improved economics in mind.

APPENDIX A

Unwinding, Line Item by Line Item

Given the broad nature of the process to unwind accounting numbers and get granular profit information, we wanted to pass on an additional layer of depth on the issues likely to be encountered. Since each line item has its own set of peculiarities, our look at those issues is also line by line. We use the structure of GAAP-based financial statements as a sort of road map, as set out on the left-hand side of Figure A.1, which summarizes the key treatments needed by each line item in the unwinding process.

This Appendix first discusses the issues involved in unwinding revenues, then moves on to address expenses and capital investments and charges.

Revenue

As we saw in Chapter 1, revenue (top-line) factors have the greatest proportional impact on cash flow and, since no other line item is more significant, we must make very sure we get the dollars apportioned accurately. No matter the market or industry, this is the most important line item, and every effort is needed to get to it right.

Fortunately, in most situations, GAAP mandates a very close tracking of all monetary receipts, and a good paper trail is required to facilitate effective auditing. In addition, the information systems that capture revenue information retain it in a way that it can be sliced very finely, typically by at least two of the four basic views we are interested in (offering, customer, channel, and geography). Although such fine granularity might not make its way to financial reporting systems, it is very likely to be accessible in various sales or other revenue management databases; and we have found almost universally that a little work here results in a very robust set of revenue information.

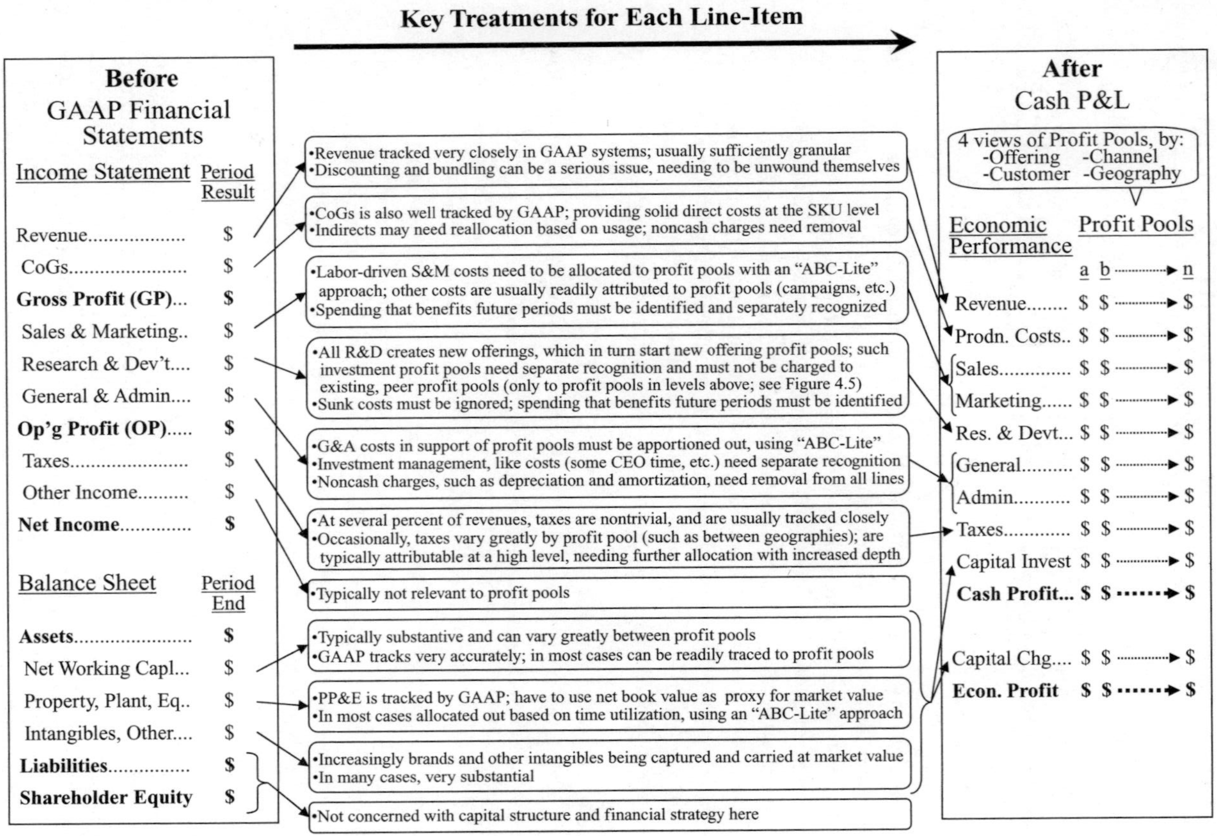

Key Treatments for Each Line-Item

Before — GAAP Financial Statements

Income Statement — Period Result
- Revenue............ $
- CoGs................ $
- **Gross Profit (GP)**... $
- Sales & Marketing... $
- Research & Dev't... $
- General & Admin... $
- **Op'g Profit (OP)**... $
- Taxes................ $
- Other Income...... $
- **Net Income**....... $

Balance Sheet — Period End
- Assets................ $
- Net Working Capl... $
- Property, Plant, Eq... $
- Intangibles, Other... $
- Liabilities............ $
- Shareholder Equity... $

Key treatments (line-by-line):
- Revenue tracked very closely in GAAP systems; usually sufficiently granular
- Discounting and bundling can be a serious issue, needing to be unwound themselves
- CoGs is also well tracked by GAAP; providing solid direct costs at the SKU level
- Indirects may need reallocation based on usage; noncash charges need removal
- Labor-driven S&M costs need to be allocated to profit pools with an "ABC-Lite" approach; other costs are usually readily attributed to profit pools (campaigns, etc.)
- Spending that benefits future periods must be identified and separately recognized
- All R&D creates new offerings, which in turn start new offering profit pools; such investment profit pools need separate recognition and must not be charged to existing, peer profit pools (only to profit pools in levels above; see Figure 4.5)
- Sunk costs must be ignored; spending that benefits future periods must be identified
- G&A costs in support of profit pools must be apportioned out, using "ABC-Lite"
- Investment management, like costs (some CEO time, etc.) need separate recognition
- Noncash charges, such as depreciation and amortization, need removal from all lines
- At several percent of revenues, taxes are nontrivial, and are usually tracked closely
- Occasionally, taxes vary greatly by profit pool (such as between geographies); are typically attributable at a high level, needing further allocation with increased depth
- Typically not relevant to profit pools
- Typically substantive and can vary greatly between profit pools
- GAAP tracks very accurately; in most cases can be readily traced to profit pools
- PP&E is tracked by GAAP; have to use net book value as proxy for market value
- In most cases allocated out based on time utilization, using an "ABC-Lite" approach
- Increasingly brands and other intangibles being captured and carried at market value
- In many cases, very substantial
- Not concerned with capital structure and financial strategy here

After — Cash P&L

4 views of Profit Pools, by:
- Offering - Channel
- Customer - Geography

Economic Performance — Profit Pools (a, b, ... n)
- Revenue....... $ $ ... $
- Prodn. Costs.. $ $ ... $
- Sales............ $ $ ... $
- Marketing...... $ $ ... $
- Res. & Devt.... $ $ ... $
- General......... $ $ ... $
- Admin.......... $ $ ... $
- Taxes........... $ $ ... $
- Capital Invest. $ $ ... $
- **Cash Profit...** $ $ ... $
- Capital Chg.... $ $ ... $
- **Econ. Profit** $ $ ... $

FIGURE A.1 Key Elements to Unwinding Accounting Obfuscation

Source: Business Intelligence Associates LLC.

One of the most significant problems with revenue often arises with price discounting. Discounting comes in many forms and sizes, and from many sources. It appears as straight fractional price reductions, channel write-downs or incentives based on performance, channel compensation for some service or cost, end-user rebates, and an infinite range of other price management techniques. However, they all do the same thing—that is, reduce price.

In many markets, particularly where nondirect channels are less significant (such as in retailing, consumer services, etc.), discounting information is typically captured and tracked on revenue management systems directly. By contrast, businesses that need to manage powerful channel and other partners have more subtle and indirect paths, and what is really discounting is frequently included within sales expenses as channel partner reimbursements (such as in the beverage industry, where a considerable amount is spent on channel "training"). In these situations, discounting information is often authorized and managed through processes that are not recorded and tracked as part of the primary revenue management system. As a result, the two information sets are separated—which, for our purposes, is a significant problem, as the only way to then assemble an accurate picture of net prices is to map the information from two different sources, thereby introducing the specter of mismatches and double counting. It usually takes a little extra resources (and patience) to get to a satisfactory level of confidence in these situations. It is not necessary to bring all of this discounting to the revenue line, certainly not for purposes of developing profit pool P&L statements, though it is useful to recognize what is happening for use in market strategy formulation.

The second potential issue area in apportioning revenues to internal profit pools comes with sales that are significantly bundled. Bundling occurs mostly between offerings, such as a software product that is only sold with implementation services; though it can occur across customers, such as a software vendor that will only sell a highly differentiated package to a company if it buys the entire suite for use by users not related to the initial sale. Naturally, the vendor in both these cases will cite reasons of ensuring a "quality" solution (or something similar) as the driver for insisting on the bundled sale, though most economists will acknowledge that it is simply a technique for extending the differentiating or other power of one offering to heighten the price or demand of another.

It is this last point that provides the key in unlocking the pricing puzzle and apportioning the revenue to the components within the bundle: What would the situation be like without the bundle? With the answer to that question comes the approach for deciding how revenue and value get recognized and apportioned.

Expenses

The review in Chapter 4 primarily looks at the issues in unwinding accounting numbers that are common across expense line items, significantly dealing with apportionment—allocations and attributions. In the following review, we examine the more typical issues that are oriented around the unique needs and situations of the key expense line items, including cost of goods, sales and marketing, research and development, and general and administrative.

Cost of Goods

In terms of line-item magnitude, cost of goods (CoGs) runs the gamut—from less significant in pharmaceuticals, to dominating in many manufacturing sectors. Fortunately, per-unit manufacturing costs ("standard costs") are tracked in GAAP-driven accounting systems with as much detail and vigor as revenue. We typically find that the controls used, and the attributions and allocations made to create standard costs in compliance with GAAP, actually results in very accurate and usable information. As a rule, *direct* cost components—which include raw material costs and labor—are attributed under GAAP about as accurately as can be achieved, allowing a relatively easy task of building up a view by stock-keeping unit (SKU). Although the SKU happens to be an *offering* view, it is so fine that it actually can be used to build up CoGs charges in other views—by customer, channel, and geography—since differences within each of these views are captured by the need for unique SKUs. For example, if a unit sold to one customer is different from that sold to another, both units will be given their own SKU (if you are familiar with production, these each have their own bill of materials), such that the SKU information can simply be compiled for those customer sets separately.

Now, in some markets, it is more than likely for there to be differences in how *indirect* CoGs need to be allocated across various profit pools; and those indirect costs have a significant chance of being incorrectly allocated in GAAP-based reporting systems. Indirect costs include factory overhead costs, such as utilities, managers, and other facilities costs, and some labor costs. In many cases, the differences in these costs between profit pools are trivial, and expenses can be apportioned quite readily in line with the GAAP-based approach (units sold or revenue). However, in many markets there is a nontrivial difference in indirect cost consumption between profit pools, and additional effort is needed to properly allocate them. Any business with CoGs over 10 percent of revenue and a substantive indirect subcomponent needs to take a close look at the drivers of indirect costs, and decide whether the standard costs metric really is sufficiently precise. Such circumstances are not unusual in capital-intensive, high-value product markets, such as airplanes, trains, trucks, and others. In these cases, the ABC-lite techniques of Chapter 4 need to be brought to production operations to allocate the key indirect costs, using reasonably accurate cost driver metrics.

While there may be some room to debate the techniques used to allocate minor cost components—perhaps amortizing electricity costs or other facilities costs over units produced, or using first in, first out (FIFO) versus last in, first out (LIFO) for materials costs—as we saw in Chapter 4, these issues typically lead to relatively trivial inaccuracies for the purposes of strategic decision making.

Lastly, there is one other charge that is often captured in CoGs and can be quite significant (particularly in capital-intensive markets), which must be removed altogether: depreciation. As we saw in Chapter 3, noncash charges have no place in cash-profit views, and must be removed.

Sales and Marketing

In the majority of markets, both sales and marketing are significant expenses, relatively speaking, and need to be apportioned to internal profit pools with care. It is unfortunate then, that most businesses apply only the most basic techniques to apportion these two highly influential line items. Techniques usually involve the allocation of high-level cost information, from GAAP reporting systems, using either revenue or units sold as allocation drivers. This leads to very significant differences between reported and actual resource consumption.

Of course, the structure and treatment of sales and marketing (S&A) expenses varies substantively from one business segment to another, and is accounted for in as many ways as there are businesses and segments. Practices range from burying marketing within the sales line item, perhaps incorporating both sales and marketing subfunctions as sub–line items; to separating marketing out as a stand-alone line item, and incorporating sales with general and administrative to form SG&A.

Whatever the structure, sales and marketing expenses are classic candidates for apportionment using a blend of direct attribution and allocation with ABC-lite. Again, where S&M expenses are substantive, and where there is a heightened lack of clarity, allocation metrics must be carefully thought out and measured with care.

While very rare, there are two areas in marketing where this need comes to the fore: advertising and PR. Usually notable in magnitude, they are paid to outside entities, and are a benefit shared across profit pools. Sales expenses are similar in nature to marketing expenses and should be treated in a similar fashion, typically comprising labor pools (sales forces), some of which may be dedicated to particular regions or perhaps products.

They also include various support functions, for mailings or the production of collateral, and so on (indeed, a department or two may actually be shared with marketing).

Certainly, each channel will have its own management capability for maintaining retailer and value-added reseller (VAR) relationships, and likely its own distribution mechanism also. Given its somewhat unique characteristics, distribution and shipping needs its own metrics for cost apportionment—even if it is included in with sales—including weight, fractions of driver time, units shipped, or others. Again, throughout the sales function, labor time is a common and critical allocation metric, while direct expenses, such as sales campaigns and the like, need to be apportioned out using the same techniques outlined for marketing.

Research and Development

Looking back on it, it is no surprise that the Financial Accounting Standards Board (FASB) typically groups these two items together, and GAAP statements squeeze them under gross profit and place them with sales, marketing, and overhead. They could obviously tell that there was some notional difference between research and development (R&D), research being more likely to be independent of existing businesses, while development is more directly relevant to them and their ongoing performance. But in the end, they decided to simply sum it all up and expense it—after all, spending on research and development needs to be included, and at a company level there is really no other spot to put them.

For our purposes, however, we are keenly interested in business performance; we aim to find and grow positive-performing areas and to neutralize negative-performing areas. Since the key to real insights lies in granular information on economic returns, it is clear that R&D spending also needs to be disaggregated, properly characterized (as enhancing an existing business or embarking on a new one), and apportioned out to relevant profit pools.

We start by acknowledging there are two parts to "research and development." The first part, as it is commonly understood, is an investment to create a new offering, around which a business model will need to be jacketed—whether or not an existing business will be used as a base in some way. Development is often involved with leveraging new research or driving new research to commercialization, and in these circumstances is simply the later stages of the research effort that creates a new offering. In other circumstances, development means extending an existing business offering—although, notably, here also that extension is itself a new offering. Since in all cases a new offering is created, we must conclude that all R&D creates some level of new offering in the business, and so must be treated as an investment, as defined in Chapter 4.

This has significant implications; in short, all R&D spending must be apportioned to the boxes in black in Figure 4.3, since they are all creating new offerings at some level—either simply a new SKU, or perhaps an entirely new line of business. To borrow from the discussion in "Is That Spending or Investing?" in Chapter 4, management must have a very clear understanding of the reasons for each of their R&D investments, and with this must know where the business will benefit from that spending.

The approach that best apportions spending that is not directly attributable is as a proportion of total financial returns; for example, if two profit pools are set to benefit from a particular project, then its cost should be prorated to them based on the relative size of their net present values (NPVs)—of course, this can be somewhat circular. With that said, it does not really matter how the cost is apportioned out. If a key strategic decision rests on it, it only matters that the project can be supported as a positive return investment by at least one business proposition.

We can summarize the treatment of R&D with a clear set of rules:

- In every case, R&D investments are intended to create new offerings, whether new lines of business, a new SKU (to enhance competitive position, etc.), or something in between. As a result, R&D spending must be apportioned out *only* as an investment in, and as a creator of, *new offerings* (called *investment profit pools*).
- Research and development spending must only be incorporated into the economics of that profit pool which it benefits; an existing profit pool can only be charged with the R&D spending from directly subordinate new-offer profit pools, and not peer or superior new-offer profit pools.
- Research and development projects may have several areas of benefit, and so may need to be apportioned out. Attributable amounts are directly chargeable to their respective profit pools, while the remainder can be allocated based on proportion of expected total NPVs (there is much flexibility here, as long as the investment has a positive return by at least one proposition).

Finally, it is not unusual for R&D projects to deliver surprises. Where unplanned benefits are generated, the economics need to be reworked to reapportion the spending to areas of the business that benefit. Similarly, in cases where projected spending needs change materially, both the economics and apportionments need to be reworked to reflect new expectations.

General and Administrative

The category of general and administrative (G&A) is frequently used as a catch-all, and its composition therefore deserves close scrutiny. In its strictest sense, it should comprise only corporate oversight and administrative shared functions, and so should be relatively small in magnitude. However, many businesses opt to include a wide range of shared functions, well beyond administration (which usually includes legal, human resources, finance, etc.) to incorporate other shared services, including purchasing (better thought of as a component of CoGs, as part of operations), distribution (likely a component of sales), and others. This is particularly true in businesses with multiple business lines, where scale economics are being widely pursued with centralization, and the accounting system is simply following the organizational structure (and the organizational structure is reflecting something else altogether!).

The guiding principal in dealing with G&A is that it all needs to be categorized in two very different areas—areas that are, again, defined by resource usage. The first is spending on resources in support of ongoing business operations—much as we have looked at in the discussions so far in this appendix—and the second is spending on resources that are fulfilling an investment-management function being conducted by the corporate center. This second category represents the role executive managers have in deciding where investments will be made (or withdrawn) on behalf of shareholders—in much the same way as a fund manager.

In the case of the first category, resources are being expended in direct support of existing business management, and the funds they are consuming are being captured centrally for some reason. As we have seen, one of the most likely reasons is that the function in question serves multiple business lines, and political and management control factors make it more expedient for it to be accounted for independently. Whatever the reason, we need to apply ABC-lite techniques to distinguish between the two categories, and to further apportion profit pool–related spending to its respective profit pools. The investment management category mostly represents outgoings only, and is not a profit pool (as it does not have any business operations attached to a business model). It may have income, as a result of investing and other activities, though it does not have any ongoing business operations and needs to be separated out.

Let's see how this applies practically, with a walk through some common components of G&A. See Table A.1.

At a high level, seven or so functions are commonly included in G&A. The CEO and his staff will spend time in both categories: investment management and business operations management. Since the entire office is usually a nontrivial cost to the business, a good approximation of where time is spent is needed to apportion this consumption of resource.

Organizationally, the corporate development function is close to the CEO, though this does not mean that this cost should be apportioned to corporate investment management. Indeed, a significant swath of the resource use is in support of transactions initiated by, and to the benefit of,

TABLE A.1 G&A Components

Function	Category 1 Investment Management	Category 2 Business Support	Discussion
Corporate Development	Some here	Some here	Does deals for business lines and corporate; allocate to both profit pools and corporate.
Finance	Some here	Some here	Both external financial reports and internal management reports; allocate to profit pools and corporate.
Human Resources		Almost entirely here	Mostly supports operations but some corporate also; allocate mostly to profit pools.
Legal Counsel	Some here	Some here	Usually provides legal support for business units and corporate; allocate to profit pools and corporate.
Office of the CEO	Should be half here	Half here	Deployed to investment management and operations; allocate to both profit pools and corporate.
Purchasing, Distribution, other shared operations		Almost entirely here	Support operations exclusively; should be apportioned to CoGs, sales, etc., within profit pools.
Strategy	Some here	Some here	Strategy efforts are conducted by both business lines and corporate; allocate to profit pools and corporate.

subordinate business units, and so should be apportioned to those business profit pools. Again, an approximation of time spent provides all the accuracy needed to apportion out most costs created here, unless there are directly attributable initiatives. Similarly, strategy functions support management at corporate and business units levels, and also need apportioning to their relevant profit pools, though their organizational structure usually makes this easier since they are often in separate units, actually located within business units, or corporate or similar organizations.

It is finance, human resources, and, to a lesser extent due to its smaller size, legal counsel where much of the apportioning effort is really needed when dealing with G&A. However, since the magnitude of these costs should be far smaller in comparison with marketing and sales and R&D, there is a proportionately reduced need for accuracy; they are not likely to have a significant impact on results, nor the story that needs to be told in the end.

This leaves the operations-based shared services. Again, these are services that are not administrative and should actually be part of other line items and included in G&A since they are organizationally centralized, and/or are reporting around the lines of business direct to corporate. In short, their spending needs to be apportioned to their correct line item. For example, purchasing needs to be rejoined with CoGs, and apportioned out to the respective profit pool that it supports. Spending here is almost exclusively labor, and resources are consumed in proportion with staff time. More likely than not, the entire G&A obligation can be addressed in a single ABC-lite effort, using high-level staff time–based metrics to apportion all related expenses.

Taxes

Of course, taxes have a great impact on returns, and can have roots in very specific parts of the business (tending to vary by geography most, though sometimes by line of business in certain regulated industries). For example, for a business with net income (NI) at around 10 percent of revenues and a corporate tax burden in the region of 40 percent of NI, taxes equate to 4 percent of revenues—a nontrivial sum by any measure of profit. Any significant variances in tax obligations between internal profit pools will cause substantive differences in economic profit (EP) performance, making the root drivers of tax obligations a critical item to understand in this process.

Capital Investments and Charges

For the purposes of figuring out charges for invested capital, and expected capital investments, business assets can be approached in two different groups: working capital and capital assets. *Working capital* refers to moneys tied up in the immediate needs of the business, including inventory, accounts receivable, accounts payable (actually a liability, not an asset), and cash on hand. *Capital assets* refers to the large physical assets that most people immediately associate with the word *asset*.

We examine both in the following discussion, starting with net working capital, which is simply working assets less working liabilities (since it is the net amount that the business needs to have as a capital investment).

Net Working Capital

Net working capital tends to have a relatively direct relationship with specific transactions and offerings, making it relatively easier to apportion to internal profit pools. Here we take a look at each of its components in terms of the key issues involved in the capital and investment apportionment process.

In most business operations, the share of capital tied up in a specific profit pool's inventory is very closely related to that profit pool's cost of goods, and as a result, in most cases we are able to use share of CoGs as a proxy to apportion out inventory capital. With that said, there are exceptions to this relatively low-effort and somewhat simplified approach, and experienced eyes are needed to identify them.

One sign that a more accurate and increased effort is needed is where material for a subset of products is purchased in bulk (perhaps driven by long lead times or similar), or where there are substantive differences between labor and raw materials content in inventory asset values. Naturally, closer scrutiny to ensure an accurate apportionment is also needed when the total investment in inventory, as a proportion of total revenue, is relatively large.

The approach used to account for inventory is another area that warrants a query, since LIFO accounting tends to substantively undervalue inventory investments, assuming that the economies around the world continue to have inflation. Even with minor amounts of inflation, the cumulative effects of valuing inventory held based on acquisition prices of several years ago can become very significant. Curiously, several industries have the problem in reverse, such as in technology. A PC manufacturer, for example, has to routinely contend with the rapid decline in component prices; by the time product reaches store shelves, many months after component purchases are made, those same components have dropped dramatically in value (hard drive prices routinely drop 40 percent annually).

Accounts receivable (AR) also tends to be relatively straightforward to apportion out to profit pools, since the terms of receivables credit afforded to customers tends to be very standardized (such as having 30 days to pay, for example) and tightly controlled. In most circumstances, AR can be apportioned out to profit pools with a relatively high degree of accuracy simply in proportion to revenues. One indication that a more involved effort is needed is where a substantive difference in credit terms granted to different types of customers (such as longer due dates for larger customers) exists. Again, the greater the total investment in AR as a proportion of revenue, the greater the accuracy needed to ensure it is apportioned such as to reflect profit pool usage. A high-level review of the profile of customer offerings and geographies is always warranted.

Of course, accounts payable (AP) needs to be netted from working capital, as it obviously reduces capital investment needs. Accounts payable is mostly an issue of trade credit for purchases of materials and labor costs, and in most circumstances can simply be allocated to profit pools proportionate to a profit pool's cost of goods (similar to inventory, described earlier). However, if there is a substantive difference in the nature of credit received between profit pools, such as differences in the sorts of materials or labor used, then a more detailed approach to apportioning AP may be warranted to make sure the difference in capital costs is accounted for.

Usually, other working capital components can be treated in similar ways (that is, they can be apportioned using revenue or CoGs as allocation drivers). When that is not the case, they tend to be relatively inconsequential in magnitude and so even more inconsequential in terms of impact after they are apportioned out. An exception might be cash on hand; a simple coverage assessment can easily give a usable estimate of the profit pool's cash needs. In most businesses today, short-term securities are actually attributable to corporate and not to subordinate profit pools, as they are being built up in support of an acquisition, or in other cases the buildup is a safeguard for potential legal liabilities (attributable to a specific internal profit pool).

An interesting example was Microsoft's $60 billion buildup in cash and short-term investments over concerns with regulator antitrust action in the United States and in Europe. It seemed that the business wanted to clearly show the equity markets that it could build cash reserves far greater than any judgment that could be handed down, and so was a continuing and safe investment. In any event, the judgments were relatively minuscule when compared with the cash and short-term assets accumulated, representing less than a percentage point of corporate value.

Microsoft was an interesting example for a couple of reasons. First, the entire buildup was attributable to a few specific profit pools accused of the antitrust behavior and not to others (not, for instance, the Xbox or ERP businesses). Second, the short-term investments themselves actually earned their own returns, which then need to be netted out for the purpose of making capital charges in deductions of economic profit. It is not that unrealistic to envisage a situation where a profit pool that was forced into building a cash reserve in preparation of legal action might actually improve performance!

PP&E and Other Capital Investments

Capital assets primarily comprise two types: property, plant, and equipment (PP&E) and intangible assets. Importantly, one of the differences with working capital is the fact that there is likely to be some significant divergence between its current value and its cost. Why is it important to know asset current values? In simple terms, because our objective is to determine capital opportunity costs, such that the capital tied up in a profit pool can potentially be released and deployed elsewhere. Capital charges need to be based on what someone else is prepared to pay in exchange for the asset—its market value.

Let's take a look at the case of a semiconductor fabrication plant, referred to in the industry as a *fab*, dedicated to making a particular kind of chip, and fitting neatly into a well-defined internal profit pool at a product model level. Constructed five years ago for $200 million, let's say that the fab is now worth considerably less, potentially yielding $130 million in an open sale. Obviously, there is no sense in pretending the opportunity cost is applicable to $200 million, since that much capital could not actually be redeployed to another use. The right course of action is to base the capital charge on the capital that can be realized with a sale—or $130 million.

Unfortunately, hard assets (or PP&E) are not recorded and maintained at market values under GAAP. Instead, GAAP initially records PP&E assets at their acquisition cost and, except for land, depreciates them over a preset timeline. For our purposes, these depreciated values are mostly reasonably close to market values, and should be used for the purpose of determining PP&E capital charges on an exceptions basis; in any case, the value recorded by GAAP is the only one available. A high-level scan of significant-value assets is warranted to detect substantive discrepancies between net book and likely market values. In general, market values exceed book values, and so capital charges tend to be underestimated. Note that in situations where alternative paths forward are being considered, liquidation costs need to be factored in (especially in cases where the asset cannot be readily redeployed internally).

In terms of apportioning PP&E assets to profit pools, the basic driver is asset time utilization; that is, an asset needs to be apportioned to internal profit pools based on the proportion of time it serves in support of each. Of course, in service and other non-capital-intensive industries, PP&E is significantly aligned with the labor in expenses under gross profit (i.e., S&M, R&D, and G&A) and is quite accurately allocated out based on staff time and head count within each of the these separate areas. However, in capital-intensive industries a more significant effort may be needed to understand what the time utilization is of each production machine or other asset by each internal profit pool; significant time studies may be warranted for particularly high-value capital assets. Note that production changeovers drive significant machine downtime, and are often sizable value drains; machine time utilization is not always the best metric for capital apportionment.

Intangible assets have typically always represented a substantive capital investment, though in the past they have mostly been expensed when purchased or created within a business, or they were capitalized and amortized over 40 years or less when acquired in a business combination. That all changed in 2001 under FASB's Statement of Financial Accounting Standards (SFAS) 141 and 142 where, for the first time, assets that are not actually touchable were recognized; if acquired externally, such as in an ordinary purchasing transaction or a business combination, they are assigned a "fair value" and booked as assets. In addition, an asset is assigned a life span and amortized accordingly over that period, or in the case of an indefinite life span, such as goodwill, its value is tested annually for impairment (that is, providing for downward changes in value only). Unfortunately, similar intangibles created internally continue to be expensed at cost and will effectively not be recognized again—a glaring example of inconsistent treatment within accounting standards.

Such is the state of the information most likely to be available to determine capital charges for intangible assets. Again, much of it will be sufficient to determine capital charges, perhaps even better than PP&E information since it starts out with a fair value, though again, a high-level scan of major assets is warranted to detect substantive discrepancies between net book and market values.

As a side note, it is worth noting that GAAP is moving closer to fair market values, which is good news for investors and business managers alike. We are in a transition, however, and there are still a great many inconsistencies in how asset values are tracked, such as ignoring appreciation and expensing internally created intangibles. The moves are in the right direction. In the near term, unfortunately, we can only use what information we have; though it is not perfectly accurate, practitioners must characterize the cost of capital employed, even if today's GAAP tends to undervalue assets (and so undercharges economic profit).

Finally, it is worth adding that for the most part, the accuracy needed in apportioning capital investments to profit pools is generally lower than that needed for the cost line items discussed here, such as CoGs, S&M, R&S, and G&A. There are two reasons for this. First, the charges that are actually made to profit pools are relatively smaller than those other line items, since only a fraction of the asset is charged (remember, the average opportunity cost for equity capital is 12 percent annually, and debt interest is approximately 6 percent). Second, the difference in assets apportioned to one profit pool versus another is much less than the differences in apportioning expenses such as CoGs, S&M, R&S, and G&A; the impact of a more accurate apportioning is considerably smaller as a result.

APPENDIX B

The Monte Carlo Simulation

The Monte Carlo simulation is a tool recommended in this book to figure out the uncertainty of business values, based on the uncertainties in the forecasts of all the inputs to the business, such as future price, volume demand, share, and other.

What Problem Does It Solve?

Intrinsic business value is a powerful measure with which business leaders can guide their companies. However, the discounted cash flow (DCF) tools that deliver expected value use forecasts of several variables (for example, price or quantity) and, as with anything that deals with the future, they are subject to uncertainty. Forecasts are typically given in terms of an expected path a variable will take over time, but the truth is there is a band of uncertainty on either side of that path (usually set to capture 95 percent of most likely estimates), and the characteristics of that uncertainty band are unique to that variable, its surrounding conditions, and even the time.

Now, a variable's uncertainty, say future price uncertainty, results in an overall uncertainty for the business's intrinsic value. Unfortunately, input and output uncertainties, though related, have very different profiles. When there are several input variables, the ability to use mathematics to quickly and reliably profile the output value uncertainty drops precipitously. Here, the Monte Carlo simulation steps in with quick, easy, intuitive, and thorough answers.

Why care about intrinsic business value uncertainty? Because some opportunities have outcomes with narrow uncertainty ranges, while others have broad value uncertainty ranges. Knowing uncertainty profiles helps in making choices, limiting risks, or capturing upsides.

What Does It Do?

The Monte Carlo simulation uses your spreadsheet DCF model. It simply applies many different numbers (called trials) to each input variable, in accordance to the probability profiles you assign them, and records the output valuations reported by your DCF model, showing how likely the value will be at the "expected" point and everywhere else. It then retroactively fits probability curves to those output values (such as normal distributions and the like), and gives average values, standard deviations, and much else. Figure B.1 sets out the simple flow of how the Monte Carlo simulation is used.

What Do You Have to Do to Use It?

Besides providing your analyst support staff with Monte Carlo simulation software, market forecasting specialists must stipulate uncertainty bands in addition to their forecasts. Most Monte Carlo software packages make this incredibly easy, with tools that profile historical patterns and offer a wide repertoire of predefined distributions. They also allow variables to be correlated with one another, with themselves (that is, autocorrelated; a random walk where the next period's amount is related to the previous period), and many other features. Forecasters can even just draw upper and lower bounds that capture 95 percent of, for example, price levels, and then apply a standard distribution curve, or even create unique ones (such as an input that has an upper value and a lower value).

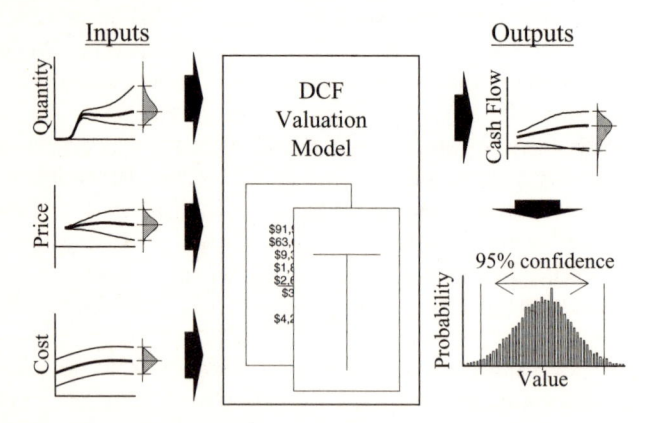

FIGURE B.1 Flow of Uncertain Inputs to Find Value Uncertainty in a Monte Carlo Simulation
Source: Business Intelligence Associates LLC.

APPENDIX C

Using Real Options
The Binomial Lattice Approach

Real options techniques are immensely powerful, and take value-maximizing decision making to a new level. Before it, the thinking that supported value-maximizing decisions was largely a static choice that went something like this: The value of investment program A is $x million, and the value of investment program B is $y million; since y is greater than x, we choose program B.

Of course, the world is not really like that. While B is valued more than A in a discounted cash flow (DCF) valuation, it may be that after you invest in A you open up an opportunity twice as valuable with a 40 percent chance to succeed. Perhaps, by contrast, B may include the opportunity to cease business operations in circumstances where the market price fizzles, or allow a switch to a more stably priced fuel source in five years. Some of these course changes can certainly be valued with DCF techniques, though their results cannot legitimately be compared; alternatives, probabilities, and risk-based discount rates are involved and need to be addressed and incorporated properly.

It is in dynamic situations like these, where uncertainty and choice exist, that real options techniques provide answers. When the values of business propositions and assets are known, real options tools bring them together in one decision regime, put a value on options to take action (like expanding a business when the market takes off more than expected), and incorporate uncertainties in how things will turn out (whether they are market, technology, or operations uncertainties).

Unfortunately, real options are not like their financial options counterparts traded in the Chicago financial markets, and so have been much more difficult to use in business management to date. They are not as cleanly defined as financial options, with fixed expiration dates, well-delineated terms, specified strike prices, and liquid markets tracking the value of the underlying asset (which is typically a high-volume commodity or publicly traded stock). Without such clean attributes, it is much more difficult to calculate fair values for real-life options, and an entire cottage industry has been built up in the last couple of decades, inventing solutions and creating tools.

With that said, real options do still refer to options and the value they represent, though they are practically very different from financial options and better thought of as decision paths mapped out in a world of uncertainties. For example, one of the first practical problems in strategic decision making is that most decisions that need to happen in the future are not even properly plotted out in the present, and so the choices themselves are not clear, let alone the timing or terms. To make things worse, the value of underlying assets is not set in highly liquid markets (a critical requirement for the now famous Black-Scholes formula solution for financial option valuations), and transactions frequently seem to have an infinite number of possible configurations. These issues have largely been resolved in recent years, and business leaders can no longer be excused from using dynamic decision-making tools in their approach to strategy and investment choices; today, future decision paths and options must be properly thought through.

This appendix discusses the most widely used real options approach for understanding decision paths, the *binomial lattice*. There are other possible solutions, including other lattice approaches, but the binomial lattice is the most robust, most simple, and the most mature in its implementation (with several software packages available that make the entire process easy for analysts; most notably the Super Lattice Solver by Dr. Jonathan Mun).

In this discussion we will not work through the mathematics underlying options or real options, or even the derivation of the binomial lattice. Although obviously critical, that knowledge is primarily needed by analysts and practitioners, and is amply dealt with in excellent works such as *Real Options Analysis* by Dr. Jonathan Mun (Wiley Finance, 2005) and *Real Options: A Practitioner's Guide* by Tom Copeland and Vladimir Antikarov (Texere, 2003). Note that any prospective student of real options analysis should be sure to study these in conjunction with updates and refinements in subsequent literature.

We do however, provide an executive-level introduction to what the binomial lattice does and how it works in evaluating real options decision paths. To do that, we use a simplified version of the example in Chapter 6 and walk through part of the first branch of the decision map for Samsung's hypothetical book printing press opportunity.

What the Binomial Lattice Does

The basic principle applied in value-maximizing real options is that decision makers will choose the decision path that delivers the highest value. The trouble is, we do not know what that path is now, since the decision is in the future and the future situation is not yet known. How can all those future paths be characterized and valued, such that business leaders can choose the one that will deliver the most intrinsic value?

Well, although we do not yet know the future, we do have the benefit of insights from experienced and skilled managers of all disciplines from our industry. These individuals have provided forecasts of technological events, market fundamentals (such as demand quantity, price, etc.), and operational performance (such as market share, costs and expenses, etc.), together with descriptions of uncertainty for each (as outlined in Chapters 5 and 6); and we believe these forecasts represent the best perspectives available anywhere. Further, analysts have taken these forecasts, together with knowledge of the business model, and have simulated the economics in a dynamic DCF model (constructed in a popular spreadsheet). As a result, we have figured out the expected value of the business proposition and, after also conducting a Monte Carlo simulation, the volatility of that value, too.

So, while we do not know what the actual future situation will be, with these two metrics we can profile the probability distribution of the business proposition's value at any year or point in the future, using a binomial lattice. And with that, we can make comparisons against the value of other choices, such as abandoning the business in favor of the value of its salvage, and identify the points where we would change paths. With a binomial lattice populated with the highest-value decisions, we have a way of capturing the decision maker's changes in course when the situation makes a more financially rewarding path available. Since we also know how likely it is to happen, we can recalculate value. Eliminating the chance of a loss, or adding the chance of a gain, has the effect of making an entire venture more valuable. For example, the option to abandon in circumstances of negative value increases the value of the endeavor at the outset—upside uncertainties are retained while downside uncertainties are removed.

How the Binomial Lattice Works

Fortunately, the binomial lattice is a very visual tool and does well in revealing what is going on intuitively. However, this comes at a price, in that multiple steps are needed (one or more per period, such as a year) to get to a result. Given this requirement, and the infinite number of ways management issues can be structured, programmers of real options software have a very complex challenge, especially if they are compiling a tool with the flexibility to cope with lengthy, multiple-step, multiple-asset valuations.

Let's look at an example. The following situation discussion briefly sets up the decision under consideration.

The Situation

We'll say that Samsung is considering a new venture in printing and needs to decide whether to invest $10 million in R&D to develop a digital printing press. It will only do so if the value of the venture is greater than zero (including the $10 million R&D investment).

Now, as this venture will be in a new market for Samsung, it will have to get access to a sales capability. Unfortunately, the investment needed to build such a sales capability from scratch is prohibitive, and the only way the venture is possible is to acquire a company with an existing market presence. If this were to happen, the price paid for the acquisition would have two elements: the base value of the acquisition (the value of its expected future cash flow from its ongoing business) *and* a premium.

Samsung isn't concerned with the first element; the expected future cash flow from the acquisition's ongoing operations covers its intrinsic value and is a wash. However, the premium is not covered, and the new venture must justify that payment itself.

At this point, Samsung recognizes that the traditional DCF valuation approach does not incorporate a very important option Samsung will have after completing the acquisition: the option to sell it off again and recoup a large part of the premium as a salvage value. Indeed, investment bankers believe that the premium will be $80 million next year (the earliest acquisition date, 2009), declining at $2 million a year thereafter. They also believe that if the company is acquired by Samsung, Samsung will retrieve the premium's value, less 5 percent after transaction and other costs.

Finally, there is the new venture's value—the digital printing press business. Estimates indicate that if launched six months after the acquisition, using the acquiree's sales capability, the new venture's cash flow has a present value today of $97 million. Uncertainty estimates give a value volatility of 18 percent. Figure C.1 sets out the decision map.

The Solution

The objective is to value the entire enterprise, including the business propositions, and all the available options. If it has a positive value, it pays for its investments and cost of capital, adds value, and warrants acceptance. There are two steps in the binomial lattice approach; Figure C.2 shows what is always the first step, an array of the broadening uncertainty of the value of the underlying asset over time.

This chart does a good job of showing how the value of our business proposition gets less certain as we move into the future. The binomial lattice works by starting at a single point origin on the left, establishing the present value of the future business proposition, and simply stepping forward one

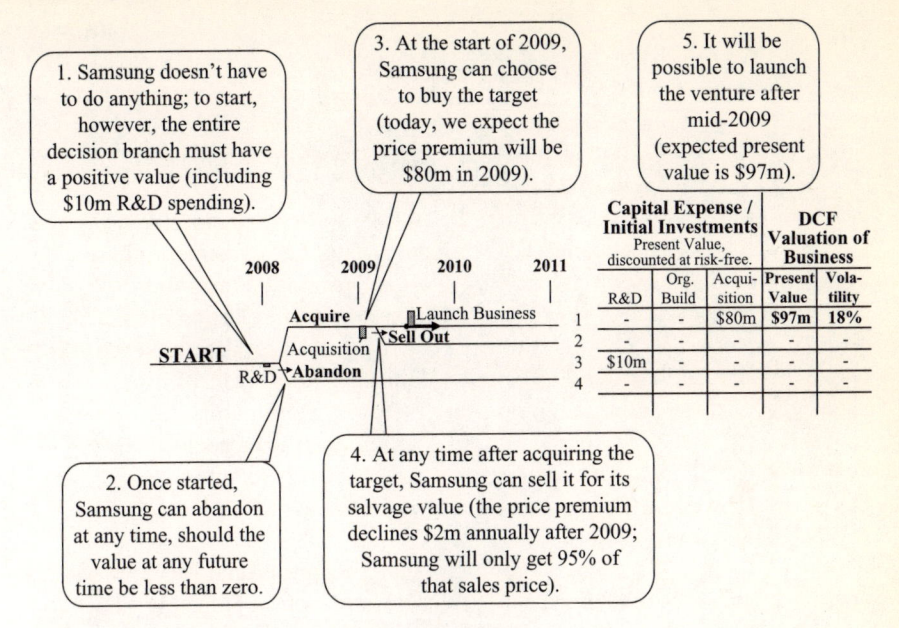

FIGURE C.1 Samsung's New Venture Decision Map

1. Samsung doesn't have to do anything; to start, however, the entire decision branch must have a positive value (including $10m R&D spending).

2. Once started, Samsung can abandon at any time, should the value at any future time be less than zero.

3. At the start of 2009, Samsung can choose to buy the target (today, we expect the price premium will be $80m in 2009).

4. At any time after acquiring the target, Samsung can sell it for its salvage value (the price premium declines $2m annually after 2009; Samsung will only get 95% of that sales price).

5. It will be possible to launch the venture after mid-2009 (expected present value is $97m).

Timeline: 2008 — START — R&D — 2009 Acquire/Acquisition/Abandon — 2010 Launch Business/Sell Out — 2011

	Capital Expense / Initial Investments Present Value, discounted at risk-free.			DCF Valuation of Business	
	R&D	Org. Build	Acquisition	Present Value	Volatility
1	-	-	$80m	$97m	18%
2	-	-	-	-	-
3	$10m	-	-	-	-
4	-	-	-	-	-

Source: Business Intelligence Associates LLC.

time period at a time to the right. As each step is made, the uncertainty of the value of the business broadens (which can be seen by the expanded range of the lattice); the degree of that expansion is a direct function of the volatility of the business proposition's value—the greater the volatility, the greater the spread in value uncertainty. (The actual formulae to calculate this are footnoted in the chart.) Note how only three factors are needed to construct this binomial spread: the value, its volatility, and the risk-free cost of capital (the return one expects from capital that has no risk associated with it, such as a zero-coupon government bond).

Using this lattice, we can map out broadening uncertainty over any period; and using the Monte Carlo–driven DCF valuation approach, many uncertainties may be combined into this one view. Indeed, all of the factors that we forecasted for the market and this business proposition's operations were put into a DCF valuation to determine an expected value for this venture; similarly, all of the uncertainties in those factors were also run through that DCF valuation model (in a Monte Carlo simulation) to determine value volatility—*resulting in this single lattice profile of likely value at any point in the future.* An incredibly useful tool!

Why is this so useful? Because now we can *clearly see when other options are more valuable* than the business proposition itself. For example,

	Now	2009	2010	2011	2012	2013	2014	2015	2016	2017	2018	2019	2020	2021	2022	2023	
																$1,443.33	1
															$1,205.57	$1,006.98	15
																$702.55	105
																$490.15	455
																$341.97	1,365
																$238.58	3,003
																$166.45	5,005
																$116.13	6,435
																$81.02	6,435
																$56.53	5,005
																$39.44	3,003
																$27.51	1,365
																$19.20	455
																$13.39	105
																$9.34	15
																$6.52	1

Start: present value of business proposition alone.

Due to uncertainty, *value can go up or down every period by an amount governed by volatility.*[1]

Likelihood of values in year 15 (a function[2] of the number of paths to each value) *reflects probability distribution.*

Here, the value of the business proposition is *lower than the salvage value* in these circumstances at these times; the acquisition would be sold off.

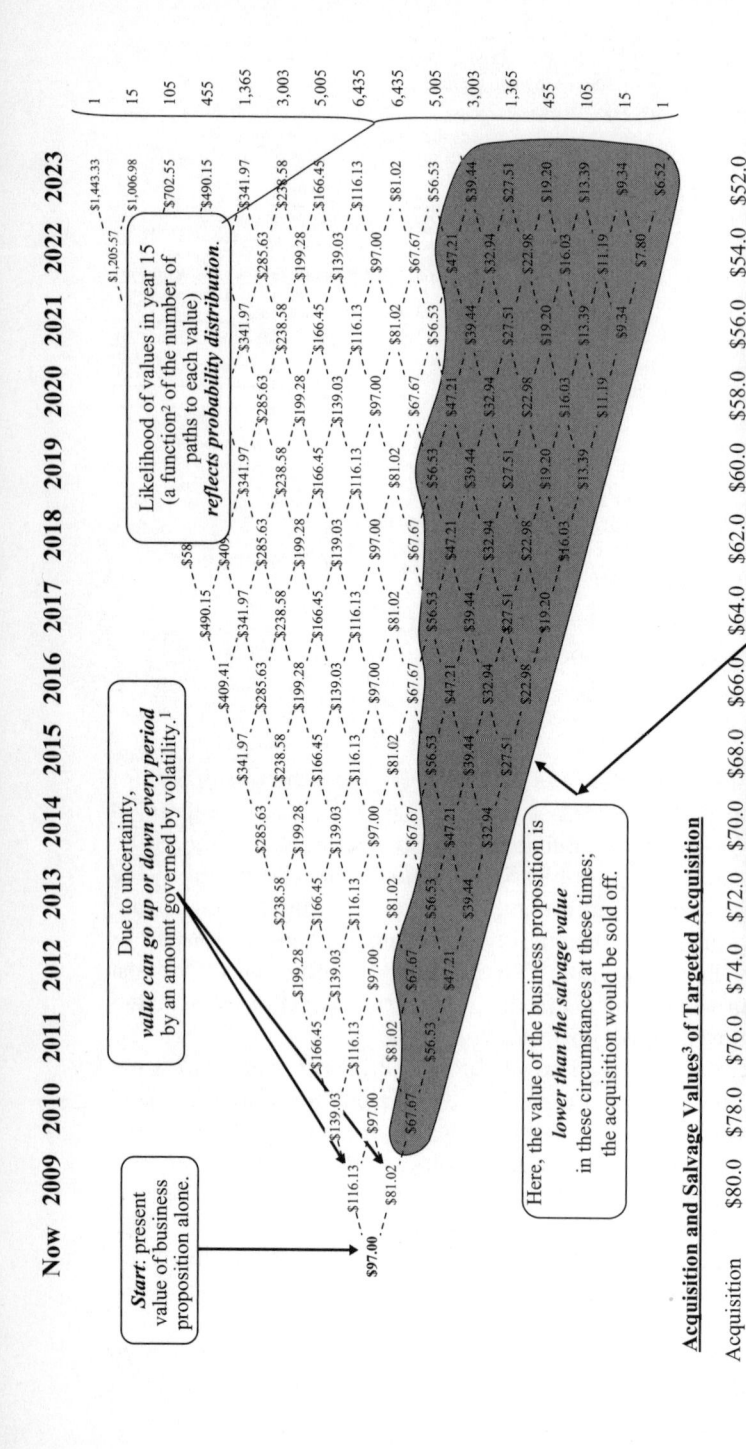

Acquisition and Salvage Values[3] of Targeted Acquisition

	Now	2009	2010	2011	2012	2013	2014	2015	2016	2017	2018	2019	2020	2021	2022	2023
Acquisition	$80.0	$78.0	$76.0	$74.0	$72.0	$70.0	$68.0	$66.0	$64.0	$62.0	$60.0	$58.0	$56.0	$54.0	$52.0
Salvage/Resale[3]	$76.0	$74.1	$72.2	$70.3	$68.4	$66.5	$64.6	$62.7	$60.8	$58.9	$57.0	$55.1	$53.2	$51.3	$49.4

FIGURE C.2 Step 1: The Binomial Lattice Profiles Increasing Uncertainty in Future Business Value

Source: Business Intelligence Associates LLC. [1]The degree of up movement in value (u) equals e^(volatility of the proposition's value) in a one-step-per-year lattice. The up move is equal to the inverse of the down move (d), or 1/d; as a result, the lattice is recombining after each step (notice how ups and downs meet at the same value). [2]Starting from the left, these are the number of paths that lead to each of the values on the right, taking many different sequences of ups and downs; for example, there are 3,003 ways to get to a value of $39.44. [3]In the Samsung example, the value of the acquired entity drops by $2 million every year, and once acquired, the resale value is expected to be only 95 percent of the original value for that year (as the pool of buyers is now smaller).

look at the bottom of Figure C.2 at the salvage value of the acquired business over time, and at the shaded area in the lattice where the salvage value is greater than the value of the business proposition itself. In these circumstances, at these times, management would pull the plug on the venture and sell the business off.

The second step in the binomial lattice approach is illustrated in Figure C.3. The lattice is shown again, this time with the lesser business proposition values substituted out by the value that would be gained in an asset sale (capturing salvage value). This is an important step, since the tool uses these new figures, this time working right to left, to figure out the value of the combined assets. The new number we have derived all the way at the origin on the left is the new *value of the business proposition with the option to abandon* the venture and sell the residual salvage value.

For those curious about the actual computations involved, the formula used by the lattice for consolidating two later period values into one earlier value is contained within Figure C.3. Additional data aren't needed to do this; it is simply a computational exercise with lots of numbers to churn through.

So far we have combined two assets into our decision path. We additionally need to incorporate invested capital to figure out the *net* present value. In our case there are two investment amounts, giving us key decision points before each is made. The first is for an immediate $10 million R&D investment to start the venture by developing the digital printing press offering itself (opening all the subsequent values and options). The second investment comes one year later; once the acquisition target has been identified and the transaction negotiated, the time comes to pay $80 million.

Since the second payment for the acquisition is in nominal (future value) dollars and is due one year from now, it needs to be included into the lattice one year in by subtracting it from the values for 2009 (that is, subtracting $80 million from $116.66 million and from $84.54 million, to give $36.66 and $4.54 million, respectively), and then brought back to today's value using the lattice approach (effectively just discounting it to today using the risk-free rate). That gives a net value of $22.56 million. From that result, now in today's value, the $10 million R&D investment is also subtracted. The value of the entire branch, with R&D and acquisition capital investments, and including the option to abandon and sell the salvage value, is $12.56 million.

To illustrate why it is necessary to approach these decisions using real options, we'll compare this valuation result with the DCF approach, where the option to abandon cannot be captured. In the (static) DCF approach, the net present value is calculated by taking the present value of the business proposition, $97 million, and subtracting the R&D ($10 million) as well as the present value of the $80 million acquisition ($76.10 million); this gives

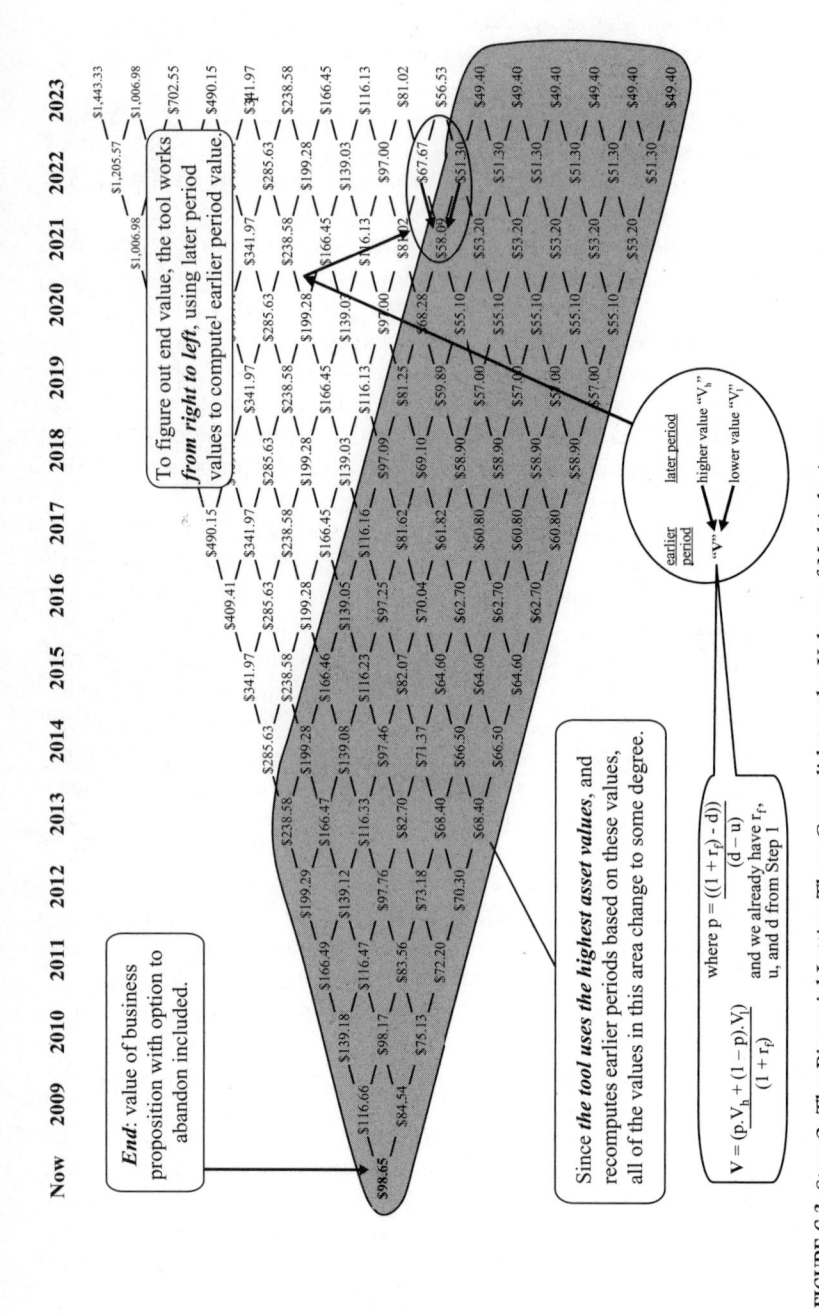

FIGURE C.3 Step 2: The Binomial Lattice Then Consolidates the Values of Multiple Assets

Source: Business Intelligence Associates LLC.
[1] Risk-free discount rate $r_f = 5$ percent throughout.

a net value of $10.9 million. The value with the option included is $1.66 million (or 15.2 percent) higher; this difference actually represents the value of the option itself. An interesting way to think about it is that management would be prepared to pay up to $1.66 million to get the option to abandon the project should the future situation turn out unfavorably.

It is also worth considering the sensitivity the decision has to different conditions. For example, if the salvage value did not decline over time, the value with the option would be $14.71 million, or 35 percent over the static DCF value.

The real options approach gives us a clearer view of the actual value of future opportunities (which seriously diverge from static DCF valuations with increasing uncertainty and additional decision paths), and allows several decision paths to be consolidated and considered in one view.

Beyond This Example

We have described the workings of the binomial lattice with a simplified illustration. In most circumstances numerous decision paths warrant review, and most of them include multiple assets and multiple time periods.

Further, we conducted the illustration with only one step per year. With some small manipulation of the mathematics involved, we can have many steps in a period—something we are likely to want to do to increase accuracy. Leveraging high school calculus, when calculations are taken to the limit the output becomes more precise. The same is true for binomial lattices: The finer the steps involved, the more accurate is the result. There is a cost to adding steps, as you might imagine, in that the number of computations needed literally grows exponentially, and trade-offs are involved between having analysis and computers spending lots of time making calculations versus the increase in accuracy. Frankly, little is gained after several tens of steps, and pursuing it into the hundreds is really only suitable for nuclear physics.

Finally, given the availability of easy-to-use software tools, much of the time needed to conduct these complex mathematical valuations has dropped tremendously in just the past decade. The software has also had the benefit of removing formula-based errors—an issue that needs to be respected, since the number of formulae in the lattice is large by any count, particularly when multiple assets and decisions are involved. Now the effort can be focused where it belongs—framing the issues and decisions. This is not an easy task, and is in fact a new skill for many executives and business leaders who are used to making such complex decisions using intuition.

Bibliography

Cooper, Robert G. *Winning at New Products: Accelerating the Process From Idea to Launch*. Perseus Books, 2001.

Copeland, Tom, and Vladimir Antikarov. *Real Options, Revised Edition: A Practitioner's Guide*. Texere, 2003.

Gadiesh, Orit, and James L. Gilbert. "Profit Pools: A Fresh Look at Strategy." *Harvard Business Review*, May–June 1988, 139.

Kapur, Vivek, and Denis Mathias. "Collaboration: Using eHubs to Create Value in High-Tech." *IBM Business Consulting*, 2002.

Kim, W. Chan, and Renee Mauborgne. *Blue Ocean Strategy: How to Create Uncontested Market Space and Make Competition Irrelevant*. Harvard Business School Press, 2005.

McKinsey & Company, Inc., Tim Koller, Mark Goedhart, and David Wessels. *Valuation, Fourth Edition: Measuring and Managing the Value of Companies*. John Wiley & Sons, 2005.

Means, Grady, and David Schneider. *MetaCapitalism: The E-Business Revolution and the Design of 21st-Century Companies and Markets*. John Wiley & Sons, 2000.

Mun, Jonathan. *Real Options Analysis, Second Edition: Tools and Techniques for Valuing Strategic Investments and Decisions*. John Wiley & Sons, 2005.

Porter, Michael E. *Competitive Advantage*. Free Press, 1998.

Rappaport, Alfred. *Creating Shareholder Value*. Free Press, 1997.

Index

Note: Figures, tables, and sidebars/boxes/examples are indicated by *f*, *t*, or *b* following the page locator.

Abandonment of opportunities, 165, 165*f*, 245, 247
ABC (activity-based costing), 72
ABC-lite, 72–77, 73*f*, 227, 230
Accountability, 198
Accounting systems. *See* GAAP
Accounts payable, 234
Accounts receivable, 233
Accuracy, 61*b*, 72–73, 73*f*, 75*f*, 79–81, 116, 236
Acquisitions, 127–128, 144, 151, 154*b*, 156–158, 158*f*, 245
Action plans, 175
Activity-based costing (ABC), 72. *See also* ABC-lite
Allocations, 72. *See also* apportionment entries
Amortization, 68–69, 71–72
Antikarov, Vladimir, 240
Apportionments of capital investments, 232–236
Apportionments of expenses:
    accuracy of, 61*b*, 72–73, 73*f*, 75*f*, 236
    cost of goods and, 226–227
    general and administrative costs, 229–232, 231*t*
    in internal profit pools, 62, 68, 72–77, 226–232
    profitability and, 44–45
    research and development, 228–229
    sales and marketing and, 227–228
    value-add and, 214–215
Apportionments of revenues, 72, 223, 225
Assets, 77–78, 232, 234–236
Attributions, 72, 75–76. *See also* apportionment entries

B2B (business-to-business) applications, 210–212
Barriers, entry/exit, 112
Binomial lattices, 163, 240–247, 244*f*, 246*f*

Blue dollar revenue, 42
Blue Ocean Strategy (Kim and Mauborgne), 98
Brand equity, 126, 126*b*–127*b*, 213
Bubble in/out approaches, 187–190
Bundling, 82, 88, 170–171, 173–174, 225
Business-building configurations, 188*t*
Business development. *See* New business development
Businesses. *See also other business-related entries*
    culture of, 184–189, 193, 197–202, 213
    objectives of, 7
    specialization of, 208–212, 208*f*, 211*f*
    structure of (*See* Organizational structure)
Business management reporting information, 40, 41, 45–46
Business models, 27–28, 48–49, 55, 123–130, 124*f*, 173, 181*t*. *See also* Game
Business operations management, 230, 231*t*
Business proposition values, 160–161, 162*f*. *See also* New business development
Business-to-business (B2B) applications, 210–212
Business values:
    calculating, 11*b*
    cash flow and, 101, 102*f*
    definition of, 10
    market strategy and, 134–139, 135*f*, 138*f*
    operational performance and, 12
    profile of, 136*f*
    uncertainty of, 237–238, 244*f*

Capital asset pricing model, 117
Capital assets, 232
Capital investments, 25, 45–46, 65–68, 77–79, 155*b*–156*b*, 157, 232–236
Cash-based profit pools. *See* Profit pools

251

Index

Cash flow. *See also* Discounted cash flow; Future cash flow
  business values and, 101, 102*f*
  definition of, 9, 9*f*, 11*b*
  driving, 59–60
  market strategy and, 148
  new business development and, 199
  price and, 14–15, 15*f*
  trajectory of, 57–58, 57*f*
Cash on hand, 234
Changes, 90–91, 177
Channels. *See* Market segments
Charted markets, 20–21, 31–32
Commercial models, definition of, 27
Company culture, 184–189, 193, 197–202, 213
Competition:
  assessment of, 113*b*–114*b*
  economics of, 33–34, 34*f*, 47–49, 50–52
  as key market force, 112–113
  market strategy and, 17, 17*f*, 18–19, 146, 147*f*
  outsourcing and, 217
  performance improvement opportunities and, 87
Competitive Strategy (Porter), 111
Control, outsourcing and, 218
Cooper, Robert G., 203
Copeland, Tom, 240
Core operating process goals, 197
Corporate renewal, 190–206, 192*f*
Corporate venture *versus* venture capital portfolios, 182–184, 183*f*, 198–199
Cost centers, 214–215
Costs. *See also* Expenses
  direct, 226, 228
  general and administrative, 229–232, 231*t*
  of goods, 42–44, 43*f*, 226–227, 233–234
  indirect, 226–227
  labor, 75–76, 228, 230–232
  opportunity, 25, 45–46, 78, 235
  overhead, 76, 226–227
  sunk, 68, 183–184
Creativity, 140–141, 150, 198–202
Cross-functional skills, 2, 52–53, 58, 61*b*–62*b*
Cross-functional teams, 199, 202
Cross-training, 58
C-suite managers, 3
Current profitability, 28–30, 35*f*, 59–60
Customers, 54–55, 114, 123–127, 125*b*, 194, 199, 204–205

Deal flow, 193, 199–203
Debt holders, 11*b*, 78
Decision paths/maps:
  market information and, 85–86
  market strategy and, 148–151, 150*f*
  populating, 153–160, 158*f*
  real options and, 136–137, 240–247, 243*f*
  summary of, 159*f*
  valuation of, 161–166
Demand, 101–109, 107*b*–108*b*, 109*b*–110*b*, 111–112, 114–116, 148
Depreciation, 26, 43, 68–69, 71–72, 227, 235
Differentiation, 18–19
Direct costs, 226, 228
Discontinuation, of internal profit pools, 81–83. *See also* Market withdrawals
Discounted cash flow (DCF):
  calculating, 10*f*
  market strategy and, 152–153, 172
  market values and, 8–14
  Monte Carlo simulation and, 237–238
  real options *versus*, 136–137, 165–166, 239–247
  valuation model, 119–120, 152–153, 165–166
Discounts, 117, 225
Disruptor strategies, 98
Distribution, 127, 128*b*, 228

Earnings before interest, taxes, depreciation, and amortization (EBITDA), 12, 14
Earnings per share, 12
Economic profit:
  calculating, 45–46
  definition of, 9*f*, 10
  gross profit *versus*, 42–44, 47*f*
  for internal profit pools, 70, 71*f*
  investment *versus*, 22–23, 23*f*, 29, 35*f*, 38*f*, 81*f*
  operating profit *versus*, 44, 47*f*
  return on investment, 182, 195–196 (*See also* Rates of return)
  value creation and, 216
Economic simulations, 89–90. *See also* Monte Carlo simulation
Economic value-add (EVA), 45
Efficiency, 213
e-hubs, 211–212
Elasticity measurements, 86–87, 148. *See also* Market dynamics
e-markets, 210–212
Employees. *See* Staff
Entrenchment, avoiding, 179–180
Entry/exit barriers, 112
Equity values, predicted *versus* actual, 13*f*
Existing markets, 20, 31–32
Expected values, 152–153
Expenses, 68–71, 69*f*, 72–77. *See also* Apportionments of expenses; Costs

Failure, 181–187
Fair values, 236. *See also* Market values

Index

FASB (Financial Accounting Standards Board), 41, 228, 235–236. *See also* GAAP
Finance and marketing skills, 2, 52–53, 61*b*–62*b*
First-mover returns, 146, 147*f*
Fixed assets, 77–78, 234–236
Flagship customers, 204, 205
Flexibility, 202
Forecasting:
   market demand, 102–109, 107*b*–108*b*, 109*b*–110*b*
   market forecast framework, 111–118, 112*f*
   market inflexion events and, 87–88, 100–109, 122*b*
   market strategy and, 152–153
   Monte Carlo simulation and, 238
   performance improvement opportunities and, 87–88
   real options and, 241
Future cash flow, 10*f*, 14–21, 32, 35, 36*f*, 116–117, 117*b*, 180
Future market inflexion events, 105–109, 105*b*–106*b*, 113–118
Future profitability, 30–31

GAAP (Generally Accepted Accounting Principles):
   cash flow and, 9, 9*f*
   new business development and, 196
   PP&E under, 235
   profitability measures with, 25, 39–47, 47*f*
   shareholder value and, 2
   unwinding, 60–79, 63*f*, 71*f*, 75*f*, 223, 224*f*
Gadiesh, Orit, 37
Game, 19–21. *See also* Business models
General and administrative costs, 229–232, 231*t*
Generally Accepted Accounting Principles. *See* GAAP
Geographies. *See* Market segments
Gilbert, James L., 37
Goals, 7, 191–197, 195*f*
Goedhart, Mark, 8
Granularity, 64–65, 64*f*
Green dollar revenue, 42
Gross profit *versus* economic profit, 42–44, 47*f*
Growth goals, 196–197
Growth opportunities, 29–30, 30*f*, 70, 84–86

Hendrix, Dexter, 186
Historical market inflexion events, 102–105, 103*b*–104*b*

Implementation, 173–175, 174*f*, 193, 205–206
Indirect costs, 76, 226–227. *See also* General and administrative costs
Individual investors, 12, 13*f*, 14
Industry specialization, 208–209, 208*f*

Information needs:
   for business management, 40, 41, 45–46
   on cash-based profitability, 52–53
   on markets, 33, 47–52, 85–86
   on market strategy outcomes, 151–160, 154*b*–155*b*
   shareholder value and, 3
   source reliability and, 61*b*
Information systems, 53
Institutional investors, 12, 13*f*, 14
Intangibles, 77–78, 234–236
Interest, 11*b*, 78
Internal operations, 128–129, 129*b*
Internal profit pools:
   capital investments and, 65–68, 77–79, 232–236
   definition of, 25
   discontinuation of, 81–83
   expense apportionments to, 62, 68, 72–77, 226–232
   granularity and, 64–65, 64*f*
   growth opportunities and, 29–30, 30*f*, 70, 84–86
   interrelationships and, 82, 84–85, 88–89, 225
   market segments and, 65, 66*t*, 74
   null-contribution, 83–84
   profitability and, 28–31
   reporting systems and, 79–80
   revenue apportionment to, 72, 223, 225
   shareholder value and, 2
   strategic implications of change in, 90–91
   synchronizing revenues and expenses among, 68–71, 69*f*
   unwinding GAAP reporting and, 60–79, 63*f*, 71*f*
   value-add and, 215–216
Internet, effect on business, 210–212, 211*f*
Interrelationships. *See also* Bundling
   of internal profit pools, 82, 84–85, 88–89, 225
   of market forces, 115
   of market segments, 60
   of market strategies, 168–171, 169*b*
Intrinsic values, 11–12, 237
Inventory, 233
Investment profit pools, 229
Investments:
   economic profit *versus*, 22–23, 23*f*, 35*f*, 38*f*, 81*f*
   management of, 230, 231*t*
   in profit drains, 29–30, 40–41, 41*f*
   research and development as, 228–229
   revenue *versus*, 21–22, 22*f*, 29
Investors, individual *versus* institutional, 12, 13*f*, 14

Joint ventures, 144

Key market forces, 111–118
Kim, W. Chan, 98
Koller, Tim, 8

Labor costs, 75–76, 228, 230–232
Lattices, binomial, 163, 240–247, 244*f*, 246*f*
Legal liabilities, 234

Managers:
   apportionment of expenses and, 76, 230–232, 231*t*
   C-suite, 3
   forecasting and, 241
   new business development and, 184–187, 186*f*, 189, 193
   reporting information for, 40, 41, 45–46
   unwinding GAAP reports, 61–68
   value of time, 219–220
Margins, 156. *See also* Economic profit; Price
Market demand, 102–109, 107*b*–108*b*, 109*b*–110*b*
Market dynamics, 82–83, 86–87
Market exit, 80–83, 143
Market forces, key, 111–118
Market forecast framework, 111–118, 112*f*
Market inflexion events (MIEs), 87–88, 100–109, 103*b*–104*b*, 105*b*–106*b*, 113–118, 122*b*
Market information, 33, 47–52, 85–86
Marketing and finance skills, 2, 52–53, 61*b*–62*b*
Market interrelationships, 88–89
Market profit pools:
   attractiveness of, 33–37, 35*f*, 36*f*
   business models and, 27–28, 48–49
   definition of, 25
   economics of, 110–118
   forecasting and, 100–109
   market strategy and, 31–33
   uncertainty of, 118–123, 118*b*–119*b*, 120*b*–121*b*
   value chains and, 37, 38*f*
   value of, 96–97, 97*b*, 100–123, 130
   vertical, 37
Markets, types of, 20–21, 31–32, 53–55, 123–127, 210–212
Market segments. *See also* Offerings
   defining, 18
   internal profit pools and, 65, 66*t*, 74
   interrelationships between, 60
   profit pool measurements by, 25, 29–30, 34–36, 48
   value growth and, 194
Market share, 32, 146, 147*f*, 148
Market strategies. *See also* Pioneer strategies; Strategic views of markets
   business values and, 134–139, 135*f*, 138*f*
   capital investments and, 155*b*–156*b*, 157
   cash flow and, 14–21, 20*f*, 148
   competition and, 17, 17*f*, 18–19, 146, 147*f*
   defining path forward in, 167–175, 169*b*
   definition of, 16–19, 17*f*
   evaluation of opportunities, 140–151, 141*b*–142*b*, 145*f*, 150*f*, 160–171, 168*b*–169*b*
   formulation process, 133–134
   implementation of, 175
   market profit pools and, 31–33
   outcomes information and, 151–160, 154*b*–155*b*
   shareholder value and, 1–4
   statement, 174–175
   value-add and, 221–222
   value growth and, 191–194
Market studies, 151, 155*b*, 157–158
Market targeting and participation, 16–19, 17*f*
Market values, 8–14, 11–12, 235–236
Market withdrawals, 80–83, 143
Mauborgne, Renee, 98
McKinsey & Company, Inc., 8
Means, Grady, 186, 210
MetaCapitalism (Means and Schneider), 186, 210
Middleware, 211
MIEs. *See* Market inflexion events (MIEs)
Milk line economic profit, 70
Monte Carlo simulation, 119–120, 120*b*–121*b*, 152–153, 172, 237–238, 238*f*, 241, 243
Mun, Jonathan, 240

Net present values, 245
Net working capital, 77, 232–234
Neutralization of profit drains, 80–83, 81*f*
New business development. *See also* Market strategies; Research and development
   creation and failure, 181–182
   enhancing processes for, 192–206
   goals of, 191–197
   investment in, 67, 67*f*
   in new markets, 20–21, 32–33, 53–55
   organizational structure and, 184–189, 186*f*, 188*t*, 193, 197–202
   survival rates, 182*f*
   typical processes for, 190–192, 191*f*
Noncash charges. *See* Amortization; Depreciation

Objectives, business, 7. *See also* Goals
Offerings. *See also* Game; Market segments
   bundling, 82, 88, 170–171, 173–174, 225
   as key market force, 114–115
   research and development creating, 228–229

Index

value growth and, 194
value to customers, 54–55, 123–124, 125*b*
Operating cash flow, 11*b*. *See also* Cash flow
Operating economics, 115–116
Operating models, 27
Operating processes, core, 197
Operating profit *versus* economic profit, 44, 47*f*
Operating values. *See* Business values
Operational performances, 12
Operations, internal, 128–129, 129*b*
Operations management, 230, 231*t*
Opportunities:
  abandonment of, 165, 165*f*, 245, 247
  economics of, 160–166, 165*f*, 166*f*, 167–171, 167*f*, 168*b*–169*b*
  evaluating and mapping, 143–151, 145*f*, 200–202
  for growth, 29–30, 30*f*, 70, 84–86
  interrelationships between, 168–171, 169*b*
  listing and defining, 140–143, 141*b*–142*b*
  prioritization of, 173–174, 174*f*
Opportunity costs, of capital investments, 25, 45–46, 78, 235
Options. *See* Real options
Organizational structure:
  apportionment of expenses and, 230
  cash-based profitability information and, 52–53
  new business development and, 185–189, 186*f*, 188*t*, 193, 197–202
  outsourcing and, 217–219
  value-add and, 213
Outcomes information, of market strategy, 151–160, 154*b*–155*b*
Outsourcing, 210–212, 214, 217–220. *See also* Third-party vendors
Overhead costs, 76, 226–227. *See also* General and administrative costs

Participation goals, 194–195, 195*f*
Partnerships, 144, 151, 155*b*, 156–158
Performance improvement opportunities, 29–30, 30*f*, 80–90, 81*f*
Pilot tests, 151, 155*b*, 157–158
Pioneer strategies, 98–100, 99*b*–100*b*. *See also* Market strategies; New business development
Porter, Michael, 111
Portfolios, 84–85, 182–184, 183*f*, 193, 198–199, 203–204
PP&E (property, plant, and equipment), 77–78, 234–236
Premiums, 242
Present value, 10*f*, 32, 36*f*

Price, 14–15, 15*f*, 146, 147*f*, 148, 225
Price elasticity, 86–87, 148
Prioritization, 72–73, 173–174, 174*f*
Probabilities, 172, 238, 241
Product Development and Management Association, 203, 205
Production costs. *See* Costs, of goods
Profitability:
  apportionments of expenses and, 44–45
  current, 28–30, 35*f*, 59–60
  future, 30–31
  goals, 195–196
  of market, 47–52
  steady state, 69–71, 71*f*, 81–82
Profit drains, 29–30, 40–41, 41*f*, 80–83, 81*f*
Profit pools, 1–4, 25, 27–30, 34–36, 39–48, 52–53, 59–60. *See also* Cash flow; Economic profit; Internal profit pools; Investment profit pools; Market profit pools
"Profit Pools: A Fresh Look at Strategy" (Gadiesh and Gilbert), 37
Profit share split ratios, 157
Profits *versus* investments, 21–22, 23*f*, 29, 35*f*, 38*f*, 81*f*
Project Management Institute, 205
Projects, managing, 193, 204–205
Property, plant, and equipment (PP&E), 77–78, 234–236

Rappaport, Alfred, 8, 11–12
Rates of return, 11*b*, 84, 98*f*, 146, 147*f*, 153. *See also* Economic profit return on investment
Real options, 136–137, 161–166, 165*f*, 166*f*, 167*f*, 172, 239–247, 243*f*
Real Options: A Practitioner's Guide (Copeland and Antikarov), 240
Real Options Analysis (Mun), 240
Reliability, of source information, 61*b*
Reporting systems, 3, 40, 79–80. *See also* GAAP
Research and development, 228–229. *See also* New business development
Resources, 175, 192
Returns. *See* Rates of return
Revenue:
  apportionment of, 72, 223, 225
  blue *versus* green dollar, 42
  investments *versus*, 21–22, 22*f*, 29
  time synchronization of, 68–71, 69*f*
Risk, 51, 98*f*, 170–172, 202

Sales and marketing expenses, 227–228
Salvage values, 157, 163, 165*f*, 245, 247
Samsung, market strategy, 138–168, 242
Schneider, David, 186, 210
Segmentation. *See* Market segments

Shareholder cash flow, 11*b*
Shareholder value, 1–4, 7–8. *See also* value-related entries
Short-term securities, 234
Siloing of departments, 2, 52–53
Simulation, economic, 89–90. *See also* Monte Carlo simulation
Skills, cross-functional, 2, 52–53, 58, 61*b*–62*b*
SKU (stock-keeping units), 40, 41*f*, 226, 229
Source information, reliability of, 61*b*
Specialization, business, 208–212, 208*f*, 211*f*
Staff. *See also* Managers
   apportionment of labor costs, 75–76, 230–232, 231*t*
   cross-functional, 199, 202
   marketing strategy and, 173–175
   new business development and, 184–186, 188–189, 199
   skills needed by, 2, 52–53, 58, 61*b*–62*b*
Stage-gate processes, 203
Steady state profitability, 69–71, 71*f*, 81–82
Stern, Joel, 45
Stewart, G. Bennett, 45
Stock-keeping units (SKU), 40, 41*f*, 226, 229
Strategic views of markets:
   business model assessments and, 123–129, 124*f*
   market profit pool values and, 100–123
   pioneer strategies and, 98–100, 99*b*–100*b*
   risk/return profiles and, 98*f*
   summary of, 130–131, 131*b*–132*b*
   traditional, 94–96, 95*b*
   value-oriented, 96–100, 130
Structure. *See* Organizational structure
Substitute offerings, 114–115
Sunk costs, 68, 183–184
Super Lattice Solver, 240
Suppliers, 115–116, 129, 129*b*

Taxes, 232
Teams. *See* Staff
Third-party vendors, 49–50, 105. *See also* Outsourcing
Time synchronization of revenues and expenses, 68–71, 69*f*
Time utilization of assets, 235

Transformation approach, 187–190
Transition problems, 218

Uncertainty:
   of business values, 237–238, 244*f*
   forecasting and, 108
   of market profit pools, 118–123, 118*b*–119*b*, 120*b*–121*b*
   market strategy and, 134–135, 136*f*, 153, 158, 160, 161, 163–164
   performance, 218
   real options and, 239–247
Uncharted markets, 21, 32–33, 53–55. *See also* Pioneer strategies
Unit sales, 14–15, 15*f*

Valuation (McKinsey & Company, Inc., et al.), 8
Value, sources of, 207, 212–222
Value-add, 45, 134, 160, 174*f*, 212–216, 219–222. *See also* Value creation
Value-added community, 210
Value centers, 214–215, 215*f*
Value chains, 37, 38*f*
Value creation. *See also* Value-add
   for customers, 54–55, 123–124, 125*b*
   implementation effort *versus*, 173–174, 174*f*
   market strategies and, 127–128
   plotting, 215–217, 216*f*
Value growth, 180–190, 181*t*, 190–206, 192*f*
Value leverage, 19–21, 20*f*
Value propositions, 114–115
Value volatility, 137, 153, 163, 241, 243. *See also* Monte Carlo simulation
Venture capital *versus* corporate venture portfolios, 182–184, 183*f*, 198–199
Vertical market profit pools, 37
Vertical performance measures, 214
Volume demand, 101, 111, 112, 114, 115–116

Weighted average cost of capital, 11*b*
Welch, Jack, 188, 212
Wessels, David, 8
Winning at New Products: Accelerating the Process from Idea to Launch (Cooper), 203
Withdrawals from market, 80–83, 143
Working capital, 77, 232–234